PO-3507
£34.99

R62785

KV-445-827

Computer Graphics for Artists II

WITHDRAWN FROM STOCK

Andrew Paquette

Computer Graphics for Artists II

Environments and Characters

 Springer

Andrew Paquette
NHTV International Game Architecture and Design
The Netherlands

ISBN: 978-1-84882-469-0   e-ISBN: 978-1-84882-470-6
DOI: 10.1007/978-1-84882-470-6
Springer Dordrecht Heidelberg London New York

British Library Cataloguing in Publication Data
A catalogue record for this book is available from the British Library

Library of Congress Control Number: 2008922190

© Springer-Verlag London Limited 2009
Apart from any fair dealing for the purposes of research or private study, or criticism or review, as permitted under the Copyright, Designs and Patents Act 1988, this publication may only be reproduced, stored or transmitted, in any form or by any means, with the prior permission in writing of the publishers, or in the case of reprographic reproduction in accordance with the terms of licenses issued by the Copyright Licensing Agency. Enquiries concerning reproduction outside those terms should be sent to the publishers.
The use of registered names, trademarks, etc., in this publication does not imply, even in the absence of a specific statement, that such names are exempt from the relevant laws and regulations and therefore free for general use.
The publisher makes no representation, express or implied, with regard to the accuracy of the information contained in this book and cannot accept any legal responsibility or liability for any errors or omissions that may be made.

Cover illustration: Steven Geisler, face, Francisco Cortina, hair and body model, and Jake Rowell, body texture

Printed on acid-free paper

Springer is part of Springer Science+Business Media (www.springer.com)

Acknowledgments

Making the illustrations for this book would not have been possible without the generous help of Mark Rein and Epic Games, W! Games, Feversoft, Robert Joosten, Cortina Digital, Bionatics, Dirk Stöel, Arno Schmitz, Perry Leiten, Sebastian Walter, Ladislav Mucina, Sebastian Mollet, Mark Knoop, Andrius Drevinskas, Laurens van den Heijkant, and Lennart Hillen/Team HARR. My warmest thanks go to everyone who contributed and to those who gave permission to reproduce existing images. A special thank you to the NHTV Academy of Digital Entertainment for their support.

Contents

3D4/Anatomy for Characters

Part II   Introduction

Illustrations List

Figure	Illustration	Source
13.5	Arm, anterior level 3	AP/Joosten
13.6	Arm, anterior level 4	AP/Joosten
13.7	Arm, anterior level 5	AP/Joosten
13.8	Arm, dorsal level 0	AP/Joosten
13.9	Arm, dorsal level 1	AP/Joosten
13.10	Arm, dorsal level 2	AP/Joosten
13.11	Arm, dorsal level 3	AP/Joosten
13.12	Arm, dorsal level 4	AP/Joosten
13.13	Arm, dorsal level 5–7	AP/Joosten
13.14	Arm, medial level 0–3	AP/Joosten
13.15	Arm, medial level 4–7	AP/Joosten
13.16	Arm, lateral level 0–1	AP/Joosten
13.17	Arm, lateral level 2–3	AP/Joosten
13.18	Arm, lateral level 4–6	AP/Joosten
13.19	Hand, palmar level 0	AP/Joosten
13.20	Hand, dorsal level 0	AP/Joosten
13.21	Hand, palmar level 1	AP/Joosten
13.22	Hand, dorsal level 1	AP/Joosten
13.23	Hand, palmar level 2	AP/Joosten
13.24	Hand, dorsal level 2	AP/Joosten
13.25	Leg, ventral level 0–1	AP/Joosten
13.26	Leg, ventral level 2–3	AP/Joosten
13.27	Leg, ventral level 4–5	AP/Joosten
13.28	Leg, dorsal level 0–1	AP/Joosten
13.29	Leg, dorsal level 2–3	AP/Joosten
13.30	Leg, dorsal level 4–5	AP/Joosten
13.31	Leg, medial level 0–1	AP/Joosten
13.32	Leg, medial level 2–3	AP/Joosten
13.33	Leg, medial level 4–5	AP/Joosten
13.34	Leg, medial level 6	AP/Joosten
13.35	Leg, lateral level 0–1	AP/Joosten
13.36	Leg, lateral level 2–3	AP/Joosten
13.37	Leg, lateral level 4–5	AP/Joosten
13.38	Foot, anterior and posterior	AP/Joosten
13.39	Foot, medial	AP/Joosten
13.40	Foot, lateral	AP/Joosten
13.41	Foot, superior, plantar level 0	AP/Joosten
14.1	Generic joint type descriptions	AP
14.2	Neck joint	AP/Joosten
14.3	Shoulder joint architecture	AP/Joosten
14.4	Elbow architecture	AP/Joosten
14.5	Hand joint architecture	AP/Joosten
14.6	Hip architecture	AP/Joosten

Author's Notes

This book is designed to be application-independent. Therefore, no application specific terms will be used, and no specific applications will be referenced. All information contained in this book is applicable to the type of projects described, regardless of which application is used to generate the elements.

This book is the second volume of a two-volume pair of books. It is assumed that readers of this book are familiar with terms and concepts described in volume one, *Computer Graphics for Artists: An Introduction*.

Andrew Paquette

3D3/Environments

Part I
Introduction

Filmmakers pay dearly for appropriate backdrops. The difference between shooting New York City on location and making a set is enormous. When it is not possible to film on location, filmmakers do their best to recreate the location they would have used if it could be done. They go to great lengths to obtain as much information as they can about the target site so that they can recreate it elsewhere. After they have the reference, they hire skilled craftsmen to build the sets. This is not an inexpensive process. Sets for the movie *Titanic* were a large part of the 200 million dollar budget.

You may wonder why, when so much is spent to hire expensive actors, even more money is sometimes used to pay for what is simply a background against which the primary action is played. The reason is that these backgrounds create a context for the action. This context enriches the story by making it believable and interesting. If this weren't true, filmmakers could simply edit screen tests of actors reading their lines before a blank wall.

When a computer graphics (CG) artist is asked to make an environment, then, it is of no small importance. It is also no small job. Environments, whether they are for film, television, advertising, print, or video games, tend to be far more complex than any characters that inhabit them. There are tricks used to design simple sets with no great loss of atmosphere, but as technology evolves, demand is increasing for ever more realistic environments. For these new demands, many of the old solutions are inadequate. It is still true that design can reduce the amount of required labor, but now the design must meet a higher standard.

Environments come in three primary types: landscape, architecture, and infrastructure. Each of these has an easily recognized generic CG solution that is highly unrealistic, but so common that it has for some people become an acceptable substitute for the real thing. It is acceptable, however, only if every single thing contained in the presentation is designed in exactly the same way. So, if a city is laid out as a perfect grid (a rarity in real urban planning), buildings are all strictly rectangular (another rarity), and every tree is a perfect sphere sitting on top of a brown cylinder (only seen in topiary) they will look fine as long as they are never adjacent to a more realistic version of the same thing. The same is true of landscapes that are nothing more than a bunch of random bumps in a large polymesh.

Real environments are highly specific. Every shape is there for a reason. If you don't understand how an object is made, then how do you expect to remake it or simplify it? For some people it is difficult to assemble furniture without instructions. Imagine how much worse it is when you cannot even decide what type of tools must be used. For a CG artist to make a convincing landscape, building, or street layout, he has to understand the subject. He has to be able to see details that are essential components to an object's likeness, and understand how those details came to be there. In Part I of this book, you will learn to see these details, and what type of CG tools can be used to mimic their appearance. Most importantly, you will learn to think like an artist as you study your source material. You will learn to see it in layers, assembly steps, tools used, textural information, and lighting.

One problem posed by environments is that their complexity demands a much higher level of optimization than other elements of a scene. Despite lavish resources, even high-profile all-CG films like *Shrek* and *Ratatouille* optimize their environments. For real-time-rendered video games, the problem is much greater. For these products, environments must be both convincing and renderable at a high frame rate. This dictates a high level of optimization. Even so, from films to games, environments can be highly realistic, and in top-quality projects, they are totally convincing.

To achieve this level of quality, an artist needs to know far more than simply how to make a clean model. For serious environment building, an artist must be observant, efficient, and able to see the invisible tools behind how a landscape came to be structured as it is.

Welcome to 3D3, enjoy!

Andrew Paquette

Chapter 1
Real-World Terrain

Terrain is the ground upon which all things will rest in your CG environment. Your *terrain mesh*, depending on your project, may be the largest single object in your entire scene. Often, these objects have half a million or more polygons, hundreds of texture maps, and cover more area than any other object. Until recently, the terrain mesh type most often encountered in CG animation was either completely flat, as in fairly early CG animations, or full of unrealistic hills and valleys based on simple randomized height maps. More recently, terrain has become highly realistic.

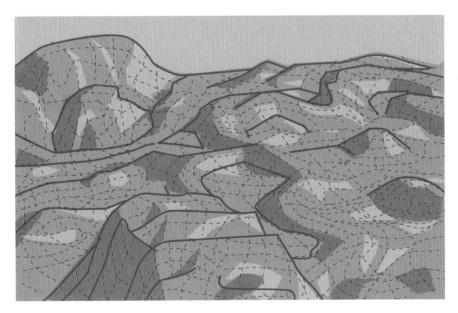

Fig. 1.1 An example of randomized terrain. Notice that it is three-dimensional, but does not convincingly represent realistic terrain

To make terrain of any kind – fantasy, realistic, abstract, or exaggerated – knowledge of how real terrain is shaped will help make your terrain more convincing (Fig. 1.1). Mountains, hills, valleys, deserts, jungles, and all other terrain-related formations have features unique to how they were formed. These features are like tool marks left behind by the formation process. It is by the presence or absence of these features that a terrain object is recognizable as belonging to a certain class.

The Grand Canyon is an excellent example of this. Most of the Grand Canyon's major features owe their appearance to one thing: The Colorado River. The Colorado River is the cutting tool that carved the Grand Canyon's distinctively deep canyons over many years of wearing away soft sandy rock. This is why the sides of the canyon are shaped like the sides of the riverbank almost a mile below the top of the canyon. The width varies along the height of the canyon, as the amount of water in the river has fluctuated over thousands or millions of years and succeeding seasons of rainfall have concentrated their erosive effect by being funneled into a progressively steeper channel.

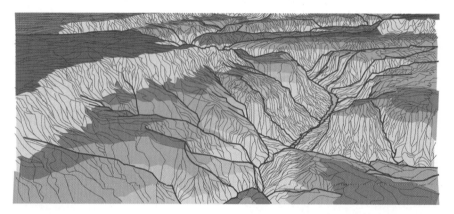

Fig. 1.2 At an average elevation of 6,500 ft, the Grand Canyon is one of the few plateaus on earth that is high enough for a river to carve out a mile-deep trench without reaching sea level

There is no need to follow every turn of the Colorado River through the Grand Canyon in order to make a convincing canyon terrain object, but if your canyon doesn't look as if it was built from the gradual wearing away of rock caused by water, or it doesn't start high enough above sea level to provide the raw material to be cut through, it won't be very convincing (Fig. 1.2).

Building terrain requires at least some knowledge of what terrain is and how it came to look the way it does. Without this, it is very difficult to replicate existing environments or to create convincing new ones. Terrain is a geological object, and for CG artists who want to build terrain, geology should be understood at least to the degree necessary to make sense of observed surface characteristics of real-world terrain.

Although water covers roughly 70% of the earth's surface, the surface itself is all land. The shape of the surface is based on conditions both above and below it. Geologic factors below the land cause it to move or change shape, and then erosion above ground changes its shape even more.

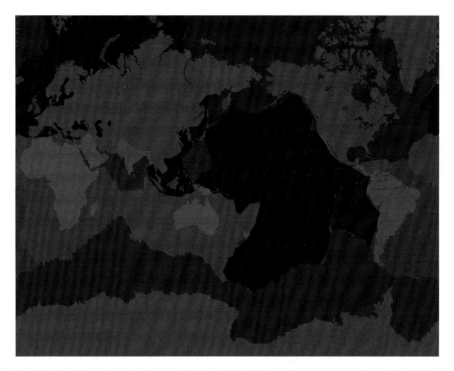

Fig. 1.3 Earth's continental plates and their major land formations are constantly moving. Notice how the boundaries of many land formations match that of continental plates. Earthquakes are common where plates collide

The Earth is divided into seven major *continental plates* and several smaller ones (Fig. 1.3). Each of the major plates is so large that several countries are located on top of each one. *Continental drift theory*, which is generally accepted as proven at this time, states that the major continental plates are constantly moving due to geologic factors existing beneath the Earth's crust. When they move, continental plates come into contact with each other. When they do, there are three possibilities: The plates will push up new mountains from both sides of the contact ridge as a *transform fault*, the plates will move in opposite directions along a common edge in a *strike-slip* fault, or one plate will push under the other from either side, causing the denser of the two plates to *subduct*, or push under, the other one. This is called *subduction*.

Volcanic events are typically centered along *subduction zones*, where magma and other molten material from below the Earth's crust finds a path to the surface through gaps or weaknesses in the rock above it. Sometimes it is ejected under great pressure, and other times it leaks out slowly at low pressure without erupting. In both cases, new rock is formed. Depending on the length of time involved and the quantity of ejected material, this type of volcanic activity can result in very tall mountains, though pressure ridges usually cause the tallest mountains when two continental plates collide. The Himalayan mountains are the tallest such pressure ridge in the world (Fig. 1.4).

Fig. 1.4 The Indian plate (in blue) presses against the Eurasian plate (in red), causing both to rise. Notice the combination effect of pressure and water. One creates the mountain; the other modifies its shape

The more active San Andreas Fault in California is a strike-slip fault located west of the Sierra Nevada mountain range. The Sierras, like most mountains, were built as a combination of subduction, pressure ridges, strike-slip earthquakes, glaciation, and volcanism (Fig. 1.5). Volcano activity is thought to be among the more recent of geologically significant events in this region, and provided much of the material required to increase the average elevation of the range by several thousand feet.

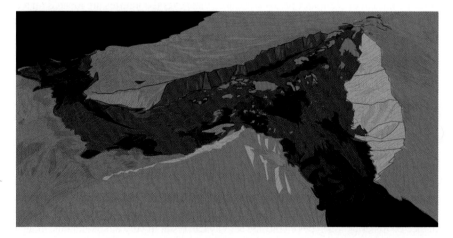

Fig. 1.5 This lava flow from Hawaii's Mauna Kea volcano cuts through less dense material and leaves a track, just like paint spilled from a bucket, and descends into the ocean on both sides of the mountain

Volcanic and continental plate collision events often cause earthquakes. Earthquakes cause secondary effects that are quite different in structure from the events that spawn them. Unlike a volcano, which creates mountains by ejecting liquid rock into a cone shape, or pressure ridges and subduction zones that press land into new positions by pushing them up or down, earthquakes send waves of force through the surface, with a variety of results. Earthquakes can cause any of the following to occur: sudden collapse of surface material along *fault lines*, tipping of rock formations, ripple effects where land is raised and lowered in alternating bands, and surface cracking, where land is separated along an area of greatest weakness.

A strike-slip earthquake causes land to move laterally in opposite directions. A *normal* earthquake causes a section of land to drop, while a *thrust* earthquake causes land to rise. Vertical movement produces the familiar effect of a land formation that appears to be tilted relative to its surroundings (Fig. 1.6). Horizontal movement can cause gaps and may split roads or other surface construction and move either side away from each other. The Great Sumatran-Andaman earthquake of 2004 was a *megathrust* earthquake. Its magnitude of 9.1–9.3 makes it the second largest earthquake ever recorded on a seismograph. The earthquake was so powerful that it caused about 10 m of lateral movement and between 4 and 5 m of vertical movement. (Keep these dimensions in mind if you ever intend to make a realistic animation of an earthquake.)

The geologic events described so far are all part of a process known as *mountain building*. The importance of mountain building to an artist, whether or not the entire mountain is ever built, is not to be underestimated. Mountain building creates the raw material that erosion sculpts into a final form. Without volcanoes, plate tectonics, earthquakes, and other factors that cause land to be produced or moved, there would be no material for erosion to act upon. With it, the endless variety of beautiful landscapes in the world becomes possible.

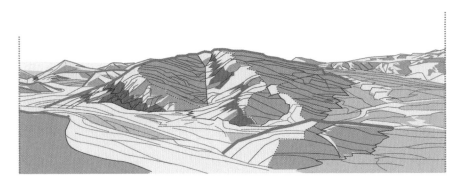

Fig. 1.6 The angle of tilt between the orange band of sedimentary rock and surrounding terrain indicates a past earthquake event

For artists, this information is not only useful for improving one's observations, but also as a resource for ideas. An environment might be more interesting if it shows cross-layering of earthquake events, particularly if combined with human artifacts.

Erosion

Erosion is a term that collectively describes a variety of natural forces that modify the shape of terrain. These forces act as sculpting tools on a terrain object. They cut material away from one location and deposit it somewhere else. What they cut away comes from preexisting material. Therefore, mountain building comes first, and erosion second.

Water may be the most powerful of all the erosion-related "tools" in nature's arsenal. One look at any hill or mountain is enough to justify this opinion, because they will all betray telltale signs of the passage of water over their surfaces. *Splash erosion* is when single drops of rainwater make contact with the ground, usually soil, and displace some quantity of soil from the force of impact. Other drops of water then carry the soil away. *Sheet erosion* is when a continuous sheet of water moves down a slope, carrying with it loose soil and rock.

Splash and sheet erosion are the first stage of water-based erosion for most mountains, because their action is required to create channels that direct water and eroded material into streams, rivers, and, if there is enough water, all the way to the sea.

Imagine it this way: Hot water is sprayed onto a cube of ice. An even distribution of warm precipitation collects on its topmost surface, but quickly settles into every small imperfection and enlarges the imperfections by causing them to melt at a greater rate than surrounding areas. The water will then pool and run over the edge of the cube, eventually wearing it away. When it runs down the sides of the cube, it will follow a path of least resistance. This path will leave marks characteristic of the passage of water etched into the face of the cube.

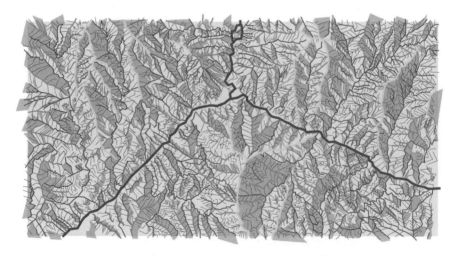

Fig. 1.7 Notice the distinctive Y-shaped branchings of these Cambodian mountain ranges. They are the most prominent structural feature of most mountains. Any artist who wants to build a convincing mountain must faithfully reproduce this effect

Because the water starts at the top of the cube and then moves downward, the greatest effect will be at the top. If the water is sprayed for a sufficient period of time, the cube will eventually be worn down to a triangular shape on either side. This is because the base of the ice cube is better protected than the top, and has less water striking it. If this ice cube were made of rock and earth instead of simple ice, differences in the composition of its elements will also cause variations in its shape. Heavier, denser objects will not be as easily moved as lighter objects, but might be more susceptible to fracture and gravity, especially if water combines with temperature extremes to cause cracking within large rock formations. The end result will be the same Y-shaped ridges we see in every mountain range, and V-shaped valley cross sections between each ridge (Fig. 1.7).

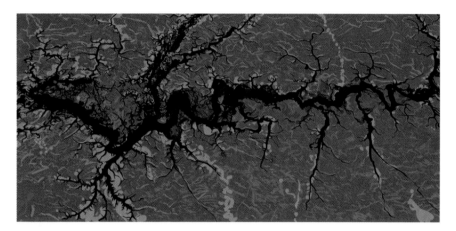

Fig. 1.8 Like the roots of a tree, the branchings of a river become gradually more diminutive the farther they are from the main trunk

As water flows towards the ocean, the volume of water in the flow generally increases. Water flows from smaller sources, and as they flow downhill, joins others and swell their size until they become large rivers with a large flow of water. Structurally, this causes the banks to gradually widen as more water enters the river.

All of the world's oceans form a single continuous saltwater body known as the world ocean. This ocean has a strong effect on land-altering weather such as hurricanes and cyclones, as well as directly eroding coastlines at sea level. If land along a coast is significantly higher than sea level, cliffs will form. Secondary erosion will then take place, subject to the cliff's material composition and ability to resist erosive forces. When the coastline is at or near sea level, beaches are formed as the ocean deposits sand suspended within it from other sources, notably particles carried to the ocean by rivers and streams (Fig. 1.8).

Ocean-related weather effects like cyclones and hurricanes do not always travel over land, but when they do, they can flatten everything in their path and cause severe flooding. Cyclones tend to cut through objects like a giant buzz saw and then redistribute the resulting fragments over large areas of land. The largest terrain-related impact of such an event is enhanced water- and wind-related erosion along the destruction path as well as property damage. Hurricane damage to terrain can be much more severe than cyclone damage, which, like tornadoes, has a stronger effect on property than terrain. Hurricanes are larger and less prone to suddenly disappear than a tornado or cyclone. Because of their larger size and greater quantity of rain content, both of which are more likely to cause flooding, terrain effects are more pronounced. Aerial photography of affected areas will show that cyclones can have an erratic destruction path, but hurricanes tend to travel directly across land until they either expend their energy or cut through to the other side. Either way, their path is clearly visible and continuous, though it may not be perfectly straight.

Fig. 1.9 When a valley glacier moves, it leaves meandering trails known as eskers behind. To either side of the esker is a buildup of debris called moraine. Both of these features significantly contribute to the shape of a glacial mountain. In this illustration, the pale violet paths are eskers

At high elevations, frozen water forms into glaciers. Because of their great mass, glaciers compact their ice into a denser form of ice known as glacial ice. Glacial ice can be identified by its characteristic blue color, a trait that results from high water-compaction levels and the very slight blue tint of water.

Glaciers are powerful erosive tools. As they either build in mass or melt (or both), they can slide down a mountain, carving it as it progresses downward. When a glacier creates a passage through a mountainous environment, it typically follows a meandering U-shaped path and pushes heaps of sediment to either side of its forward moving front, much as a boat casts spray from either side of its bow as it travels over water. Sediment deposited in this manner is called moraine and can be identified by the fact that it forms a ridge along either side of a glaciated path, also known as an esker (Fig. 1.9).

The temperature-related erosive impact of a glacier is not small. Even if the glacier is immobile, it can still cause a great deal of erosion simply by causing the nearby rock to alternately freeze and thaw. This causes long vertical cracks to form in rock, and eventually leads to gravity-assisted erosion when these cracks become large enough to cause rock on the weaker side of the crack to collapse and fall.

The primary source of erosion producing water in the world is from rain and the oceans. Between the two lies all the world's land. Rain falls first on the highest points and then races to the oceans, carrying part of the mountains with them as sediment. Sediment has a tendency to settle, and then become compacted into sedimentary rock. Sedimentary rock looks like striped bands, and are almost always nearly perfectly horizontal. When this is not true, it is generally because of disruption to a horizontal band by earthquake. The range of disruption varies a great deal, from a simple tilt to a writhing snakelike curve.

When you see sedimentary zones in a landscape, it means that a high volume of water was once present there, even if that is no longer true. The deserts of Arizona and Utah display ample signs of having once been entirely submerged then lifted due to belowground activity, both volcanic and tectonic.

The effect water has on an object's shape is dependent on the material the object is made of. Soil will crumble more easily than granite, composite rock will have an uneven bumpy wear pattern, and very hard rock may crack and split when stressed but be highly resistant to water and wind.

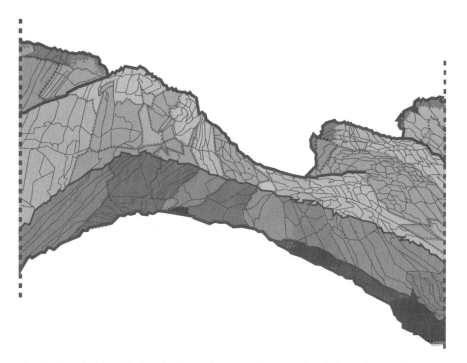

Fig. 1.10 Arch, New Mexico; fragile sandstone erodes easily in wind, causing weaknesses in rock that in turn allows gravity to pull large sections out of a formation. In this primarily wind-created arch, gravity has played a part, as is evident by looking at the underside of the arch, from which large blocks of stone have fallen. Notice that the shape of the underside of the arch is formed of several overlapping concave sections

Wind, though invisible, has a substantial impact on the shape of any land it passes over. Strictly speaking, it is nothing more than the movement of air. But it works in much the same way as water. At sufficient speeds, wind is capable of striking and lifting particulate matter from one object and then carrying it to another, where an erosive impact occurs and creates more particles to be carried elsewhere. The overall effect of wind-related erosion is the smoothing of rock, as if by gigantic sheets of sandpaper. Unlike gravity erosion, which tends to cause sharp borders around concave sections of rock, wind erosion causes smoothly flowing borders across rocks (Fig. 1.10).

The tendency with wind, beyond smoothing surfaces it comes into contact with, is to flatten. In areas with very strong wind-related erosion, the landscape is generally flatter than areas where water erosion is more prominent. Where the Grand Canyon is a good example of water erosion, nearby Monument Valley has many excellent examples of wind erosion. In Monument Valley, large wind-created buttes and spires stand surrounded by vast plains of wind-driven gravel and pebbles.

In arid regions, wind is particularly powerful because there is very little to impede its force. In deserts, entire mountains are worn down to dunes. This is because vegetation acts as an effective *windbreak*, blocking and disrupting a wind before it ever reaches its target or reducing its impact significantly when it does. Deserts have very little vegetation to protect soil and rock, and also contain the most striking examples of wind erosion available on the planet (Fig. 1.11).

Wind is capable of reducing entire mountains to nothing more than a great shifting sea of sand. Although rare, all of the world's major deserts contain areas dotted with thousands of sand dunes, the most extreme form of wind erosion.

Fig. 1.11 Unlike other types of terrain, sand dunes change their shape rapidly and often. They cannot be counted on to remain in place for long, and only the most prominent features have any longevity

Erosion requires gravity. Without it, water does not travel from higher to lower elevations, wind will not deposit sediment on successively lower surfaces, glaciers would not move, lava would not flow down, avalanches and landslides would not occur, and rocks split by extreme cold would not fall. Keep this in mind if you are designing an environment that either does not have gravity, or that has a different level of gravitational effect. Erosion is more powerful the stronger the pull of gravity is, and vice versa.

Gravity erosion is also called mass wasting. Mass wasting is the downward movement of rock and soil, caused by the attraction of gravity. Depending on the type of landscape in question, you may see strong signs of mass wasting, or none at all. Generally, limited elevation change over a large area would indicate low incidence of mass wasting, but it is also possible that a broad plain at approximately the same elevation is itself the result of mass wasting.

Fig. 1.12 Butte, Monument Valley, Utah. The gradual buildup of fallen rocks around this butte creates a debris skirt at its base. The result is a 3D feature well known in the American southwest, a butte emerging from a wide base of loose rock and boulders. Over time, the butte will be reduced to spires, then to gravel

Like water, rock (and everything else) will fall or roll until it reaches the lowest point it can reach before its passage is obstructed. Rock is more easily blocked than water, making it far less mobile, and limits its spread more than water. Nevertheless, rock falls can cover very large areas of land (Fig. 1.12).

Strong gravity-related terrain modification is visible in mountainous regions, where fallen rock accumulations are found at the base of steep elevations. It is also visible in other, less obvious places. Mudslides are caused partly by gravity and partly by temporarily enhanced fluidity due to infusion of water into soil. Another common effect is a *slump*, where land will spontaneously drop towards a lower point, causing a crescent-shaped ridge on the upslope end of the collapse, and an accumulation of soil at the bottom.

The effects of erosion described here are not meant to be comprehensive, but to enhance your observation skills as a terrain artist. Keep this material in mind the next time you design a terrain object, and you may be surprised how much more interesting the result is.

Scale

As it relates to environments, scale is very important to understand. Unlike architecture, vehicles, and the props we use in daily life, our planet and the terrain it is made of are not human scale. Compared to the scale of human needs and human activity, terrain is vast. Where a human can be accommodated luxuriously in 500 m² of living space, most landscape features extend unchanged for thousands or even tens of thousands of meters.

A typical "steep" slope in an environment is a grade of about 6%, or 6 ft of vertical elevation for every 100 ft of lateral movement. This would hardly be noticed at the human scale of a house or an office building, but it can tax the engine of an automobile or train. The reason something so small can have such a strong effect is because of the overall size of the slope being so much greater than something that could be manufactured at a human scale (Fig. 1.13).

CG artists, being human, tend to frequently underestimate the size of terrain features.

Fig. 1.13 Mesa, Prescott, Arizona. This distinctive landscape is convincing partly because the level of dimension contrast is correct

Dimension contrast is the degree of difference between any two or more dimensions. A 1-m length compared to a kilometer is a high degree of contrast, but 2 mm compared to three is not as great. In terrain models, dimension contrast tends to be strong. A ridge of steep hills or mountains can suddenly punctuate plains that extend for hundreds of miles. Mountains may have bases measured in the hundreds of kilometers, but terminate in ridges that might be only a few meters across.

Sensitivity to the size of terrain elements is an important skill for a CG artist to develop. When terrain models are exaggerated, unless carefully controlled by a consistent design or rule set, they will not be convincing. Sometimes an artist will want to edit a model to create local changes on a scale similar to characters that inhabit the environment. This tends to result in too many surface modifications per meter, particularly elevation changes. An object built like this will have wild terrain bumps of unbelievable dimensions located unnaturally close to each other.

This type of error may be related to an artist's level of familiarity with topographic, as opposed to flat, maps. Most people, including artists, are less familiar with topographic maps and contour maps. Instead, less expensive and more easily obtained flat maps that contain information on roads and boundaries, but very little elevation information is their only reference point. Regardless of the cause, terrain that is built without sufficient regard for scale will always be less convincing than it could have been.

So far, this chapter has described relatively large-scale terrain effects: continental drift, earthquakes, volcanic events, glacial erosion, and large-scale water and wind erosion. This is fine for terrain in the distance, but what about terrain that is close to your camera? This must also be represented, if for no other reason but to provide a plausible bridge from near to far terrain elements. Without it, your terrain might appear as empty as a painted billiard ball.

Fig. 1.14 Rocks and boulders such as these can add tremendous realism to a scene

Near detail then, although it might be built separately from the primary ground surface, is still part of your terrain. The kind of near detail you may be inclined to build will be close up models of rocks, boulders, hillsides, and anything else that is visible at less than 30 m or so. Slumps, small creeks, minor changes in terrain height, gullies, crevices, and many other features can all be important additions to your model (Fig. 1.14).

To build detail, both near and far, requires an ability to distinguish between different elements. When you observe terrain reference, you should be capable of tracing a boundary around each distinctive feature of the object. If there is a pressure ridge, you should be able to delimit its boundaries. If it has a slump against its side, you should be able to identify that and draw a boundary around it, and so on for every other independent feature. This is important because features that are either of different types, spawned by different events, or that are location distinct, will have self-contained characteristics that identify them as different from their surroundings (Fig. 1.15). If surrounded by a border and dealt with as separate objects, the structural contrast of these sections will be enhanced, along with the realism of your model.

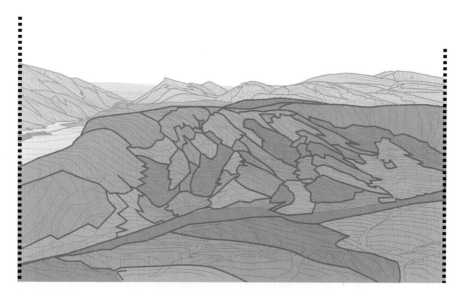

Fig. 1.15 Each area outlined with a heavy line may be treated as a separate object for the sake of understanding structural differences unique to distinct geological events

Once you have learned to recognize terrain characteristics crucial to creating a likeness of that terrain, you are ready to begin building it in CG. Until then, the best you can hope for is a clean model that doesn't look right.

Chapter 2
CG Terrain

Fig. 2.1 The problem with terrain is that no matter how close or how far away you are, there is always more detail (Copyright Bionatics)[1]

Real-world terrain is so complicated that there is no practical way to reconstruct it with full fidelity in CG. Much of the work of building terrain models is optimizing the model and textures for rendering, either for a real-time render engine or pre-rendered frames. The first step is to know what the model is supposed to look like, as discussed in the previous chapter, and the second is to optimize what you see into something your renderer can handle (Fig. 2.1).

---

[1] IGN Paris authorization 2006CUCB0235 - all rights reserved

The first question you need to answer is whether the terrain will be built for a real-time renderer (RTR) or be pre-rendered as a series of individual frames. The type of object you build will be radically different depending on which type of renderer you select. Objects created to be rendered as frames have fewer limitations imposed on them than objects built for a real-time renderer. Objects built for real-time rendering, particularly the all-important and extremely large terrain object, must be carefully optimized to work in your game engine. This doesn't mean that objects designed to be rendered as frames don't have to be optimized, but the requirements are less strict and based more on aesthetic than technical requirements.

History of Terrain in CG

Large terrain objects were a rarity in the early days of CG, and many productions had no terrain at all. Instead, games took place entirely indoors (Fig. 2.2), and film FX crews did not use CG to represent environments. Instead, they used CG only for props and occasional characters. As computing technology improved, the complexity of CG production increased. First, we got the dinosaurs of *Jurassic Park*, and then we got the fur from polar bears in the famous Coca-Cola polar bear advertisements by Rhythm & Hues. After this, hair was introduced in *Final Fantasy, the Spirits Within*. The first commercially appealing example of CG trees came in *Toy*

Fig. 2.2 The first fully 3D engines used simplified interiors, sometimes going so far as to make exteriors into interiors by enclosing them with polygons, as in this image, to reduce the number of distant polygons taken into account during rendering

Story. As each of these innovations was introduced, they were immediately absorbed into every other production and became commonplace. More recently, full-blown architectural environments have been included in live action/CG features like *Spider-man.* Fully realized, high-resolution, large-scale terrain models however, have only recently been introduced in films like *Shrek 3, Cars,* and *Ratatouille.*

Videogames have been using fully 3D environment models (mostly indoors) at least since the release of the first *Tomb Raider* game, and used simpler versions of them to represent large outdoor spaces before that. However, the spaces represented were always tightly confined and heavily tiled with repeating textures. Even a highly optimized terrain mesh can be so complicated that the amount of real-world space it is meant to represent must be kept to a minimum.

As the hardware technology these games ran on improved, terrain meshes became larger and larger. At first, you had a series of interconnected interior spaces, as in *Tomb Raider.* In those early 3D games, you would occasionally have a glimpse of the outdoors, like in *Banjo Kazooie* or *Spyro the Dragon,* but these were glimpses of very small sections of terrain. Later games showed more and more. *Halo, Medal of Honor,* and *Assassin's Creed* are all examples of games that contain what appears to be fairly complete terrain. It is not immediately noticeable how much is missing from these environments, but they are highly optimized. Racing games seem to show even more terrain, but carefully optimize how much is built, as opposed to simply indicated, by ensuring that the player's camera cannot leave the race track. New render engines however, are now capable of rendering truly enormous landscapes in real time.

Currently, large-scale terrain meshes can convincingly represent over $400\,km^2$ of territory in real time. This is so much terrain that if you were to simply drive a real-time vehicle around its perimeter at a $100\,km$ an hour, it would take $16\,hours$ to complete the circuit, and you wouldn't have seen any of the interior of the terrain mesh!

This increased rendering capacity means that terrain modelers will not only have to work with much larger models, but they must also build them to a higher standard of quality and optimization (Fig. 2.3). So, the second question you must ask yourself is this: "How much terrain needs to be in my model?"

Your decision should be based on what is meant to appear in the scene, regardless of how the scene is going to be optimized. This is just the first step of the optimization process, so you needn't worry about later steps now. To begin, you must have some idea of what you need. This might be in the form of storyboards, *animatics* (a crudely animated storyboard), or a game design document that provides specifications for the environment.

The specifications should look something like this:

  (i) Close up interior, house
 (ii) Exterior, road outside of house (village seen to either side)
(iii) Castle on hill
 (iv) Castle moat
  (v) Interior, castle

Fig. 2.3 A forest of quads can be very detailed if the landscape is large enough (Copyright Bionatics)[2]

Shot List

Using this *shot list*, you should be able to figure out what must be present in your terrain. The list above does not provide any information on what the specific items look like. You should have an idea of this from production sketches on your project, or if you are inventing it, you should commit your design to paper before starting. If your environment is meant to be realistic, you may want to explore a globe to see what type of terrain you want. This is the "big circle" moment, when you take a big marker and draw a big outline on a map (or draw your own map) and say, "I want this."

---

[2] *IGN Paris authorization 2006CUCB0235 – all rights reserved*

Optimization

Once you have selected what you must see in order to get the shots you want for your animation, you should decide which parts can be faked, and which parts must be built as a fully realized 3D terrain. Faking terrain can be done in a number of different ways, the most popular of which are these:

- Background mattes (BG mattes, or just "mattes")
  - These are backdrop paintings or photographs, usually static, but sometimes attached to geometry
  - Sometimes these are renderings of CG geometry
- Billboards
  - A polygon mesh with a texture map, usually in combination with other billboards in different locations for a *parallax effect*. The map will have an alpha channel for transparency to eliminate the silhouette of the polygons it is attached to.
- Texture maps
  - Bump maps, displacement maps, and normal maps

Real-time graphics have user-controlled cameras. This gives the user enhanced ability to view your environment from unanticipated angles. For this reason, environments built for real-time engines are optimized differently than for pre-rendered output. One of the more obvious differences is that real-time geometry is less likely to contain gaps than pre-rendered geometry. Real-time objects are usually built as solid. If they have gaps, they are blocked by something else, or the missing polygons are well outside the *active camera range* (Fig. 2.4).

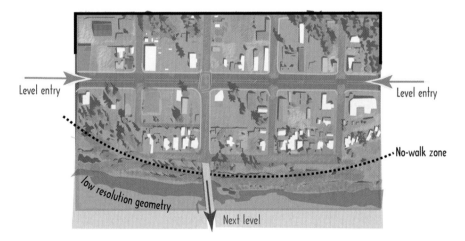

Fig. 2.4 In this diagram, a significant section of the environment is identified as outside of the walk zone, and therefore as low-resolution geometry. Making decisions like this before geometry is made can save considerable time

Real Time/Pre-rendered Graphics

For pre-rendered graphics, you do not need to worry about a player peeking behind objects and spotting missing geometry. You may, therefore, build only those things that are visible to your camera. You can take this to ridiculous extremes by eliminating objects, or parts of objects, that are just barely outside of camera range. If you do this, you must be very careful to finalize camera animation before you optimize your model or the missing items may become visible problems. Another common optimization technique with a flaw is eliminating polygons that face away from the camera but are within your frame. The reason this can be a problem is that even if they are not themselves visible, they may contribute to the lighting in your scene, or be reflected in something else that is visible or contributes to the lighting.

After you have determined what you want to be able to see in your environment, you need to define either *active areas*, or the active camera range. Either option amounts to the same thing: you need to know where the camera can go, whether it is free ranging or not, and how far it can go. An active area, also known as a legal *walk* zone, is an area defined by *flagged* polygons that designates where a player character can walk. This defines where the camera can move as well, and will tell you exactly what you need to know to construct your environment.

For this, it is a good idea to create an environment map. Your map should define the entire border of your terrain and everything it contains. You should have all major locations marked and named, and active areas marked. With this done, you can analyze your document to find optimization opportunities.

Keep in mind that when terrain is rendered, its border may be visible. If it is a square, as many artists unwisely like to make it, the corners of the square will be visible from some angles (Fig. 2.5). If you would like to disguise this (in most cases, you should), you may want to try one of the following:

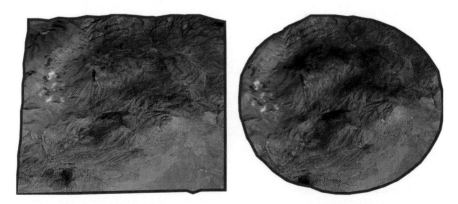

Fig. 2.5 A circular terrain border, as shown here, eliminates corners visible on the horizon in renders

- Use a circular terrain border

This will eliminate any corners and provide a consistent horizon from any view. It may also be visibly bent. This can be desirable because it imitates horizon curvature, but if the scale of your model is small, it will appear exaggerated.

- Use an irregular terrain border

This is not an uncommon solution for both games and pre-rendered graphics. An irregular border will also hide the edges of your terrain, but you must be careful both of its shape and how it blends with background elements

- Raise the edge of your terrain above that of your active area, preferably in the shape of mountains or other natural obstructions.

This is not always the most convincing solution because some environments require a view of the horizon. If yours does not because it is a Swiss village in the Alps for instance, then this will work for you.

Reference acquisition can be the most difficult job for a terrain artist. First, most artists will need *bare earth* elevation measurements that eliminate elevation "noise" from trees, buildings, and other ground cover. The data is known as a *digital elevation map* (DEM) (Fig. 2.6) and can be purchased from various vendors. Some DEM databases are free, and if you are lucky, they represent the kind of terrain you want. Acquiring this data can also be done with various freely available planet-viewing software packages, but it can be tedious to use because you have to sample elevation values and then somehow transfer the data to paper and then back to your model.[3]

Fig. 2.6 A digital elevation map (DEM) is responsible for this 3D model of the volcano Maat Mons on Venus (Image courtesy NASA/JPL)

---

[3] Recently, some software vendors have included import/export tools to acquire GIS data from various Internet sources to create topographic models

Digital Elevation Maps

A more old-fashioned but perfectly reliable method is to use *contour maps* of the territory you are interested in and then translate this into a CG model. Sometimes these maps will also provide some information on terrain composition, but this is not always the case.

It is easy to measure terrain elevation from a flat surface, but because the earth is spherical, it is incorrect to do so. Surface curvature is not easily detected at near distances, and beyond about 100 km not only is the curvature visible as a curved horizon, but orientation of surface objects also becomes clearly affected by the curvature of the earth (Fig. 2.7).

Fig. 2.7 A gently curving horizon may be used to telescope great distances and to hide edge-of-the-earth boundaries. If the curvature is pronounced, the effect is cartoony (Model courtesy of Andrius Drevinskas and Julian Fries of team Sorrowstead)

Even if your terrain represents a smaller area, you may want to consider starting all of your elevation measurements from a semi-hemispherical base. This will in most cases add a subtle degree of realism. If this effect is overdone it will first betray a cartoon influence, and then simply appear extremely distorted, so do be careful how you apply this technique (Fig. 2.8).

Sometimes it is desirable to compress space in order to reduce overall poly count. If you want distant mountains but do not want to make them out of billboards, nor do you want to extend your terrain for many miles, what you can do is compress the space your terrain occupies. To do this, you can create concentric rings that define the scale of objects within a certain distance range of the center. For each successive ring, you can change the scale. If you are consistent about how you apply the scale changes, and the rings are spaced to match, it would look something like this:

1st ring: 0–50 m; 1:1 scale   4th ring: 351–750 m; 8:1 scale
2nd ring: 51–150 m; 2:1 scale   5th ring: 751–1,550 m; 16:1 scale
3rd ring: 151–350 m; 4:1 scale   6th ring: 1,551–3.1 km; 32:1 etc.

Fig. 2.8 Natural terrain features, such as the river in this city, affect where housing can be built, and where it is desirable to build. The highways affect the way fields are divided

Space may be compressed a great deal in this way. If you elect to use this method, you will probably also want to build from a hemispherical or spherical base, to show the horizon curve because you will be able to easily represent extremely distant objects, including the horizon.

Land Use Maps, Texturing

A *land use map* defines regions to be filled with a certain type of object or activity. An example of this might be to show farming activity near a small city, as traversed by a highway. Examination of a map of this type will tell an artist what goes where, but will go several steps further and also define optimization measures to be taken for each object. For instance, will the camera enter any buildings? If not, are interiors necessary for any buildings? Buildings with transparent windows visible to the camera might need interiors. These buildings might be described differently from those that do not require an interior treatment. Here are some of the questions you might ask, to assist in determining how to describe the elements for your basic terrain model (leaving aside architecture and landscape for the time being):

What is the distance to camera, at its closest, of this element? Stratify this based on fixed distances. The greater the distance, the more optimized the object can be (Fig. 2.9).

Will this object be animated? If so, detail essential to its animation may not be omitted.

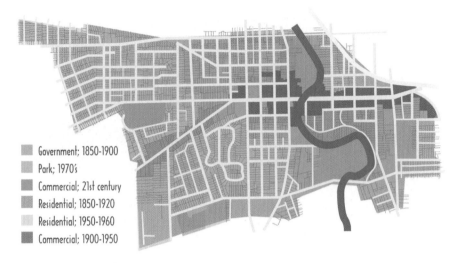

Government; 1850-1900
Park; 1970's
Commercial; 21st century
Residential; 1850-1920
Residential; 1950-1960
Commercial; 1900-1950

Fig. 2.9 A land use plan, like this one, can be a useful planning aid when designing your environment. It can answer global questions about your set, instead of looking at each building individually

Does the detail represent a geologically distinct event? If so, consider using the same optimization treatment for all similar portions of the terrain.

Does this object contain detail that may be adequately conveyed with texture maps?

What kind of maps? At a great distance, the effect of surface-distorting maps may be less visible than color maps. This distinction is important to make in the planning stages of a terrain object because of the strong effect it has on later results.

Must the object be built in 3D, or is it just as effective as a BG matte or billboard?

Is it close enough to the camera to warrant a high level of detail both in geometry and mapping?

You should have a fair idea how objects in your terrain will be built based on your map design for the terrain. Some artists, and some projects, will opt for using the same resolution for everything, regardless of camera distance, but this is a minority solution. The purpose is to provide animators and renderers the greatest possible flexibility for their jobs, but it is also extremely expensive to do.

Procedural solutions,[4] or solutions that are automatically calculated based on parameters provided by artists, can have a very high level of detail throughout, but discard details as soon as the camera is beyond a certain range, and recalculate lower resolution detail as a stand-in when this happens (Fig. 2.10).

---

[4]Procedural solutions are heavily dependent on custom software, and often require some programming knowledge to use properly.

Fig. 2.10 This landscape from *Landjuweel, the game* is made primarily with the use of a small number of blended tiling textures (Team HARR/Lennart Hillen. With permission)

Title Sets

One very popular solution for artists engaged in constructing terrain is the use of *tile sets*, or groups of tilable textures, usually square, that can be placed beside each other to create a wide variety of patterns out of a comparatively small number of tiles. When done well, these are nearly indistinguishable from a natural arrangement of texturable elements. 3D elements may also be tiled in this way (Figs. 2.11).

For the simple purpose of imitating surface detail too fine to be represented polygonally, normal maps have become very popular. Once too computationally heavy for common use, these maps are increasingly important, particularly in games.

Unlike a displacement map, which is used to calculate the height of surfaces based on gray scale information, normal maps use rgb data to calculate normal orientation. This allows for a far more complex surface definition than offered in the single-axis displacement model (Fig. 2.12).

Creating normal maps requires the creation of both a high- and low-resolution version of your object. More correctly, it requires a target object, whose texture coordinates will be used as the basis for the normal map, and an origin object from which surface information will be taken. The origin object is high resolution, and the target object is low resolution. You then must render the map by selecting the objects and invoking your application's normal map render tool.

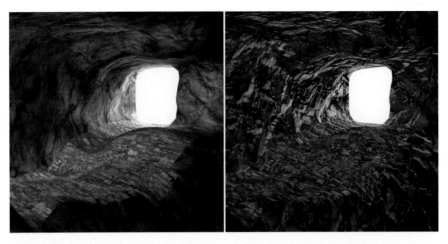

Fig. 2.11 A cave rendered without normal maps and with normal maps (Courtesy Arno Schmitz)

Fig. 2.12 Buildings from the game Gears of War, with heavy and beautiful use of normal maps (Copyright © 1998–2008, Epic Games, Inc. All rights reserved)[5]

The end result is calculated for you, and will not easily be edited by hand. This means that if you want to be sure your map is tilable, you have to be careful to make tilable geometry to begin with. Trying to modify a normal map after your renderer generates it can be very difficult.

Although displacement maps are less commonly used today in favor of normal maps, they are still used, as are bump maps. Both require only single channel images and so are a great deal less demanding of memory resources and CPU bandwidth, and both are calculated more quickly. This is only a meaningful difference when a large number of maps are involved, or maps of exceedingly high resolution, but bump and displacement maps still have a place in terrain models.

[5]Epic, Epic Games, Unreal, the "Powered by Unreal Technology" logo, the Circle-U logo, and Gears of War are trademarks or registered Trademarks of Epic Games, Inc. in the United States of America and elsewhere.

Sometimes, a single axis of projection is all that is needed. Also, adding a bump map to a normal map, particularly if not always applied to the same UV set, can create an interference filter to break up any visible tiling. The same may be done with color maps to further obscure tiling. This is desirable because tiling is unnatural, and will compromise realism.

If you want the textures you make to fit properly, you will have to design the triangulation layout of your object to match. Because texture maps are always rectangular, a topological limitation of their definition, your terrain should be broken up in such a way that it can accommodate that shape. If you intend to use a set of tiling maps, you must ensure that your terrain is broken into contiguous quadrilaterals, preferably matching the aspect ratio of the maps you intend to use on them.

Tiling texture sets are the primary reason for high poly counts in terrain objects. Although the shape of most terrain is often enough to justify the poly count, even a completely flat terrain object will usually be broken into hundreds of thousands of quads, to make the best use of either procedural or tiling textures. Think of each quad as a picture frame for your texture maps. Within each frame, you may rotate or flip your map to create up to 16 variants for each tile. For your tiles to work properly though, they must be designed well. If they are designed well, most viewers will not be able to find the seams between textures, and probably won't have any idea they are looking at hundreds of small square maps (Fig. 2.13).

Fig. 2.13 In this terrain, polygons are a little less than a meter square (Image courtesy of Team HARR, Lennart Hillen)

A set of texture tiles does not have to be interchangeable at every angle with every other tile, but every tile should tile on all four sides with one or more maps. Every map should represent every detail you wish to represent in your terrain. For example, you may want to have several different maps to represent different sections of a road. Some could be muddy, others full of puddles, and some dry. In other places it might curve out of the frame at a 60° angle, or in another place at 45°. All of these variations must be represented so that you may create every tile configuration that you need (Fig. 2.14).

Fig. 2.14 These three maps are together responsible for all of the terrain in the previous illustration (Images courtesy Team HARR, Lennart Hillen)

For purposes of organization, tiles may be divided into the following categories:

- One material Corner
- Two or more materials/blended
- Angle
- Straight

The fewer materials represented in each tile, the more flexible the tile will be. For borders between irregularly shaped materials like grass and mud, *blend tiles* are needed. A blend tile defines the edge between two materials, whether hard or soft, and disrupts the straight-edged pattern made by polygon borders.

One method to blend tiles is to create a *blend map*. This map blends maps based on color values contained within it. This method may be used in combination with custom tiling (Fig. 2.15).

Colors in each tile should not contain *high contrast (HC) adjacent pixels* unless they are a specific requirement. HC adjacent pixels cause noise patterns in renderings that are both distracting and unrealistic. To avoid them, work within a carefully defined hue and tone range, and do not sharpen or otherwise manipulate the image in such a way that contrast is increased.

When you are happy with your tile set and the geometry it will be mapped to, it is time to apply the tiles. Doing so can be time-consuming, depending on the number of individual quads that must be mapped. Just like laying tile in a bathroom, the more tiles there are, the longer it will take. For terrain objects, you may want to

Fig. 2.15 On the left is an image of a blend map projected onto the terrain it controls. On the right is the result of the blend map; blended tiled textures, with the tiling pattern effectively disrupted by the blend map (Images courtesy of Team HARR, Lennart Hillen)

introduce a certain amount of randomness to speed up the process, but within carefully defined limits. One way to do this is to trace out border areas that cannot be random, and then fill the interior of each border with the same tile. After assigning the maps, you can randomly select polygons and modify the orientation of their UVs to adjust the overall mapping. Depending on the tilability of your maps, this method can work for large sections of terrain (Fig. 2.16).

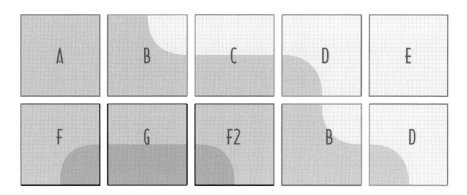

Fig. 2.16 Of the ten tiles represented here, seven are unique, two are direct copies of others in the set, and one is a copy that has been reversed. The tiles are designed so that each edge (tile) will match up with at least one other tile. Edges that are tilable are highlighted in the same color

You may want to build sections of terrain that are tilable in 3D, like hillsides, caves, or other natural features. If you do, the objects should be positioned in such a way that the tiling effect is not clear to the viewer. If the tiled sections of terrain are large enough, their repeated use may be disguised, though usually a change in orientation or displacement from similar objects is required.

Terrain geometry is the floor of your world. Everything sits on it or is contained by it. It is where most shadows land after the lights have been flipped on. Terrain provides context, atmosphere, realism, and even beauty to your scene. By itself, without anything added to it, it can be very interesting. Most contemporary projects do require more, a great deal more. After building terrain, the next step is to add the trees and other plants; next stop, digital gardening.

Chapter 3
Plant Life

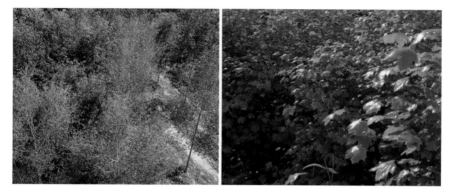

Fig. 3.1 In these two renders, the complexity of each scene is staggering because of the vegetation. No matter how much you limit your view, or expand it, there are ample opportunities to fill your screen with millions of triangles (Images by Martin Hinrichs, courtesy of Fryrender)

The movie *Toy Story* introduced the world to the first convincing fully CG trees. At the time, they were truly amazing. Any given tree in the movie had about 10,000 leaves, and any street had 600,000 leaves on the trees standing on either side of it. Despite the large number of details, it wasn't *natural* detail, but a highly optimized approximation. Later movies, like *Shrek 3*, had much more detail, and it was optimized as well.

A single tree can contain enough detail to keep a CG artist busy for years (Fig. 3.1). Optimization, then, is a requirement for any artist who wants to build models of plants in a reasonable period of time. To do this, a real plant can be used as a reference, but what are you going to pay attention to? Most plants have so many parts that it is difficult to know where to begin. Will you try to rebuild it leaf by leaf, or will you use your observation skills to figure out how the plant grows? If you do the latter, you will not need to make as many observations as you would otherwise, and the end result will be just as convincing, even if it is not an exact representation of

A. Paquette, *Computer Graphics for Artists II: Environments and Characters,*
© Springer-Verlag London Limited 2009

a specific plant. Instead, think of plants in generic terms, as species with specific traits rather than individuals constructed of specific details.

To understand a plant as a species, you must understand your subject. Just as some knowledge of Geology is important to the terrain artist, botanical information is of use to an artist in the business of making CG landscapes. This is true for artists who are responsible for defining or modifying *procedural variables* and those who model from scratch, using knowledge of plants combined with observation for realistic results.

For an artist, the purpose of knowing something about plants is to be able to recognize those qualities that make one plant recognizably different from another. Plants are distinguishable on many different levels, from cellular to leaf structure, to the way they reproduce, grow, where they grow, and what they need to survive. Each of these things affects the final appearance of a plant and may be used to differentiate between plants and to help guide you in designing what type of plants to include in a scene.

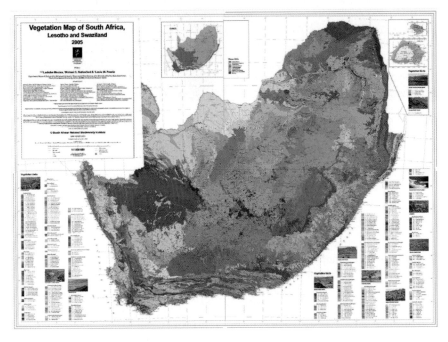

Fig. 3.2 A vegetation map such as this is an invaluable aid when deciding which plants go where in your environment (Map © 2005 Ladislav Mucina, Michael C. Rutherford, & Leslie W. Powrie)[1]

---

[1] From the book 'The Vegetation of South Africa, Lesotho and Swaziland Strelitzia 19' published by South African National Biodiversity Institute.

Geographic factors

Plants grow where they do based on mostly predictable variables. Tropical climates have the greatest variety of plants, and Polar regions have the least. Some botanists believe that polar and temperate zone trees are more resistant to adverse climatic conditions than plants in tropical regions. This theory works for many plant species, but not all of them. For a CG artist, however, it is generally true that as terrain moves away from the equator, the plants in that region are less diverse and less sensitive to adverse climate conditions (Fig. 3.2).

A *tree line* defines another type of boundary for plant growth. A tree line is a boundary beyond which trees will not grow. Other plants, like scrubs, grasses, and mosses, will grow beyond tree lines. There is more than one type of tree line. It is most commonly thought of as the highest elevation up to which a tree may grow. A tree line of this type is easily seen from a distance when looking at high mountains. There will be a blanket of trees ascending its slopes until they reach the tree line. Beyond this altitude, the mountain is bare. Other sorts of tree lines are defined by characteristics other than strictly elevation. In some arid regions, there is a line below which trees cannot grow because of the intense heat and aridity of the soil. This is a *desert tree line*. Another sort of tree line is based on whether a mountain slope is facing either North or South (reversed depending on which hemisphere). With this type of tree line, shade on one side of the mountain is greater than the other, and has a different climate. This limits tree growth on one side, and encourages it on the other. Trees cannot grow at all above the Arctic tree line or below the Antarctic tree line because of intense cold. Both of these lines occur at varying latitudes due to local variables. Other limiting factors are related to conditions such as proximity to volcanic activity, severe wind exposure, and excessively swampy soil.

Because tree lines vary depending on a variety of factors, they are not consistent across the globe, at least not when measured against any one factor. When looked at in combination with other factors, they become more consistent. For instance, the highest tree line in the world is in the Bolivian Andes mountain range. Although the tree line does vary even within the Andes, it varies depending on which direction any given slope is facing and becomes more predictable. At its highest, the tree line is 17,000 ft. As you move south or north from this point, the tree line becomes gradually lower. It is 13,000 ft in New Guinea, 6,500 ft in the Australian Alps, and only 4,000 ft on South Island of New Zealand. Moving north, it works the same way. It is 14,400 ft in the Himalayas, 11,800 ft in Yosemite, 7,000 ft in the Swiss Alps, 3,600 ft in Norway, and 2,600 ft in Sweden (Fig. 3.3).

Whatever the climate in your environment is, it will have an impact on the type of plants that can grow there. Just as a fish must have gills to breathe under water, plants must adapt to their environment in order to survive. If you include plants that are mismatched to their environment, giant redwoods in the middle of a sand dune for instance, they will look out of place to viewers. If you do this intentionally, it may require an explanation of some sort. If it is not intentional, please keep in mind that it may be noticed.

Fig. 3.3 The tree line of this slope in Yosemite is about 11,000 ft above sea level

Latitude, altitude, and rainfall are primary determining factors that decide what type of plant will grow in a given location. Secondary factors are these: soil type, wind, evaporation, and disturbances such as storms, volcanoes, mudslides, fires, and flood. Many *biomes* are defined by these factors. Below is a list of some of the more common biome types.

Alpine	Temperate grasslands
Sub-alpine	Chaparral
Desert	Temperate grasslands
Sub-tropical	Temperate deciduous
Tropical forest	Coniferous forest
Arctic	Tundra
Antarctic	Lakes
Savanna	Wetlands

In each of these, the type of plants that can grow within them is defined by characteristics of the climate and local environment. If you are sensitive to this when planning how to add plants to your environment, the finished product will be more convincing (Fig. 3.4).

Once you know where your plant can grow, you should have an idea how the species is distributed within that range. This is called a plant's *spatial pattern*, the way it places itself relative to other plants. A plant's spatial pattern is very important because it affects the health of individual plants as well as entire populations.

For an artist, if the spatial pattern is incorrect, plants will appear to be unnaturally positioned, too close, or too far apart. A good way to check on real-world spatial patterns is to examine aerial or satellite photography.

Fig. 3.4 Natural arrangement of maple in a temperate deciduous forest

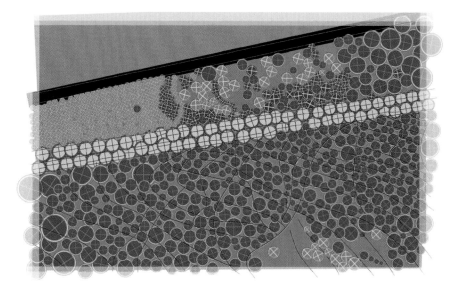

Fig. 3.5 Notice the two parallel rows of trees at the upper edge of the forest. Unlike surrounding trees, these have been planted on either side of a dirt road in the forest. Although this part of their pattern distinguishes them from surrounding trees, they occupy the same amount of space as their neighbors

Fig. 3.6 The view from inside the spatial pattern; the same allée as seen in Fig. 3.5

One thing you will notice is that even when plants are positioned in orderly rows by humans, they will if possible follow the same spatial pattern they do in the wild. Therefore, they are the same distance from each other that they would be in a natural setting. If they weren't, it would most likely affect their viability as an organism. Landscape architects are aware of this, and take care to accommodate the requirements of various plant species (Figs. 3.5 and 3.6).

Building a plant, as opposed to simply selecting the species and deciding where it belongs, is the hard part of working with plants in CG. It doesn't have to be that way. If you understand how they grow, what the parts are called, what they are for, and what affect various conditions have on their shape, building a plant can be fairly easy even if the end result appears to be complicated because of many repeated elements.

Plant Classification

Botanists classify plants based on many different factors. For artists, the clearest divisions may be made between the following:

1. Nonvascular plants. These plants do not have a circulatory system and are entirely dependent on receiving moisture from their environment. Mosses are an example of this type of plant. Mosses and other nonvascular plants reproduce by spores, and do not have flowers. They can be found growing on trees and rocks, or along the ground like a carpet in forests.

2. Vascular plants. These are plants with a circulatory system. This classification contains two major categories:

(a) Plants that reproduce via spores
   (i) Ferns and related plants are included in this group.
(a) Plants that reproduce by seeds
   (i) Conifers. These are plants that reproduce by means of an uncovered seed,[2] usually within a cone-like shape. Some, like the juniper, have a seed inside a hardened berry-like structure. Conifers do not flower. They have needle, scale, or awl-shaped leaves, and bear pine cones or berry-like seed packets. Pine trees, redwoods, junipers, and the ginkgo tree are all conifers.
   (ii) Monocots. Monocots have parallel vein structure in their leaves; they start growth with a single seed leaf. Grasses, grains, wheat, taro, coconut, banana, pineapple, and many other food crops are all monocots.
   (iii) Dicots. A dicot plant has a two part divided reproductive system. The seed grows inside of an ovary, and the ovary is inside a flower. After the flower has been fertilized, it falls away and then the ovary grows into a fruit. Apple trees, most other fruits, vegetables, and beans are all examples of dicot plants.

Leaf Structure

Identifying plant species can sometimes be accomplished by observation of the type of leaves and leaf structure of a plant. Because it is possible to identify a plant in this way, it follows that an artist should be sensitive to this very important feature of plant anatomy (Fig. 3.7).

Leaves grow from *nodes* on a branch. All leaves have an *axillary bud* at this location, but only some have a stem, or *petiole*. This is the first major difference one will find between plants: those that have a petiole and those that do not. Leaves that grow from a petiole are called *petiolate*, and those that do not are *sessile*. A sessile leaf literally grows directly out of its node on a branch. To compare with human anatomy, a sessile leaf looks something like a human with a head but no neck.

Some leaves are *simple*, and others are *compound*. A simple leaf is a single leaf that grows from a single node, or petiole. A compound leaf is made of many *leaflets* that look like a leaf except that they all grow from a common *rachii*, or second stem-like structure that grows from the petiole instead of a branch. Compound leaves are divided based on how the leaves are arranged along the rachii. *Even pinnate* leaves grow as two rows of leaflets along either side of a rachii, and terminate in a

---

[2] "Uncovered" refers only to whether it is covered by an ovary. Clearly, they are covered by the structure of the cone itself.

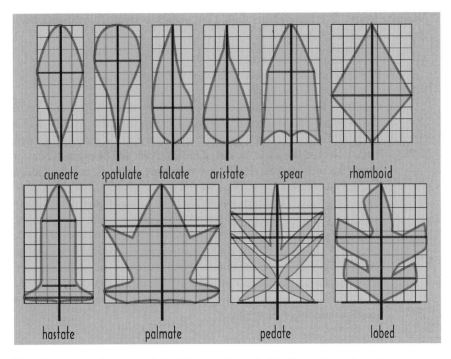

Fig. 3.7 A group of leaves, as defined by gross shape. In this illustration, red crossbars represent position of widest point, and grid size is a reference for leaf aspect ratio

leaflet pair. An *odd pinnate* compound leaf is the same as an even pinnate until the very end, where an odd pinnate leaf terminates in a single leaflet instead of a pair. A *bipinnate* leaf has pinnate compound leaves branching from a central rachii, with each of these producing their own leaflets. A *palmate* leaf terminates in five leaflets that grow from a common position at the end of the rachii, roughly in the shape of a hand, hence the name, palmate (like the palm of a hand). A *trifoliolate* leaf also grows from the terminus of the rachii, but instead of having five leaflets, it has three.

Leaves absorb light energy from chlorophyll in the exposed surfaces of their leaves. To enhance their ability to collect as much of this energy as possible, several different leaf arrangement designs are used. An *alternate* arrangement is when leaves alternate which side of the branch they grow from as they move from its base towards its terminus. The angle between leaves on either side of the branch is approximately 180°. An *opposite* pattern is when a leaf pair grows from the same position along a branch, but each successive pair is rotated until the terminus is reached. The rotation value varies depending on the plant, but is consistent within any specific plant. A *whorled* growth pattern has three or more leaves per node, all arranged around the branch in a roughly circular arrangement. The effect is that of a rosette (Fig. 3.8).

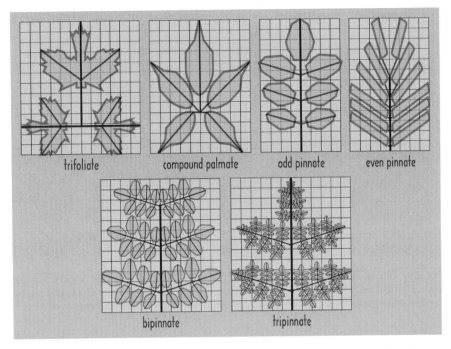

trifoliate   compound palmate   odd pinnate   even pinnate

bipinnate   tripinnate

Fig. 3.8 Compound leaves are those that grow as leaflets from a central stem, or rachii. The type of branching pattern defines compound leaves and how many times the rachii branch before leaflets appear

Leaf Shape

The widest cross-section of a leaf, as measured against its central vein, is used to determine whether a leaf is *ovate, obovate, elliptic,* or *oblong*. Each of these leaf types is defined by the position of the widest cross-section along the central axis of the leaf. If the leaf is widest at its base, it is ovate. If it is widest at the furthest end of the leaf, it is obovate. If the leaf is widest at its midpoint, it is elliptic. A leaf with parallel, as opposed to convergent, sides is called oblong (Fig. 3.9).

Leaves have *margins* just slightly within the border of the leaf itself. This is an area of discoloration that follows the edge of the leaf. Most leaves have one of the following margin types (Fig. 3.10):

1. *Entire*: this is a smooth outline, uninterrupted by cuts or subdivisions.
2. *Lobed*: a series of rounded ends around the leaf's vein pattern, ordinarily less than half as deep as the distance from the outer edge of the leaf and its center vein.
3. *Serrate*: a series of sharp triangular teeth-like projections around the edges of the leaf where the serrations are asymmetrical and point towards the leaf tip.
4. *Dentate*: like serrate leaf margins, but each triangular projection is roughly symmetrical and points away from the central vein of the leaf.

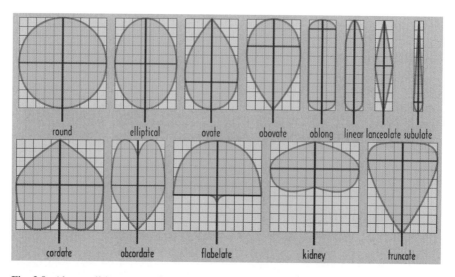

Fig. 3.9 Almost all leaves may be described as belonging to the shape types contained in this illustration and Fig 3.7. These shapes, however, are only one variable of many. Margins, venation, borders, and whether compound or whole are other factors that affect plant identification

5. *Crenate*: a row of semicircular arcs, usually small, around the entire edge of the leaf.
6. *Erose*: a ragged edge, something like a combination of serrate and crenate, with irregular cleft depth.
7. *Palmatifid*: follows the palmate structure of the leaf, with smooth edges, as in a leaf with entire-type margins. Clefts are very deep, and reach almost to the center of the leaf.
8. *Pinnatifid*: similar to Palmatifid, but with a pinnate pattern.
9. *Parted*: Deep clefts in a palmate pattern, with sharp or angular edges.

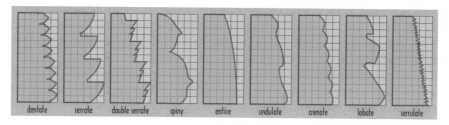

Fig. 3.10 The edge patterns represented here can appear on any leaf type, considerably increasing the number of possible combinations

Venation is the vein pattern within a leaf. This is not visible from a distance, but in close up shots is an important identifying characteristic of any leaf. There are three types of venation (Fig. 3.11):

Pinnate: a central vein from base to tip of the leaf, with a branching pattern of secondary veins at an angle from the central vein. The pattern is similar to that of a feather.

Palmate or *digitate*: veins originate from a central location at the base of a leaf and project outwards towards the tip of each lobe of the leaf.

Parallel: veins originate from a common location at the base of a leaf, extend from this position radially to a limited extent, and then travel nearly parallel to each other through the length of the leaf before converging at the leaf terminus.

dicot   reticulate   pinnate   arcuate   parallel

Fig. 3.11 Within each of the three major venation types: palmate, pinnate, and parallel, there are many subtypes and variations

Growth Limits

The tallest tree known in the world is a sequoia from northern California. It is 112.5 m tall, though some trees have grown to be somewhat taller.[3] According to research conducted by George W. Koch of Flagstaff, Arizona, even in ideal growing conditions, trees are not likely to grow above 130 m due to the mechanical difficulty of raising water to that height within the circulatory system of a tree. He found that at the top of the redwoods he studied, the upper portions of the trees exhibited signs of drought-related ailments. Because of this, photosynthesis was reduced and further growth inhibited.

All plants have a growth limit that constrains the individual to within a maximum size. The growth limit might be elevation related, as in the case of the giant redwoods, or caused by some other factor. Whatever it is, it is good for a CG artist to be aware of this, or risk making wildly mis-scaled plants.

---

[3] A tree from Australia is thought to have been between 143–150 m tall

Fibonacci Numbers

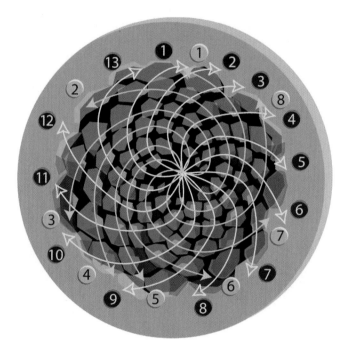

Fig. 3.12 Fibonacci numbers can be found in the number of spirals in a pinecone, 8 in one direction and 13 in the other

Leonardo of Pisa, also known as Fibonacci, considered the problem of how many rabbits would result from a single pair over time. The result is the Fibonacci number series. It was later discovered that these numbers not only had application to exponential growth in rabbit populations, but also could be found in the growth patterns of many (though not all) plants. The numbers appear in a couple of different ways, the most common being the number of elements that grow along spirals, such as in the seed pattern of a sunflower, scales on a pine cone, or the number of leaves at each successive stage of growth, regardless of whether they grow in a spiral.

Examples are not difficult to find. The Fibonacci sequence is as follows: 0, 1, 1, 2, 3, 5, 8, 13, 21, 34, 55, 89, 144, 233 ... and so on. Each successive number is the product of the two before it. The number of leaves required to make a complete revolution around a branch for instance, is often a Fibonacci number. The number of petals on a daisy, regardless of the type of daisy, is usually a Fibonacci number. The number of seeds in a sunflower, the number of scales on a pinecone, or even the number of petals on almost any flower will be a Fibonacci number. If you draw a line connecting the 1st, 2nd, 3rd, 5th, 8th, 13th, etc. scales on a pinecone, you will trace one spiral row of scales. Offset your start position by one scale and you will do it again (Fig. 3.12).

There are a number of theories regarding why so many plants are jam-packed with Fibonacci numbers. The number of leaves in any given revolution around a branch is thought to be arranged to accomplish the greatest exposure to light and that the Fibonacci sequence helps accommodate this. On the other end, some say that Fibonacci numbers allow leaves to be more closely packed than any other leaf arrangement. Whatever the reason, any artist should be able to see these numbers recurring in botanical subjects for himself. Because it can be observed, it can be included in any work based on a subject known to contain Fibonacci numbers.

Landscaping

Fig. 3.13 The quantity of foliage in this section of a major city is not unusual. Although manmade elements are visible in this scene, they occupy a minority of the area in the image

Plants are commonly found in all environments, from deserts to large cities like New York and Los Angeles. No matter how plant-free you might think a given location is, if you get any reference on it, you will see there are a great many plants. Los Angeles, for instance, is so heavily planted with large eucalyptus and palm trees that trees of one type or another block one's line of sight in nearly any direction. New York City, the "Asphalt jungle," famous for its lack of trees, has many tree-lined streets and numerous tree-filled parks. The Sonoran desert in Mexico and Arizona teems with plant life, and so do most other deserts. Death Valley in California and certain parts of the Gobi and Saharan deserts might seem like exceptions, but even they have plants. They don't have as many as other places, but they do exist even in these places. Whatever your location is, you should expect to include some plants, and quite a few of them (Fig. 3.13).

Level of Detail

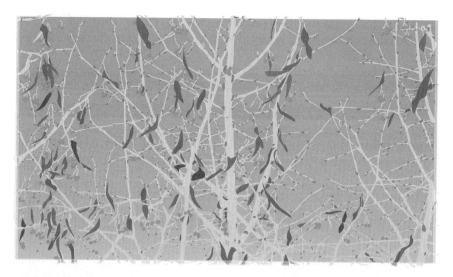

Fig. 3.14 This close-up view of a few branches from the same tree contains enough detail to keep an artist quite busy. Expand this to a long shot with many similarly detailed trees, and you have an optimization opportunity

Plants have so many separately distinguishable parts that you'll be lucky if your model simply manages to represent each of those details, regardless of resolution. Indeed, the number of parts is so great that if you merely use a single triangle to represent each item, as long as the triangles are scaled and positioned correctly, the end result may be recognizable as your target object. Normally, a plant model is not so drastically reduced in detail as that. Normally, some details will be ignored, and others represented with many more than one triangle. If you make good choices, the end result will not draw attention to the missing parts, nor will it be obvious that the level of detail contained in parts that are represented is low (Fig. 3.14).

For recognition, it is important that you start with the correct relationships between parts. To accomplish this with a plant, imagine the plant as it grows from the roots up to simplify the problem. How many branches does its trunk have? Some grow directly out of the ground as five trunks in a palmate pattern. Is your plant doing this, or is it just one trunk? Where does its first node appear? How many nodes rotate around the tree before one full 360° rotation has been achieved? How far apart are the first node and the last in a 360° revolution? Do the nodes appear as scars on the trunk, or do branches emerge from them?

The series of questions listed above is a starting point, and they are very important questions if you are to have any hope of understanding what you are doing as you begin your model. You want to think of every step one part at a time, without considering how complicated the end result will be.

One thing that can complicate your project early on is if you try and build naturally curved geometry for your trunk, nodes, and other parts. At this stage, you should be more concerned with the other details mentioned above. For now, you can build your trunks and branches as perfectly straight sections of geometry. Later, after you've answered many of these questions and built the raw geometry, you can bend them in whatever manner needed, but do not do that yet. Plants are organic objects, and as such have a high level of symmetry. It will be easier to maintain this during the modeling process if everything remains aligned with the global axes for as long as possible.

The answer to question #1, "How many trunks?" will tell you if you need to rotate your trunks away from each other to fit them into the right space. Do not rotate them yet, but simply note the information for later. Build only the first section of one trunk for now. Duplicate it later, after you have finished with some other steps.

Next, find the nodes. The first one you need to worry about is the one appearing at the lowest point on your plant. You may not want to build all of the nodes, particularly in high detail, but it is useful to create them anyway as markers to help you position other parts. If you have a very large tree with large nodes left from broken off branches, you will have to build them or the tree will not look right. For now then, it is a good idea to make a simplified representation of a node scar, even if it is just a three-sided pyramid. Scale this to the right size for your plant and position it in Y at the right height.

Find the number of nodes per full revolution and divide a full 360° circle by this number. Check the Y distance between the first node, and the next two nodes that define the start of new 360° revolutions. Call these nodes A, B, and C. Check the ratio of the distance between AB and BC. BC will either be less than AB, or so close that you can't tell the difference. If the latter is true, measure between a larger number of revolutions and then the next set of the same number of revolutions. This ratio will tell you by how much you must reduce the scale of each successive revolution in Y in order to recreate your target. You may also want to check the width of distant scars, to see by how much they scale down as they move up the trunk of your tree. Understanding this scale factor is crucial to building your tree properly.

Where is the lowest branch of your plant located? Is it at the first node or higher up? Wherever it is, you may want to build this first branch as a section, from its point of origin on the tree to its first branching point, oriented to match one of the global axes. Does the branch extend undisturbed, regardless of curvature, with smaller branches extending away from it? Or does it change direction every time it splits into a smaller group of branches?

You will find that heavily pruned plants, like fruit trees and rose bushes, can sometimes be difficult to understand. They have had so many branches removed that their nodes are growing one atop the other in a confusing clutter. If this describes your object, ignore it for now, and try to find the original branching pattern prior to pruning. When the branch splits, how many subbranches does it split into? Is it three, like parsley, or two like a rose bush, or is it something else? This branching pattern will be consistent throughout your plant. Once you have determined what it is, you need to only know by how much each split reduces the diameter and length of the next section proportional to the original. If this sounds confusing, it isn't. Just look at the illustration, you'll see it isn't so complicated.

The questions you've answered so far give you the raw material to build most of your branches for the tree, but with two notable exceptions: the angle of rotation between each branch and the trunk, and the position of the horizontal axis of the tree. The rotation angle is important to note, but you should not rotate your branch and copy it until you are satisfied with your model. You want to work on one branch only until you are completely satisfied with it. Otherwise, your model may become so complex that you lose the ability to work with it further.

The horizontal axis of your tree is very much like the horizontal axis of a leaf, and comes in pretty much the same varieties. The position will vary in Y, and your plant may have two axes, one atop the other, to create roughly parallel sides for a section of your plant. Whatever the case may be, this information will allow you to set the duplication and scaling factors for your branches to ensure that the resulting plant has the correct overall shape. This is again, information you should note, but not use yet.

Next, you need to build your leaves. If you answer the same questions as you have for the branches, and build your first leaf accordingly, you will be ready to apply foliage to your tree when you have completed just a couple more setup tasks. Does your tree have flowers or fruit? If so, build one of each, place them where they belong, and make sure you take note of attachment angles. So far, everything you have built should be oriented along one of the global axes, but you will have to know at what angle each successive piece rests relative to its parent before you populate your plant with branches, leaves, fruit, and flowers.

Please take the time to properly apply texture coordinates and texture maps now, before you have so many parts that it would be a nightmare to do so. At this stage, you may wonder why, even if your goal is to build a low-resolution object, so many detailed questions are being asked. The reason is that one of the best methods for building a low-resolution model is to make renders of a high-resolution object and then apply them with alpha maps to a very low-resolution representation of your plant. Either way, the high-resolution object is required.

Once you have the basic parts built, you are ready to extend your branches all the way to their termination point with full leaves, etc. After you have done this with one branch, you may want to adjust your object to seamlessly blend all of its parts, instead of having a rough assembly of interpenetrating parts. Plants are so complex that self-penetration may not be noticeable, but if you can fix it now without much effort, it isn't a bad idea to do so. Check your texture coordinates after you have done this, to make sure they still make sense (Fig. 3.15).

Now you should copy and rotate your branches all the way around their trunk (or trunks) to the top, by following the nodes upward in a spiral pattern. The resulting plant will have a very high level of detail, probably too much.

Many plants have broken or missing branches, dropped fruit, and only partial foliage and flowers. Now is the time to prune your plant. For broken off branches and twigs, you should have a texture map ready to represent the color difference at that location. Once you have done this, you will have a very nice-looking tree that is difficult to render because of its high level of detail. Now, you must optimize.

Fig. 3.15 With just a few simple variables – leaf type, branch type, node location, twig pattern – you can create extremely complex plants simply by copying and repositioning a small number of core elements, as in this branch with leaves

Optimization

Fig. 3.16 A low-resolution natural environment from the game *My Horse and Me* makes extensive use of various optimization techniques to represent what would otherwise be a very complex scene (Courtesy of W!Games)

The most brutal level of optimization available is to make a render of your tree with an alpha map, as an *rgba image* and then apply it as a texture map with transparency to a single quad. This type of optimization is called a billboard and can be used for many things besides plants. The most common use of *billboards* is for distant trees, but they can be used for any type of distant object that has a fixed location. These should not be part of a background image because they would then remain in the same position relative to the camera no matter which direction the camera is pointing. A billboard is a true 3D object fixed in 3D space, so camera movements will affect whether the billboard is in view or not to a semi-realistic standard. If the billboards are far enough away, and successively closer objects have successively greater detail, it is unlikely that any viewer would notice that they have no volume.

Other types of billboards simply require more polygonal surfaces upon which texture maps with alpha channels are projected. After the flat billboard described above, the next most common is made of two planes that intersect at the trunk. Each plane has a render of the tree attached to it, but from two different views, usually X and Z. This is called a cross billboard and is useful if the tree or plant is close enough to the camera that a totally flat billboard would draw attention to itself. Both these billboard types exist at the extreme low end of the resolution spectrum. They were the only type of trees encountered in early 3D video games, but with modern consoles, they are now used almost exclusively for far distant objects (Fig. 3.16).

Intermediate range plants can be made from a larger number of billboard planes, all the way up to several thousands per plant. Again, distance from camera governs the level of detail more than anything else. If you can get away with ten planes instead of a hundred, you should, but if you need more, don't be afraid to use them. One method that works very well is to build the trunk as a simplified polygonal object and then use alpha-mapped billboard polys for each branch, or each branching section. A hybrid model of this variety will have several hundred triangles at a minimum, and might go up as high as 10,000 triangles, depending on the level of detail you need. If this is the method you will use, do be careful to start with one complete node-to-tip branch, to make sure it looks right before you multiply it to fill out your plant.

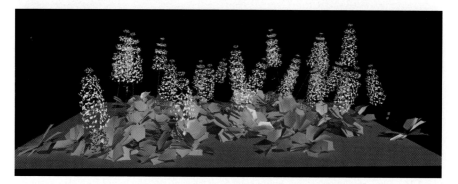

Fig. 3.17 This close-up has 48,000 triangles despite having no more than 8 triangles in any given part. For botanical subjects, even for close-ups, they still need to be optimized

For video games, billboard mapped polygonal plants of up to 3,000 triangles can be acceptably realistic in most situations. For film or even extreme close-ups in games however, you will need to build your model at a natural or nearly natural level of detail. In this case, your best option is to be careful when modeling the plant in the first place, and then edit it well as a 3D object before completing it and then filling out your environment with geometry-laden copies (Fig. 3.17).

For most scenes, you will probably use a variety of resolutions for the various plants it requires. You may have sheets of billboard grasses just behind a few blades of polygonal grass. These might surround a hybrid billboard tree that is in front of large groups of cross billboard shrubs and even some distant single quad billboard objects. In the near foreground, you may have highly detailed models of leaves, flowers, and fruits. With all this vegetation sitting on your terrain, you should have a convincing landscape. If people are to inhabit it however, you may need to deal with a few roads and buildings.

Chapter 4
Civil Engineering

Fig. 4.1 Highway bridge, Prescott, Arizona

Before a single architectural element is placed in an environment, it is not a bad idea to ask how it got there. Did a truck drop it off? If so, where is the road? Was it built on the spot? If so, how did the builders arrive at the location? These questions are answered by the work of civil engineers, specialists who design the skeleton of a city; its roads and sewers, tunnels, bridges, canals, streetlights, and any other manmade thing that allows the navigation and habitability of an environment.

CG projects that ignore the work of a civil engineer will not be convincingly realistic, and opportunities for more interesting environments will be lost. In some cities, nearly half the area is given over to traffic-related structures. Architecture is important to any CG artist who builds a city, but it is not the only thing required. For architecture to be convincing, it must be attached to its environment in a convincing way. This usually requires the creation of some amount of infrastructure: roads, sidewalks, gutters, stoplights, street signs, etc. (Fig. 4.1).

If you move outside of a city, you may find large public works projects like dams, canals, bridges, and tunnels. Parking lots, utility buildings, maintenance access, and roads will surround any of these structures. Each complex of this type can be like a self-contained city and a very interesting addition to an environment. Usually, small towns or cities are located nearby, to provide a workforce for the project, whatever it is.

A. Paquette, *Computer Graphics for Artists II: Environments and Characters,*
© Springer-Verlag London Limited 2009

Below are some examples of the type of structures built by civil engineers within differing specialties:

1. Structural engineering:
   - (a) Tall buildings   (c) Dams
   - (b) Bridges   (d) Towers
   - (e) Platforms   (g) Foundations
   - (f) Retaining walls   (h) Stadiums
2. Waste treatment:
   - (a) Sanitary waste treatment   (c) Potable water
   - (b) Industrial waste
3. Transportation:
   - (a) Highways   (d) Roads
   - (b) Railways   (e) Parking
   - (c) Airports   (f) Traffic control
4. Geotechnical:
   - (a) Rock and soil analysis for load bearing properties
5. Water management:
   - (a) Drainage
   - (b) Retention ponds
   - (c) Waterways
   - (d) Levees
   - (e) Dams
   - (f) Lake

History of

Until the late eighteenth century, civil engineers and architects were nearly interchangeable. You could hire either to make just about any type of structure. It was only during the Industrial Revolution that civil engineering became a separate profession and was recognized as such. From that time on, architects built buildings, and civil engineers built everything else. If you want an airport, a civil engineer will design almost everything except the main building, which will be designed by an architect to fit within the confines of the civil engineer's design.

Most environments, especially cities, are crowded with multiple layers of civilian infrastructure. Sewer systems, traffic control, artifacts of public transportation like bus shelters, police call boxes, public telephones, and many other things installed for public use by multiple agencies, peacefully coexist in most environments (Fig. 4.2).

The size of civilian infrastructure is easy to underestimate. Large structures can be located in remote hard to access locations, while nearer examples are so commonplace that most people hardly notice them. Without a special reason to do so, why would anyone take note of how many electrical junction boxes, sewer covers, street signs, and mail boxes there are? More importantly, after seeing these things every day, who goes to the trouble of paying attention to them anymore?

Fig. 4.2 Street fixtures, however few, add tremendous character and realism to a scene

They become as much a fixture of an artificial environment as a ground cover of fallen leaves in the forest, and who goes to the trouble of counting the leaves?

For a CG artist tasked with building an environment, knowing the size and number of elements to be contained in that environment is very important (Fig. 4.3). An artist who does not take the trouble to discover the answers to these questions will have a lower quality environment than one who does.

Depending on how old the city is, you may find evidence of a broad range of time periods represented in its infrastructure (Fig. 4.4). You might have a subway system

Fig. 4.3 In some locations, civilian infrastructure can use as much as 50% of available land

built in the early twentieth century, "new" entrances to it built in the 1960s, even newer signage from the 1980s, and twenty-first century trains running on the tracks, right alongside much older trains. Any scene that does not take this into account risks a lack of credibility with its viewers. If you want a credible environment in your CG scene, like the artists at Disney and Pixar, you're well advised to do as they do and research the entire environment, not just the focal points that are necessary for story purposes.

Fig. 4.4 In this image, evidence of multiple eras is visible. Old brick sidewalks beside asphalt, modern signage and eighteenth century ironwork contribute to make this street more interesting

The first step in any project is to prepare the surface for construction. To accomplish this, the soil will be analyzed, then surveyed, and then graded. The analysis will determine whether the land is suitable for certain types of construction, the survey will fix the boundaries of construction elements, and earth moving equipment is used to *grade*, or shape the earth into usually level ground for construction (Fig. 4.5).

The grading process can be significantly more complex than simply flattening terrain, depending on what is being constructed. For a complex structure built onto a steeply sloped terrain, the earth (and rock) may be removed from one part of the lot and moved to another to make a kind of large open-air sculpture in the exact shape demanded by a structure that may require such complexities as a gently curving switchbacked rail transport cavity etched into the side of a mountain.

Ignorance of the importance of grading by an artist can cause him to miss important details in a model, such as sections of hillside that are removed to make space for a home, the level lot that is thus created, and the retaining wall built to prevent landslides from overwhelming any structure built on the site.

Another important detail is the *natural slope* of any hill. Different types of rock and soil have a natural slope, or a maximum angle beyond which the slope cannot increase without risking soil slippage or landslide. After such an event, the

Fig. 4.5 An environment made exclusively of elements from the same era can be interesting, but the lack of variety will be evident

likeliest outcome is that the soil and rock will rest at its natural slope angle again. This is one reason why hillsides that are made of the same type of material and that are exposed to approximately the same conditions will have the same slope angles.

Slopes create a tricky problem for engineers to solve. If they need to traverse a slope, but they can count on the slope eventually reverting to its natural slope angle, potentially destroying their work in the process, what can they do to ensure the longevity of anything they construct? To solve the problem, engineers employ a wide range of techniques, some more effective than others. They can build retaining walls, switchbacked roads, or simply level the least stable portion of a slope. The best techniques are sometimes the least invasive, but not always. The number of techniques available is much greater than suggested here, all of which may be easily observed if you are looking for them (Fig. 4.6).

Slope is defined as the amount of elevation change, or *rise*, over the *run* of a slope. It is most often expressed as a percentage derived from the formula:

$$m = \frac{\Delta y}{\Delta x}.$$

Where Δy is the rise and Δx is the run. To determine the change for each, use:

$$m = \frac{y^2 - y^1}{x^2 - x^1}$$

where the y coordinates are the start and end elevation values and the x coordinates are the start and end values in the horizontal axis. The end result of this equation is a *ratio* that can be converted to a percentage, the most common way to describe angle of slope. In American roadways, a slope angle, or *grade*, of 6% will warrant a warning sign, primarily for slow-moving vehicles that might overheat over long grades. Steeper grades

Fig. 4.6 Most slopes are unstable at greater than 35°. In this illustration of Mitchell's Butte, a rock formation in Monument Valley, Arizona, the upper portion of the debris pile has a 40° slope, but the lower portion is a much more stable 17°

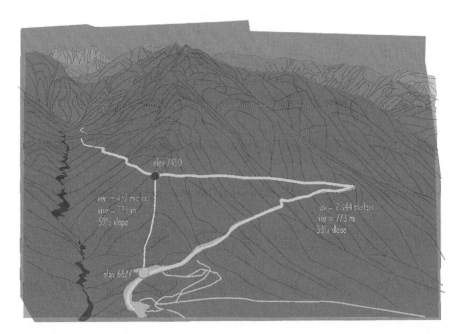

Fig. 4.7 In this switchback road on the slopes leading to Mount Whitney in California, a 59% slope is reduced to a 33% slope by making the switchback. It remains an extremely steep slope, but it possible for vehicles to drive up what would otherwise be impassable. To reduce the slope even more, additional switchbacks would have to be added

of 10% or more can result in steep switchback roads (Fig. 4.7). At even steeper grades, trains may not be able to pull themselves upwards by engine power alone, and will be attached to pull cables for especially steep sections of track. A grade of 18% is illegal for almost any kind of construction in the US, though paved roads at this grade and greater do exist, either as the product of early construction or builders who ignored the law.

Some land formations force engineers to build around them, or to otherwise incorporate them into their project. A variety of factors can cause this to happen, and most engineers and architects assume that for almost any project, especially for new construction on previously undeveloped land, that some accommodation will have to be made to the local terrain. This can be as simple as rotating a building's major axis to match a local feature, or it can be as complex as changing a structure's shape to make it match a contour line on a hillside.

Aerial photography of most cities, particularly older ones, will show that the shape of the land closely governs their infrastructure (Fig. 4.8). Steep slope angles cause a reduction in the number and size of constructions, while a shallow slope angle allows larger constructions and more of them. Roads frequently follow irregular terrain features such as rivers, hill perimeters, and ditches. Connected streets radiate outward from them, and form themselves into neat grids only after some distance.

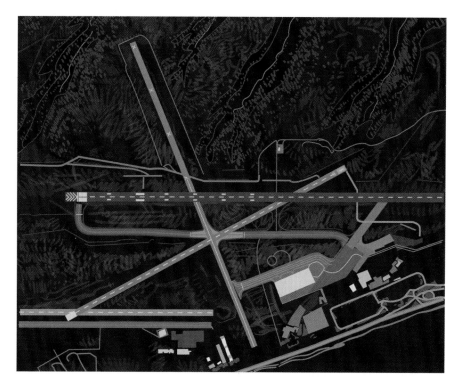

Fig. 4.8 In this image of the Yellowstone, Montana airport, note how runways are laid out, to make the most of terrain that is repeatedly punctuated with deep ravines

As CG matures, making environments that are more specific becomes increasingly viable. Where once all streets were laid out in perfect grids and even watercourses and hills were aligned with them, film and game projects are now beginning to incorporate more natural layouts. The effect of this is that the minimum standard of quality for realistic environments has been raised to include features such as terrain-specific street layouts.

The equipment used to shape terrain for construction projects is in itself interesting to look at, but can also provide information to the CG artist how certain structures are formed. Most earth-moving equipment is large, and some of it is, compared to human-scale, enormous. Regardless of the finished size of these machines, at some level they are always human-scale (Fig. 4.9). This is because they are built and operated by humans. Therefore, a bulldozer, crane, or even a massive coal-mining machine will not be convincing if it does not contain human-scale elements.

Fig. 4.9 In this crane, from the smallest to the largest parts, are found human scale elements. These are either the small components from which the larger machine is built, or housings and controls built for human operators

Surface Preparation

The materials used in construction are often simple shapes that are easy to make in CG, like cylindrical pipes or rectangular flat sheets of stone or wood. If you build your object out of its base components, you may find that you have little need for any but the simplest tools in your 3D application. If you build an object in this way, however, it will usually lead to an unwieldy number of elements that will reduce the renderability of your scene.

Working from base construction elements can be used to make an initial version of a structure that is then used as reference for a lower-resolution object, but this is

Fig. 4.10 Notice the simplicity of the materials found on a construction site. Apart from the complexity of how these and similar elements might be assembled, the base parts are not difficult to make

an unusual technique not often used by professionals because the large number of pieces slows down the construction process too much. More importantly, knowledge of these basic construction shapes will give you the ability to more easily detect natural boundaries within your subject, making the end result more believable (Fig. 4.10).

Transportation is a major area of interest to civil engineers, and possibly the most prominent examples of their work may be found in this category. They make roads, bike paths, highways, signage for roads, traffic signals, utility structures, airline terminals, airports, marinas, train stations, and just about any other permutation of a structure meant to somehow facilitate transportation.

Construction Materials

In games and film, transportation facilities are important parts of any project. From the rough-hewn country paths of *Shrek 3* to the New York avenues of *Spider-man*, or even the fanciful flying vehicles and invisible portals of *Harry Potter*, transportation is often spotlighted in CG projects. One aspect of these facilities that is often incorrect is scale. This is more often true of video game projects than films, but the error can be found in both.

There are several reasons for this. The easiest to identify is that the larger a structure is, the more detail is required for it to remain convincing as a CG object. More detail translates into more polygons, and the structure eventually becomes too large for the game engine. This is not true of film, where polygon count is less of an issue, yet even in film it is possible to find examples of contracted infrastructure objects. This happens most often with interior shots, even when the CG interior is created specifically because it would be cost-prohibitive to build an actual (*practical*) set of the desired dimensions.

One reason for this can be that the CG structure is actually an *extension* of a practical set, and must be scaled to real-world elements. More often, this can come from sheer ignorance of real-world scale. This is not the kind of error most film set designers are likely to make, but art directors or designers with a good knowledge of dimensions do not always directly supervise CG artists. Instead, they are given drawings to build from that certain structural information without dimensions. If their model looks like the production sketch, they've done their job, even if the scale is wrong.

On the other end, a storyboard artist who knows nothing of dimensions may have composed a frame that forces the filmmakers to apply the wrong scale factor to a CG element in the film. This happened fairly often in the movie *Space Jam*, where, because storyboard artists at Warner Brothers did not maintain a fixed scale standard for the objects contained in their storyboards, CG artists at Cinesite were forced to use inconsistent scales to accommodate the storyboard frames. For example, the Nerdlux spaceship in the film was scaled so that in some scenes it is the size of a 747 jet, but in others is closer to the size of a municipal bus. This was the only way the compositions in the approved storyboards could be maintained. Changing the scale to an accurate, or at least consistent, one would have forced the filmmakers to redesign many of these shots.

CG Application

In CG, it isn't just size that matters, but dimension contrast. Dimension contrast is when very small objects are immediately adjacent to very large objects. The tendency in CG is to avoid this situation because it creates a rendering problem where detailed models of small and large objects must coexist. This happens when the point of view of the camera or player is near to the small objects, thus requiring a certain amount of detail in those objects, but the larger structures are also visible, requiring in turn even greater detail.

The problem described for film is especially common in games, where very few artists have any knowledge of dimensions or the scale of civil engineering projects. Although it is undoubtedly true that some environments are deliberately small due to poly count limitations, this is an increasingly thin excuse as video game engines and the hardware they run on can even now accommodate extremely large numbers of polygons in any given scene.

In real-world terms, some of the largest covered structures in the world are transportation facilities of one kind or another. The largest such structure is currently terminal 3 of the Beijing capital airport in China. Whether or not your project has room for that specific building, surely there are projects that would benefit from the inclusion of buildings like this. Simply being aware of the existence of such facilities is an important step towards bringing them into CG entertainment products, and by doing so, significantly expanding the variety of sets that are traditionally used (Fig. 4.11).

Artists draw subjects from life and conduct research to see things they wouldn't otherwise notice. Other than the designers of this structure, who else could imagine it without seeing it first?

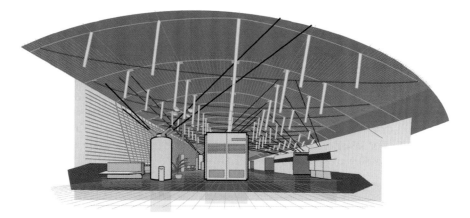

Fig. 4.11 Pu Dong airport in Shanghai was, at the time it was built, the world's largest covered structure. It is so big that a person standing in the middle of the central aisle can look to either side and not be able to see the far wall because it disappears behind indoor atmospheric haze

Transportation

After a large transportation facility is designed, that is, after the major features have been designed, *signage* is made to provide information and guide visitors through it. Signage is a very important part of the design of any facility, and you will notice if you take the trouble to examine one, that there are a large number of informational markers placed throughout any modern facility, and even some older ones. The ancient Romans used *milestones* to mark the perimeter of roadways, and also to provide distance information and directions to other locations at junctions. Modern engineers

Fig. 4.12 In this image of the St. Exupery airport in France, near Lyon, a large number of small repeated elements combine into a very large, but simple (and unexpected) "winged" shape

use a variety of techniques to assist travelers who need quick, easy-to-understand information to help them navigate easily and safely to their destination (Fig. 4.12).

Today, we have large digital displays, painted symbols on walls, pavements arranged into graphic patterns to provide directions, large signs hanging from poles, and more. All of this signage is important not only to an artist who intends to build a convincing environment, but also for an intrepid artist who wants to go a little further than simply including it in his work, real signage can be observed, and the artist will discover that it is more interesting and unique than it first appears (Fig. 4.13). For instance, some signs meant for outdoor placement are designed to resist wind, so they are not easily knocked over.

Fig. 4.13   In this example of overdone signage from the CERN laboratory in Geneva, Switzerland, there is an apparent radiation hazard

To accomplish this, some designers suspend the sign on flexible hinges from above, allowing the sign to swing in a breeze, and allow wind to pass through it without knocking it over. Others are supported on the bottom by strong but flexible struts. This allows the sign to bend forwards and backwards, also without knocking it over. These and other design features add interest to your objects and in many cases will not significantly affect their poly count.

Signage

Placement of signage is also an important issue. In a newly built environment, signage is usually very neatly arranged, but as time passes and new signage needs are found, it can become cluttered. The way in which the clutter accrues is important to note. Sometimes it is not the result of age, but that different people, none of whom are making any effort to make their addition, integrate with preexisting signage, putting up signs. They are asked to post a "no smoking" sign because of a new law, and they put it wherever it is most convenient for them at the moment. Before long, there is a multitude of messy signage. This is an easily observed attribute of almost any modern city.

Sometimes engineers are called in to help design specific devices for large projects, like the world's largest particle accelerator, the Large Hadron Collider, at the CERN laboratory in Geneva, Switzerland. The LHC is a nearly 17-mile-long circular underground tunnel through which subatomic particles will be projected for various scientific experiments. One of the more interesting attributes of the CERN facility, and the LHC itself, is that neither looks as anyone would expect, at least not if your knowledge of how facilities of this type are designed comes from any form of popular entertainment (Fig. 4.14).

Fig. 4.14 Parking restriction signs attached to a lamp post in Phoenix, Arizona. Although these have been designed to accommodate additional signs, it is already beginning to look cluttered. Any modern city would look bare without such a cluttered lamp post, and many of them

In contrast to the sleekly designed and completely clean, white, steel, and glass laboratories we are familiar with from movies such as *Fantastic Four*, *Paycheck*, and *The Incredibles*, CERN is neither perfectly clean or white, nor is it made of sleek materials. Instead, the colors of its parts, when painted at all, are painted garish colors meant to aid in clearly identifying the equipment, not to create a scientific ambiance. Large concrete blocks covered with the graffiti of scientists and construction workers lie everywhere in crowded heaps. Although everything from the tangles of cable, cryogenic equipment, magnets, detectors, tunnels, and so on are all being expertly assembled, it is clear that no interior designer had anything to do with the project. Comfort was not the guiding force in the design of CERN so much as functionality. For that reason, it resembles the Hoover dam more than Reed Richard's fancy Baxter Building laboratory, despite the fact that its function is much closer to that of a comic book superhero than that of the dam.

Civil engineers and architects are not only design professionals, but they are also very creative. They are far more likely than any CG artist to come up with something unexpected in their design. Computer graphics, as was discussed in the previous volume, *Computer Graphics for Artists: An Introduction*, is a profession that requires design solutions by artists who often do not have design training. It is for precisely this reason that it is worth the trouble for CG artists to study the work of people who do have a design background (Fig. 4.15).

Fig. 4.15 This is one of the many magnets for the Large Hadron Collider, CERN laboratory, Geneva, Switzerland. The concrete monolith in the foreground is made of just a few of the many such radiation shielding blocks housed by the laboratory

It may be argued that the work of a CG artist requires a type of creativity that is unfettered by concrete links to real-world sources. This is not only false, but demonstrably so. Many games require highly realistic settings, like in *Full Spectrum Warrior*, *Resident Evil*, and *Lord of the Rings*. The same is true of film. Some of those settings, like in *Lord of the Rings*, are fanciful, but they are still based on recognizable style elements that have a real-world history that can be researched, documented, and measured. For that reason, even the most imaginative production designers in film and games will devote considerable effort to the task of discovering all they can about their subject. If that subject happens to be an environment, it will include at least some, and possibly quite a lot, of civil engineering. It will also contain architecture.

Chapter 5
Architecture

Fig. 5.1 Architecture, though it can be represented as a series of cubes with simple textures, for truly beautiful results, more effort is required (Model and render by Arjan Oosthoek)

CG architecture was once the exclusive domain of architects who used CAD software. It hasn't been that way for more than a couple of decades now, but one thing that is still true is that architectural subjects in film and games are not built with the same level of detail as their counterparts in CAD. When an architect designs a building, he designs everything, every detail of the structure, from the roofing tiles to the studs, wiring, and plumbing in the walls, to hinges, doorknobs, and other things. They specify every material used, and sometimes go to the trouble of listing suppliers for every article needed to build the structure (Fig. 5.1).

Buildings that are built at full detail are not render-friendly; not that they can't be rendered, but that they aren't efficient. Most entertainment products do not require detailed 3D structures inside every wall, and CG artists certainly do not need to know exactly where to buy all the requested materials.

Unlike architects, who put in too much detail for most entertainment projects, the problem for CG artists is that, while they generally know how to optimize an object for whatever their specific use might be, they are not always experienced enough with architectural subjects to avoid obvious likeness errors. Some studios, both large and small, make an effort to have at least one person with an architectural background on staff, but this is not true of all studios, and even with those that do, it isn't always enough to deal with the quantity of architectural files that are needed.

Architecture presents special technical problems to the typical CG artist who does not have an architectural background. Architectural subjects can even be, and frequently are, more complicated to build than characters. This might surprise some readers who are in no way intimidated by the regular box-like forms of a typical building, but if you think about it in a different way, the problem should be immediately evident. It is true that organic shapes have complex curved forms that are not always easy to describe, but in most cases, there are only a small number of these shapes. In a human figure for instance, there are four limbs, a head, and a torso. That's it, six pieces. It isn't much to keep track of in comparison to the tens of thousands of details that many buildings are made of.

On one recent blockbuster film, a major FX studio was given a large contract to make the majority of *vfx* shots. Their bid was primarily based on a large number of complicated character animations that would have to be done. The digital sets, largely made of box-like buildings, were bid at a much lower figure, which is an evidence of how much the studio underestimated the work. In the end, they lost money on that part of the project.

This is the problem of architecture for CG artists: it is harder than it looks. If you become good at it, it can be a lucrative specialty. To use the previous film studio example again, it is easy to see the probable origin of the miscalculation: Up until then, most projects did not require fully realized cities in CG. One movie, *Final Fantasy: The Spirits Within*, famously spent no less than $125,000,000 to make, but on that project, it was difficult for other studios to extrapolate where the money was spent. Was it spent on the extensive sets, or was it the numerous realistic human characters and animations? On other projects, architecture was either a simple set extension, or just a few buildings. The difference between that and an entire city was greater than simply the increase in number of buildings would suggest.

Until about the year 2000, it was not feasible to have large digital sets due to the render times involved. Now, we are seeing more and more projects that have them, but they remain deceptively difficult to make. The aim of this chapter is to help students appreciate the special difficulties of working with architectural subjects, and learn some techniques to improve their work. This chapter will not make architecture less complicated, but should make the subject easier to deal with for the student.

Architecture is complicated not just because it contains a large number of individual elements, but also because most of the elements it is made from have already been reduced to their minimum level of complexity. When you have an object that is built of squares and cubes, unlike a character, you cannot simply change the level of curve detail to simplify the structure. Instead, you must remove structural information altogether. If you were building a character and found that it was a few thousand polygons over the budget, you wouldn't remove an arm or a leg, but would instead try to remove a certain percentage of polygons from every part, so that in the end the curve detail is consistently reduced, but all of the functional parts remain intact. With architecture, this is not always possible. You cannot remove even a single vertex from a cube without radically altering its shape. In such a situation, it may be a good idea to get rid of the entire cube.

Fig. 5.2 Very small objects with minimal poly counts can be heavy in aggregate if multiplied enough times. This building uses 3,410 triangles for dentils that have only ten triangles each

For buildings, there are several different levels of resolution likely to be encountered in a CG project:

1. Less than 500 polygons: Extremely low resolution
2. 501–2000 polygons: Low resolution
3. 2001–5000 polygons: Medium resolution
4. 5001–15,000 polygons: High resolution
5. 15,001–50,000 polygons: Very high resolution
6. Above 50,000 polygons: Extremely high resolution

Each of these resolution levels has their own problems, but as a rule, the higher the poly count, the more difficult it is to make. Depending on how the buildings are made, it is possible for the number of polygons to be almost irrelevant. You can have buildings adjacent to each other with no apparent difference in their level of detail despite huge differences in poly count. This is possible because different buildings do not always have the same number of parts. A complex neo-classical structure can have half a million polygons and be adjacent to a 1,000 polygon modern garage that is made of just a few flat shapes without any resolution contrast.

Any human character will have the same number of limbs. This is why it is possible to make a generic polygon budget for "characters" on a project. Now think of a character budget where the "characters" could be anything from humans to scorpions, millipedes, whales, dragons, or multi-limbed aliens. The budget won't make any sense in such a situation because the number of parts varies from creature to creature. The same is true of architecture (Fig. 5.2).

Another reason the poly count could be considered irrelevant is that texture maps can be used in place of polygons. In this way, some very high-resolution buildings are made, not of high numbers of polygons, but of extremely high-resolution texture maps. In the movie *Jurassic Park*, multiple 4096 × 4096 (4 k) maps were used for the

T-rex dinosaur. In *Space Jam*, four 4 k maps were used for the floor of the basketball court. For other movies, multiple 4 k and even 8 k maps are used to represent surface detail on models that have only a few hundred polygons.

Video games cannot use high-resolution texture maps, so they rely on higher poly counts to make up the difference. For this reason, buildings in video games are beginning to have higher poly counts than their counterparts in film. An interesting variant, and not an uncommon one, comes from SimCity. The poly count for individual buildings in that game are kept as low as possible. Ironically, while this is true of the in-game models, the artists at Maxis first go to the trouble of making extremely high-resolution buildings with hundreds of thousands of polygons apiece, and then render low-resolution maps based on them for application to the low-resolution stand-ins, or imposters.[1] This is not an uncommon solution for low-resolution architecture (Figs. 5.3–5.5).

Here, then, are a number of resolution solutions:

1. Low poly, 1 map
   (a) This solution is best suited to situations where you need to make dozens or hundreds of buildings and the level of detail in individual buildings is less important.
2. Low poly, exchangeable maps
3. Medium poly, multiple maps
4. Hybrid, low-poly/high-poly rendered maps
5. High poly, etched tiling

Fig. 5.3 In this model, a higher-resolution mapping solution requires multiple maps. If a single map were used instead, it would be too large to easily load into memory (Model courtesy Dirk Stöel)

---

[1] Interview, Ocean Quigley, Art Director *SimCity*4. http://simcity.ea.com/community/events/chat_oceanquigley_121902.php

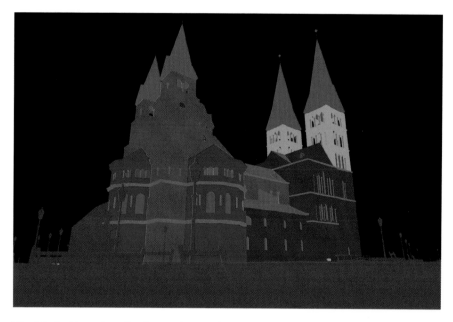

Fig. 5.4 In this render, all polygons that use the same map have been flood-filled with the same color. By counting the colors, it can be determined that the building has four texture maps

Fig. 5.5 By etching a tile set pattern into the structure of your geometry, you can easily reduce the total number of texture pixels needed to map your object

As in SimCity, high-resolution models are rendered into color and normal maps, and the maps are applied to extremely low-resolution geometry.

6. Full detail

Any of the above techniques may be mixed for various results, but these are the seven most commonly used methods for compressing the detail of a polygonal building into a renderable object. Nurbs geometry is not often used for architecture

Fig. 5.6 In architectural renderings, nothing is left to the imagination. Although it is not always true, architectural renders like this one generally contain a much higher level of detail than found anywhere else. So much detail, that it can be difficult to render a sequence of frames in a reasonable period of time, although they are perfectly suitable for still images (Image by Jose Manuel Linares, courtesy of Fryrender)

because there are few advantages in doing so, and several disadvantages. Nurbs can be effectively used during the design or construction process, but only in a few limited situations does it make sense to make a finished structure out of nurbs (Fig. 5.6):

Cast Concrete/Nurbs

This category includes any model where smooth curved surfaces are desired. It does not include such things as arched walls made out of flat sections, but structures with full, not segmented, curvature. Cast concrete is sometimes used to create organic forms in architecture, but it is not the only material used to achieve this. Nurbs can definitely be useful for constructing this type of object, but leaving it as nurbs makes less sense unless it is needed for lighting or texturing.

High-Resolution Lighting/Nurbs

Because surface normals are calculated at every sampling point on the surface of a nurbs patch, lighting on nurbs objects tends to be much smoother than for polygonal objects. For high-resolution renders, this sometimes makes good sense. On the negative side, unless great care is taken during the construction process, mapping objects built in this manner may be difficult.

As you can see from the examples given above, the primary question you are faced with as an artist when determining the resolution of your architectural subject, is how to balance the texture size and number of textures against the number of polygons in your model (Fig. 5.7). In some cases, technical limitations will drive your decision, in others, aesthetic factors. If your game engine cannot handle large texture maps, your options become limited. If you have to be more careful how many textures you use, they become even more limited. Aesthetically, you may need a certain amount of detail, or not. These are the factors that tell you how to weigh your decision about which type of model you make.

Fig. 5.7 The small building in the foreground has almost 70,000 triangles; the large building behind it has 30,000. Size doesn't always determine the number of polygons needed for a building, but the amount of detail in the building itself does

Modern buildings, especially very large ones, can have parts of their internal *superstructure*, or skeleton, clearly visible. Leaving these elements without any form of sheathing can be a matter of style or a way to reduce costs, but either way, it presents a problem for the CG artist. Any time the internal structure of a building is visible, the level of detail in that area increases dramatically. Clever use of opacity maps can mitigate the problem somewhat, but if the camera gets at all close to the superstructure, it will have to be modeled or risk not being credible (Fig. 5.8).

Once you have decided at what resolution to make your building, you may want to consider how to organize its many parts. This is not difficult for medium or low poly treatments, but for anything more, it is wise to break your building into easily managed sections. This may be done on three levels: tilability, object type, and direction.

Any object that is repeated elsewhere without change to its structure is a tilable element. You may want to keep all original tilable parts together as a tilable section. This is a backup in case you need to make changes to the base object later, a very common occurrence.

Fig. 5.8 The vault of this auditorium from the Lyon convention center begs to be built, both because it is interesting and because it covers such a large span that to leave it out would create a likeness error

Windows, dentils, brackets, and doors are distinct object types. If you keep such things together, you can very quickly derez an object based on the object types you allow to be visible. All you have to do is select object groups based on the size of their individual components and make them invisible if they are below a size threshold.

The edges found in architectural subjects are often either parallel or perpendicular in two dimensions. This can easily lead to visual confusion unless you take steps to prevent it. Elements that face front can be grouped together, just as elements that face back, up, or to either side should be kept separate. Grouping by direction allows you to quickly turn on only those parts of the object that face the camera at any given time. This also allows you to work on discrete sections without any visual interference from parts that are oriented differently.

When working with a modern building that has a simple overall design, be careful to look for the details. It is a rare modern building that is as simple as it first appears. As a CG artist, if you miss the less obvious details, your building risks being less interesting, and possibly less credible, than it would otherwise be (Fig. 5.9).

In the case of a typical skyscraper "cube" for instance, look for the exact spacing of windows, specific dimensions of floors, and check for patterns within the larger window grid. Sometimes they really are simple, but make sure you've checked carefully before you accept this first impression. In the illustration below (Fig. 5.10), glass panels that are not easy to see when looking at the center of the building are evident at its boundary. This is an interesting and unique detail that is worth including in the model if your poly count budget will allow it.

An interesting problem presented in some buildings is what to do with interiors. Unless your structure uses mirrored glass, you should expect to be able to see inside of the building at least to some degree. Building a full interior for a building is usually

Fig. 5.9 The wireframe of this building would be difficult to understand if more than one wall is visible at the same time

out of the question due to resolution limitations. What, then, is a CG artist supposed to do?

There are a few rote solutions that represent, if not the entire range of possibilities, at least a reasonable sample of options that have proven effective in various contexts.

1. Reflective opaque windows. This is the easiest and cheapest method. There are two versions of this: one is to have truly reflective windows that reflect whatever is in front of them; the other is to use a reflection map that is based on another image. Either way, a view of the interior will be blocked, thus relieving the artist of any obligation to include an interior.
2. Box interior. With this method, simple interior geometry, such as a rectangular prism is placed against the opposite side of every window. This provides an impression of walls, ceilings, and floors. With proper lighting or texture maps, this can be a very effective substitute for the real thing. For it to work, the box must be closed to prevent any possibility of a gap in the interior.
3. Plane interior. This is similar to the box, but with fewer polygons. For this solution, a render is made of anything from a box interior to a fully detailed interior, and the result, usually a 180° view, is used as a texture map on a plane that is positioned behind each window in such a way that it is very difficult to see that there is no floor or ceiling.
4. Partial interior. Depending on how close the camera is expected to get to a building, the amount of detail within may be small with no loss of credibility. For long shots

Fig. 5.10 When looked at from most angles, it is not immediately apparent that most of this building is sheathed by small glass panels

where a camera is both close enough to see inside a window, and is expected to remain in position long enough to obtain a clear view, some detail is necessary. For these situations, a lightly dressed interior is made, but without anything approaching full detail. Low-resolution furniture and simple architectural detail are enough.

5. Full interior. This is reserved for shots where the camera is close enough to enter a room. When this is true, a full interior is not usually made for more than one room, though depending on the purpose, it may be more. A full interior is the equivalent of an entirely new set as far as detail is concerned, so it should only be used in those circumstances when it is absolutely required. To do otherwise is a waste of time, resources, and rendering bandwidth.

Many buildings have special edge treatments. This is sometimes for structural reasons, sometimes as a matter of style. Either way, buildings that possess this characteristic have at least one advantage over buildings that don't, at least as far as a cg artist is concerned: It is easier to light them so that their structure is easily understood. This is of particular importance in video games, where an undistinguished edge in a fast-paced game can cause a player to run directly into it, not realizing it is the corner of a building, as opposed to a flat wall some distance away.

An edge treatment, or even a *contrast edge*, a condition created by the contrast between two adjacent objects, has the effect of outlining or highlighting structural information in your building. Because this can be so helpful, it makes sense for artists to be on the lookout for opportunities to use them. Sometimes they are not easy to see, as when a brick pattern abruptly changes at the corner of a building, but the bricks are the same color as all the others. Even a change as subtle as that is

Fig. 5.11 Edge contrast between adjacent walls
and outlined edges help viewers understand the
structure of a building from a distance

helpful for a viewer, and worth putting in, but you might not see it yourself in a wall
made of thousands of bricks, unless you first tried to find it (Fig. 5.11).

A common mistake made for low-resolution buildings, and occasionally for higher-
resolution buildings, is to ignore *flashing* on rooftops. Flashing is either aluminum,
lead, or tile placed on edges of the roof to help direct the flow of water and to prevent
leakage. The effect is of outlining all the edges with whatever material the flashing is
made out of. When flashing is not included in the model, as a texture or polygons, the
edges of the roof are lost and it can be very confusing to look at. This is truer the more
complex the roof structure is (Fig. 5.12). For simple flat roofs, this is a non-issue.

In architecture, many parts of any building are *framed* in one way or another;
doorframes and window frames are just two examples. Ledges, or moldings, can

Fig. 5.12 In this image, notice how flashing aids in clarifying the structure of each roof

have the effect of framing the space between floors, clocks are usually either set in front of a buildings' façade, or set within a recess built especially for it. Either way, it is framed. This is handy for the CG artist, because this habit of framing distinct elements of a building (for structural reasons, usually) make it easier to clarify the different parts without having to resort to a great deal of detail. A first level of detail may only be a simple cube with a simple roof that occupies the same spatial volume of your target building, a second level of detail would possess all major features, like windows and doors, and at the third level of detail, framing (of all types) should be added to your building, if only at a simple level of detail.

Decoration can be another way to frame parts of your building. Statues may flank a window in neoclassical architecture, or a sculpted pattern of intertwined grape leaves may traverse an entire face of a building in a continuous horizontal band. Decorative elements, particularly sculpted ones, can be very complicated to make. For this reason, in combination with their size relative to the entire structure, they can usually be represented with *normal maps*[2] instead of actual geometry (Fig. 5.13).

Fig. 5.13 Architectural framing has the same effect as outlining; it clarifies the structure of the building

---

[2] More on this in the next chapter

Architects, particularly those who receive commissions to make large public structures, make every effort to create interesting designs, without straying beyond the limitations of the project. Modern architects sometimes do this in an understated, but highly effective way: they create uniqueness through repetition. What this means is that they will start with something regular, like a grid, and then will build irregularity into it, but without disrupting the grid (Fig. 5.14).

This stylistic trait is easy to miss when the overriding pattern is prominent, and will cause an artist to make careless mistakes if he isn't observant. If you are working with a modern structure, keep a sharp eye for variations within the overall pattern.

Fig. 5.14 Although this building façade is based on a simple grid pattern, the contents of each grid square are not the same

Sometimes a building design has been reduced to a minimum number of unique elements, with very little repetition. This is frequently found in freestanding buildings, with no walls shared by adjacent structures. If this is the kind of building you are working with, instead of having repetition at a gross level and variation at a fine level, it is reversed. Details will be repeated, but large structural elements will be either completely, or at least significantly, different from each other (Fig. 5.15).

The incidence of repeated elements in a building is important for an artist because it can have a pronounced effect on the effort required to make the model. The more repetition there is, the fewer unique parts need to be made. A problem with it however, is that architects frequently vary the number of repetition. What this means is that a *dentil* may be repeated 200 times along a ledge where a window is repeated only 5 times, and the windows contain elements that repeat only twice. Because the sections have different repeat values, a measuring challenge is presented to the artist, who has to measure everything carefully or nothing will fit together (Fig. 5.15).

Fig 5.15 In its smaller parts, like the fire escapes and distances between window sections, this building has some repeated dimensions and angles. In its larger parts, the undulating roofs, the way the rear of the building is divided, the parts are different

Measurements in Gothic architecture, as well as the Islamic architecture that partly inspired it, is often made by *geometric subdivision*. What this means is that all measurements are broken down from the same basic geometric elements. A circle is squared, and then subdivided. Center points are found by drawing intersecting lines through the corners of each square; new circles are drawn, etcetera. In a Gothic cathedral, you can clearly see how the measurements of the parts are related to each other in this manner (Fig. 5.16). Knowing this can make it easier to ensure that your measurements are correct, even when working with a building that you have no measurements for.

Architectural styles vary considerably between different regions, especially in archaic architecture, where primitive transportation forced builders to use local materials. The style of architecture will also reflect the climate for which the structure is made. Buildings in Northern Europe, Japan, and the American northwest, all make frequent use of steeply pitched roofs because of heavy rain in those areas. On the other hand, buildings in Arizona, Spain, and the south of France make extensive use of flat roofs due to low rainfall. Houses in Cambodia can be built on stilts to avoid flood damage, and caves are made use of by the Anasazi tribe of North America as a natural form of protection that comes with its own form of air conditioning system embedded in the rock it is made from.

Even modern architecture, where technology has to an extent reduced the impact of transportation and availability of resources on building design, buildings still retain stylistic influences from their predecessors in that regions' architectural design history. Just as European neoclassical architecture looks back to ancient Roman styles for inspiration, modern Islamic architecture reflects the forms and patterns of ancient Islamic architecture. The same is true of modern Japanese, Chinese, Indian, and the work of architects in other countries (Fig. 5.17).

Fig. 5.16 Each window is composed of a number of discrete elements. Each of the dimensions of these parts is based on subdivision measurements of the outer border of the window, which is in turn based on a subdivision of an exterior wall

Fig. 5.17 These buildings in Monaco are built into extremely steep cliff sides that could not be easily modified. Instead, the buildings are positioned around the deep chasm between two sheer cliffs. Tunnels connect roads on either side

What all this means is that the architecture in your scene should be stylistically consistent with the region it is meant to be a part of, and appropriate for the climate. Knowing this can significantly speed up your project because the questions you are answering when doing your research can be more specific. Instead of simply looking for interesting buildings, you first narrow the search by deciding on a region.

The age of your environment is another consideration to keep in mind. Generally, the older the settlement is meant to be, the more likely you are to see a range of that civilization's design history represented in its buildings. In modern Antwerp, for instance, there is a mixture of older Dutch architecture alongside eighteenth century French, twentieth century European structures and twenty-first century signage mixed with seventeenth century decorative elements.

This is an important consideration and opportunity for artists. In production design, the layering of age and style influences is not often seen. Most often, everything in a scene is from the same era, as if each successive generation destroyed entirely the artifacts of their previous generation. Natural disasters, like the 1906 San Francisco earthquake and fire, can have this effect, but if you intend to do this in your design, please keep in mind that it is a rare occurrence indeed, to have all of a civilization's history swept away at once, leaving no option but to rebuild everything from scratch (Fig. 5.18).

Fig. 5.18 Antwerp train station, built between 1895–1905, is an excellent example of heavily decorated Art Nouveau architecture

Fig. 5.19 Some buildings aren't perfect, like this example from Amsterdam

When designing or selecting buildings for your digital sets, please remember that many buildings show signs of wear over time. Including stressed buildings from time to time can enhance the realism of your sets and make them more interesting. This can be anything from the occasional sagging barn in the countryside to the exposed shell of a building after a fire. Be on the lookout for opportunities to acquire reference of these structures, because they rarely remain in a distressed state for long. They will either be repaired or demolished and your chance to get reference will be lost (Fig. 5.19).

Without architecture, most environments wouldn't make much sense. Like almost every other aspect of building a CG environment, they are so complex that at least some optimization takes place. A large part of that for any project is accomplished with texture maps.

Chapter 6
Texturing

Fig. 6.1 Texture maps substitute for structural detail in this image from the game *My Horse and Me* (Courtesy of W!Games)

Textures add a variety of different types of information to your model: color, bump, specularity, subsurface scattering, displacement, normals, fur, glow, and more. The reason textures are used to convey all these different types of information is that a texture map provides an artist with a convenient method of sampling points on the surface of his model. With a texture map, instead of using only the vertices or faces of the model as reference points, you can modify renderable qualities of your object within a face by using the pixels of a map attached to it (Fig. 6.1).

The power of textures, then, extends well beyond a paint job; it gives you the ability to modify the way your model behaves on a sub-face level, and to do so at a very high sampling rate, depending on the resolution of your map. It is important to keep this in mind before you begin the job of texturing any model. Unless you think of your map as information, it is very easy to put the wrong type of information into your map, and reduce the quality of your final rendered output.

The most common texture channel used is for color, and the most common type of texture map for this channel is a photo-based texture. This is also where many texture problems originate. The reason is that a photograph contains much more information than the color of an object, even though all the information it contains is represented as colored pixels. A thermal image of an intruder on a security camera measures body temperature and ignores all other information. The result is a colored image that looks like a person. It is accurate as an impression of the temperature of that person, but it says nothing about actual color that we might want in a render.

Photographs record the end result of a myriad of interactions that affect how light travels within a scene. Because they do not measure the color of objects, but reflected color based on numerous variables in addition to the *intrinsic color* of on object, not only can the colors be incorrect, but also photos are usually polluted with considerable *channel interference*. The first step towards extracting the information you need from a photograph is to learn to recognize the type of information it does contain, and how to separate it into different channels so that you can clean it up.

Perspective/Lens Distortion

The shape of your lens will cause straight lines to bend as if curved. The shorter your lens length is, the greater the distortion will be. Most cameras are sold with a 50 mm lens. This lens length is short enough to cause severe distortion when photographing subjects at close range. This is the first channel of information, the lens channel that must be fixed if you intend to take any fixed measurements or texture maps from the photo. To do this, many photo-editing tools have filters that allow you to pull points on a lattice superimposed on your photograph to modify their position relative to each other (Fig. 6.2). Depending on how much distortion there is, this may be accomplished quickly, or only with some effort.

To improve the odds of acquiring a usable image, care should be taken at the time the photograph is made to align the camera at a perpendicular angle to your subject, with its sides parallel to the edges of your image plane. The longer your lens is, the less distortion you will have, but it will also require you to be farther from the subject. Another solution is to use a multi-plane camera. A camera of this type is very expensive, but if you have access to one, you will be able to photograph a subject from a near distance with almost no distortion at all.

Fig. 6.2 Even in this close-up texture shot on the left, perspective distortion is evident and must be fixed

Monitor Calibration

In film vfx studios, all monitors are recalibrated frequently. In game studios, it almost never happens, and some studios don't do it at all. If your monitor is not calibrated (and if you aren't sure, then it isn't) then you cannot trust the colors you see on your screen. This is true even if you have a brand new, straight from the factory, never-adjusted monitor. As I type this, I have two such monitors in front of me, and images on one, when transferred to the other, do not match. This means that at least one is wrong, but more likely both are. For photo editing, a color-calibrated monitor should be used instead.

An improperly calibrated monitor can result in amazingly poor-quality images. For example, on the videogame *Full Spectrum Warrior*, a programmer decided to test textures on an improperly calibrated monitor. He did this with the idea that if the textures looked right on that monitor that they would look good on properly calibrated monitors also because a good monitor produces better results than a bad one. The problem is that this theory couldn't possibly work. If you calibrate your art to a poorly calibrated monitor, it will only look good on monitors calibrated the same way. If all monitors are calibrated to the same standard, or an attempt is made to do so, as happens during manufacturing, then the results should fall within a predictable and acceptable range. On *Full Spectrum Warrior*, the results of the test led the programmer to modify the textures so that they would look right on his test monitor. Once he had done this, they looked wrong on every other monitor in the studio.

If you have access to monitor calibration equipment, you should use it. If you don't, you should get it.

Color Shift

The colors recorded in any photograph are an approximation of color values reflected from an object, as interpreted by your camera, based on various settings and unique characteristics of your scene. The color and intensity of any lights in your environment will affect the color of your subject.

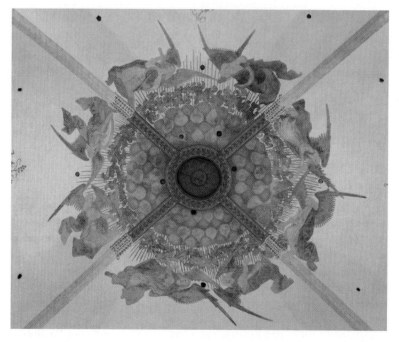

Fig. 6.3 In this image, all of the colors have shifted towards yellow orange due to lighting conditions present when the photo was taken. Using a digital white balance can sometimes eliminate this error. In this photo, the hue shift is so strong that it will be difficult to fix by retouching

The intensity of your light source will have a strong effect on the saturation of colors in your scene. At low light levels, saturation of colors is high, but intensity is so low that saturation levels are difficult to measure, making them appear to be low, though this is the opposite of what is happening in the scene. At a medium level of illumination, your objects' saturation levels will be relatively close to what they should be. Lighting that is any more intense than this will reduce the saturation of your colors, eventually bleaching them all to zero.

The intrinsic color of your object is the pure color of your object, as it would appear if lit completely evenly, without atmospheric interference, reflectivity, or any other effect to modify it. Lighting affects the apparent intrinsic color of everything it comes into contact with, by adding its own color to that of the object (Fig. 6.3). This is why, when a photograph is taken at dusk, every object in the photo has a strong hue shift towards red. The hue shift is so strong that photos taken at this hour without filters are unusable for color information. The effect takes place regardless of intensity, color, or time of day, but is sometimes neutral enough to produce good results. The color shift will be evident in both the lit portion of your photo and the shadow side of objects in your scene.

If you take your shot indoors with carefully controlled lighting, or outdoors at mid morning on an overcast day, you can avoid the worst of this problem. Regardless, you will have to do some color and saturation editing of your work in an image-editing program to eliminate lighting artifacts. It is vitally important to remove lighting artifacts because they are the equivalent of *baking* lighting into your texture map. This is not good because you cannot avoid taking your photos in differing lighting conditions that will not match the CG lighting in your scene. Because the lighting will not match, when lit by CG lights, unedited photo textures will tend to have whatever color errors are present within them highlighted by your CG lights. A texture shot in an environment with yellow lighting will have a yellow cast to it. If it is adjacent to a texture shot in violet lighting, it will have a violet cast to it.

This is not immediately evident to artists who are not trained to recognize color shift, because every color in the scene will be affected in exactly the same way, to exactly the same degree. This will *equalize* the colors to your eye, and make them appear normal. It is only when they are placed beside images taken in different lighting conditions that color errors become obvious.

Mosaic images made of photographs are an excellent example of this. Photos are each given a slight hue shift across the entire image, and then assembled with other images into a pattern where the hue shift alone defines another image, like a celebrity portrait. This is exactly what happens to texture maps when the hue shift isn't adjusted, they become like a dirty flake of paint that is recognized primarily by the color of the lightsource and less by the colors of the subject.

Light Gradient/Falloff

The farther light must travel, the less intense it becomes. This is known as *falloff*. Depending on how much light is present in your scene, it can be difficult to detect a *falloff gradient*, or a gradient *tone shift* along a surface in your scene that is related to a lessening of light as it passes over your subject. We are so accustomed

Fig. 6.4 Notice the pale yellow white gradients in each triangular section. They are all painted the same color, but in this photograph they are represented by many colors arranged in a complex gradient. Which color of the thousands present in these areas represents the true color of the ceiling?

to seeing this in our environments that, unless we are looking for it, it is difficult to detect (Figs. 6.4 and 6.5).

The result of having a falloff gradient in your photo is that it becomes difficult to know the actual color of any given object in your picture, because it gradually changes from one end of the picture to the other, even if you know the color should be completely even all the way across.

If, for instance, you are looking at a wall that has been painted yellow, and there is a diagonal gradient falloff from one corner of the wall to the opposite corner, you will have a number of yellows to choose from. Depending on the *bit depth* of the image, you might have millions of yellows to choose from. You know the entire wall is a flat yellow because a fresh coat of paint has just been evenly applied, and it has dried perfectly. What do you do?

At the paint store where the paint was purchased, they have an exact definition of that yellow. It is based on a mixture of exact quantities of different paints. This definition will be more correct than any pixel in your photo of the wall. A scan of a swatch of the paint would be an improvement, but if you don't have one, you are left with your photo. If you take a photo of the scene with a reference *grey card*, you can calibrate the color on the card in the photo, which is a known grey of exactly 50% intensity, 0% saturation, with the other colors in your scene. This will correct many of the color problems, but will not eliminate the gradient.

For a flat yellow wall, the best solution may be to pick what appears to be the most accurate color and then flood fill the entire region with it. If the region has a highly complex variety of colors, as in a graffiti covered wall, this will not work very well. In that case, you are best off either using a gradient mask to reverse the gradient in the shot, or repaint the scene with flat colors, based on information in your reference.

Fig. 6.5 In this image, most of the contrast is derived from small pits best represented by a bump map. There are noticeable color changes that appear to be actual intrinsic color changes within the surface represented, but over this is a shadow gradient moving from the lighter upper left portion of the image to the darker lower right corner

Contrast

Contrast is the degree of difference between colors and tones in an image. If contrast is weak, individual colors are more difficult to see. If contrast is strong, color differences are easier to see, but the image may be difficult to understand.

Depending on your camera settings, contrast in your photo may be anything from practically none, to perfect, to extremely strong. For use as a texture, you want the most accurate representation of the colors needed for your map. To achieve this, you are often better off not editing the contrast of your picture very much (most digital cameras have good contrast settings) unless you are certain there is a contrast error. If there is, you will have to adjust the contrast values based on your own ability to determine when it looks right. To practice doing this, you may want to photograph some objects near to your computer and then edit the photos while looking at the subject, to guide you in your edits. After a bit of practice, you should be able to edit contrast without needing reference (Fig. 6.6).

Fig. 6.6 In CG, it is more common to have not enough contrast, as in the left portion of this image, than too much, as on the right. The reason is that lighting almost always reduces the natural contrast of the objects in your scene. Compensating for this is more than a simple white balance operation

Shadows

The stronger your light is, the stronger the shadows in your scene will be. The most prominent shadows will be *cast shadows* that are cast by nearby objects. These will be hard edged in strong light, and will cover large parts of the objects they are cast upon. These must be removed entirely from your photo if it is to be usable in a CG environment. You do not want shadows cast by a lightsource that doesn't exist in your scene, or based on an object that also doesn't exist in your scene.

Another type of shadow, but one that is often allowed to remain in textures because it is so difficult to remove, are the fine shadows on the surface of an object caused by slight irregularities. Wood grain, plaster walls, small pits in bricks, drips of paint on a painted wall, and many other things are good examples of this type of shadow. If you have the time and can paint them out, it is best to do so. Before you do, however, you may want to first trace off their shape into another layer as a guide for making a *bump map*.

If you do allow these shadows to remain in your maps, do keep in mind that they will not change based on lighting in your scene, and if they are prominent, it will be clear that these textures are double-lit. Shadows can be the most easily spotted texture error after hue shift, so great care should be taken with them if they exist in your source images.

Bump Maps

If you use shadow impressions from a photo as reference for a bump map, as is often done, remember that a bump map uses the intensity of pixels in a map to determine their height. If you use the shadow information from your photograph exactly as is, you will not get the result you want. You will have enough information to paint it correctly, but the values in the image are not intensity values based on height information, as your finished map should be, but intensity values based on a 2D projection of a 3D scene. Because it is not the same information, it will not yield the same result.

The outlines of each bump area can give you an idea of shape, just as intensity values can give you an idea of height, but the correct values and shape are something you will have to extrapolate from the data in the photograph. If you use a single cylindrical bump on a wall as an example, with a strong light hitting it from one side, then the opposite side of the cylinder will have a crescent shaped shadow, and the side the light hits will have an arc shaped highlight. In between will be a tonal gradient, unless the bump is too small for a gradient to be represented. When rendered as a bump, you will not get a raised cylinder, but a crescent-shaped crevice and an arc-shaped wall, with a short ramp in between. This is true for any bump or displacement map (Figs. 6.7 and 6.8).

Fig. 6.7 When a section of the color photo on the left is turned into a grayscale bump map, the end result is noticeably different from the goal, even though the outline of the complicated pattern of stacked stones is retained

Fig. 6.8 Most of the detail in the bump map on the left is not easy to see because the value changes are too slight to be readily recognized by the human eye. To paint a height map properly, the full range of desired height difference, in this case from about 0–6 cm, must be scaled to the full 0–255 grayscale values possible in a bump or displacement map. Notice how much more realistic the render on the right is than the previous render based on a photo-derived map (Map courtesy Lennart Hillen)

Atmosphere/Fog

Any environment, even an interior one, contains small specks of particulate matter suspended in the ambient atmosphere. Light collides with these particles, and is affected by them. At near distances in a clean environment, the effect is nearly invisible. At greater distances, or those with higher concentration of airborne pollutants (natural or otherwise) like pollen, dust, smoke, etc., the change in color values can be dramatic. At great distances, the effect is so strong that it can be literally impossible to distinguish between one color and another, even between two colors that are exactly opposite, like red and green. Instead, everything in such a scene will take on the colors of whatever ambient light and shadow is present, with details distinguishable only by tonal differences.

This is important to know if you are taking reference photos from a long distance, like of a building façade with a long zoom lens. Even if you can zoom in close enough to fill your frame with your building, your camera is no closer to the object, and the atmospheric interference will still be present and will affect your colors. A picture taken this way will not contain usable color information, though it may have good structural information.

Reflected Light

Reflected, or *bounce*, light, is light and color bounced from one object to another. Bounce light does not require a highly reflective surface like glass or polished metal. Almost anything will bounce or receive bounced light, even a furry teddy bear. Therefore, in any scene, you will have colors from neighboring objects bouncing from one to the other. If you put an orange pail beside a black teddy bear, you will see an orange tinge to the fur nearest the pail, and a dark patch on the pail beside the bear, even if shadows are being cast in the opposite direction (Figs. 6.9 and 6.10).

It is good to be aware of this so that in those situations when reflected light noticeably changes the colors in your object, you can remove it by editing.

Fig. 6.9 Overall, the bricks in this photo have a high specular value due to being wet from rain, and have prominent highlights as a result. The high specularity of the bricks causes reflections in the image that an artist is well advised to strip from his texture maps

Reflections

Reflections, like shadows, are easily spotted. Unlike reflected light, which can create a subtle effect, actual reflections are not subtle at all. A reflection error is a full reflection of something in your scene, usually in a hard polished surface, and it

Fig. 6.10 If you want your object to have a high specular value, use a specular map; do not bake them into your color channel. In the example above, a specular map is enough to make the stones appear to be wet (Map by Lennart Hillen)

must be removed or your map will not make sense. There is a narrow exception to this. When you want reflections in your scene but cannot build the reflected object in 3D, you may want to photograph the reflection into your textures. However, if you do this, it is often better to instead shoot the reflected object itself and add it to your shader as a reflection map.

Blur

If your camera or subject moves while the camera shutter is open, the resulting image will have some blur. If the camera moved, the entire frame will be blurred. If something in your shot moved, then it will be blurred. Unless you desire a special effect of some kind that requires blur, you will not want to use a map that has been blurred in this way. If it is a slight amount of blur and you no longer have access to the subject, it may be worth the trouble to retouch it from the image, but usually it isn't. To avoid blur in your texture reference photos, you should use a stable shooting surface, like a tripod, and your subject should be motionless as well.

Blocked View

Certain subjects cannot be photographed without some amount of interference of this type. If you are taking a picture of a building, not only might pigeons get in the way, but if the building has enough decorative detail, the decorations themselves may block the view of other parts of the building. If you can avoid this by careful framing, it is worth the trouble to do so. If a moving object, such as an animal, blocks your view you can take several photos. Even if the animal is in each of the photos, if its position is changed from image to image, you can cut and paste the photos together to eliminate the blockage.

Sometimes you will have to take separate shots from different points of view. This can be effective if you have an immovable object in the way. You will probably pick up noticeable lens distortion, because you will be photographing your subject from an angle, but after adjustment, you should have a good idea of what belongs in the blocked area.

If you cannot get to the blocked material, but need it, you will have to make it up based on your best guess from the existing reference.

Resolution

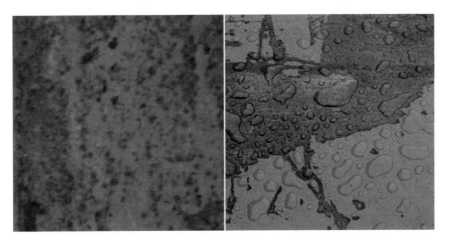

Fig. 6.11 Even though the two maps above are the same resolution, the scale of the detail in either map is different. Because it is different, one is too sharp or the other isn't sharp enough. Either way, it is a problem

The resolution of maps that are meant to be adjacent should match. It is difficult to accomplish this in the field when acquiring photos, but if you keep it in mind when you shoot, and use the highest resolution possible for your camera, you will get what you need in most circumstances (Fig. 6.11).

Once you have a good-quality cleaned-up photograph, you can either use it as-is, or use it as reference for a painted texture. There are two schools of thought on this, with parties on either side holding strong opinions. On one side, there are artists who prefer to use photo texture. The idea is that they are more realistic because they are more detailed and accurate than painted textures. On the other side of the debate are artists who prefer to paint their textures. These artists object to the various types of information pollution that occur in photo textures, and prefer to paint their textures from scratch to prevent clogging any one channel with information from another.

Both methods have their strengths and weaknesses. It is unquestionably more work to paint a complex texture by hand, such as a mixture of stains on a porous surface, than to photograph it. A photograph of this texture would, however, be highly prone to contain unwanted information. This is why using a combination of the two methods is not uncommon among professionals. A combined workflow requires a source photo that is first cleaned, and then used as reference for painting. Sometimes a completely new image is made, other times the photo is simply *retouched* to clean up the most obvious problems. For artists who require only the cleanest maps, there is no substitute for making them by hand. If time is an issue and extremely complex maps are needed, photos can work very well. If you are making *The Incredibles*, you will probably want to paint your maps, but for *Spider-man*, a good argument can be made for using photos (Fig. 6.12).

Fig. 6.12 This texture map was made as vector art based on a photograph of a pattern on the wall of a cathedral. It may be used as is, if the paint job is meant to be clean, but if dirt is desired, a dirt map will be added. Because the art is vector-based, the colors may be easily changed to create variations. With the addition of bump and specular maps, this texture can be made to be highly realistic

Color

Bit-depth is a term that defines the number of bits of information that are stored per pixel or per channel. The more bits there are, the finer the resolution of specified color information can be. A 24-bit image has 8 bits of information for each of the three red, green, and blue channels. Over 16 million different colors are possible at 24-bit color depth, more than the average eye can detect. This doesn't mean that a 24-bit image will have this many colors, but that it can represent this many colors. A 32-bit color is the same as 24-bit, with the addition of an 8-bit transparency channel.

Many maps have fewer than 256 colors, or as many colors as can be represented at 8-bit depth, but without careful palette control, the colors represented at 8-bits may produce *banding* because the colors needed cannot be represented with either the palette used, or the bit-depth. This is why 32-bit color is the most common bit depth used in texture maps for console game and film textures.

Regardless of the accuracy of color representation, you should make an effort to be aware of how many colors are actually needed for your textures. Use too many, and you risk making it dirty or cluttered. A good rule of thumb here is to analyze the subject of your map for the minimum number of unique intrinsic colors.

For a label on a bottle, this might be as few as two main colors, red and white for instance, and a number of colors in between for anti-aliasing. If the label has a coffee stain, then you add the color of the coffee to both the red and the white, plus a range of transparency, perhaps 100 levels, resulting in 202 colors, plus anti-aliasing. If you think of colors this way, as white paper plus red ink with a coffee stain over it, instead of simply a group of 202 semi-related colors, your colors will be cleaner than they would be otherwise. It is always easier to lay down colors accurately in layers than to try and figure out the final product pixel by pixel.

Fig. 6.13 How many textures, and of what kind, are required to make a realistic 3D representation of the objects in this scene?

Texture design

There is no one solution that will work for every situation when texturing 3D models. Some solutions work in some situations but not in others, and vice versa. If you want the highest possible quality, but are working with a renderer that cannot use alpha maps, you will not be able to have transparency and will be forced to build certain types of structures in polygons instead of creating the effect with maps. This is the primary tradeoff: between unique, high quality textures, and poly count. Sometimes it is either cheaper or better to use textures instead of polygons, and sometimes it isn't. Learning to differentiate between the two is not an exact art, but with practice, you will be able to come to agreeable compromises that render quickly and look good (Fig. 6.13).

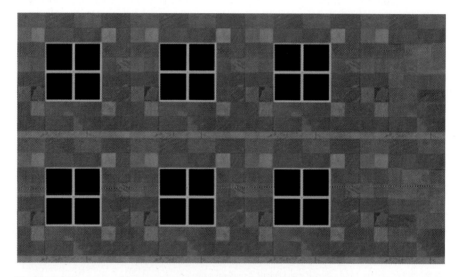

Fig. 6.14 This map is clearly reusing the same stones in a pattern that repeats eight times. It would be better to make a couple of variations and then place them to disrupt and disguise the repetitions found here. Doing so would produce a more appealing result and could use fewer pixels overall, because a unique map to cover the entire area is unnecessary

The first compromise is whether you intend to use unique textures for every element in your scene. If you do, you will have bigger texture maps than you would otherwise. You may also have more maps. The advantage is that viewers will not see any repetition in your map's patterns (unless it is supposed to repeat), and your scene will be more convincing because of it (Fig. 6.14).

If you cannot afford to sacrifice render speed or memory for large numbers of unique maps for every object, you could go to the other extreme and reuse your maps as much as possible by *tiling* them. When tiled, a small texture map repeats itself in a grid-like pattern. The result is that a very small map may cover a large area, but it does have an aesthetic drawback: the tiling pattern is usually easy to spot and tends to make objects less convincing to a viewer. This can be mitigated somewhat if the tiling effect is carefully hidden by careful control of the map's major features, but even this usually isn't enough to disguise the tiling. Tiled textures may also create disturbing *Moiré* patterns on your screen. This is when a regular pattern, your map, is viewed through another regular pattern, your monitors' pixel grid, and an *interference pattern* is created where they cross. If you do not want a Moiré pattern, you will have to use a different solution.

A middle ground is to use *texture tiles*, not to be confused with a *tiling texture*, to have as many unique maps as possible, reduced chance of interference patterns, and a better disguise for repeated use of the same texture map. A texture tile is an image that is not repeated mechanically based on having its UVs stretch beyond legal UV space. Instead, the tile pattern is literally etched into the model, and each quad is mapped to fill 0–1 UV space. A *Tile set*, or group of tilable maps is then created and assigned to each quad. This method increases the poly count of your object, but has the advantage of allowing a great deal more variety in the mapping solution because you can now mix and match the positions of each tile. This simple attribute is usually sufficient to completely disrupt any Moiré pattern, and at the same time makes it very difficult for any observer to detect any repetition. For variety, you can also flip or rotate the textures (Fig. 6.15).

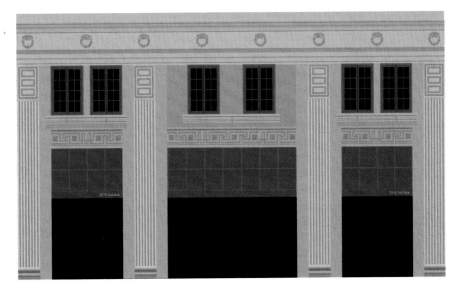

Fig. 6.15 In this example of a texture tile set layout, there are several repeated textures separated by polygons. As long as there are polygons in your model to hold each of these textures, only one of each is required

Some artists use *blend textures*, texture maps that define what percentage of any layers of texture maps beneath them, is visible at any given location. These maps allow static Moiré inducing patterns to be blended in such a way that it is very difficult to spot any repetition. This technique is particularly effective with landscape terrain, but it can also be used in other things, like this architecture example from *Gears of War* by Epic Games (Fig. 6.16):

Fig. 6.16 Normal, color, diffuse, and specular maps add a great deal to this geometry from the game *Gears of War* by Epic Games, Inc. (Copyright © 1998–2008, Epic Games, Inc. All rights reserved)[1]

Normal maps change normal information based on an RGB image that is created by projecting the normals of selected high res geometry onto the UV layout of low-resolution geometry. Texture maps made in this way may be edited afterwards by hand, but it is not easy to do because of the difficulty of matching different colors to normal direction values. Normal maps do not create new geometry as displacement maps do, but change the way light affects existing geometry. This means that, just like bump maps, an object with normal maps applied will have exactly the same silhouette it has without the maps.

---

[1] Epic, Epic Games, Unreal, The "Powered by Unreal Technology" logo, the Circle-U logo, and Gears of War are trademarks or registered Trademarks of Epic Games, Inc. in the United States of America and elsewhere.

Normal maps have specific texture layout requirements (overlapping UVs are not allowed). These requirements may force you to use more than one *UV set*. For other reasons, it may also be advisable to use more than one UV set. For example, what if you have a brick wall where all of the bricks are arranged in the same repeating pattern, but the colors on the bricks don't match that pattern, or don't repeat in the same sequence? When faced with such a problem, you may want to use multiple UV sets. What this allows you to do is have a tiling pattern for your tiny repeating brick pattern, but several larger textures for the more unique color pattern (Fig. 6.17).

Fig. 6.17 These bricks tile in three separate tilable sections, within each of which, a repeating texture consisting of only a few bricks is sufficient to represent the structure of every brick in the pattern, the colors in each of the three sections does not repeat at all however, and demands a separate UV treatment

Weathering

Many surfaces will look unnatural if they are too clean. For an architectural rendering or an advertisement, you will probably want your objects to be pristine, but for almost everything else, you will want dirt maps. Dirt maps don't have to actually represent dirt, though they often do, but any form of weathering at all.

This can be rust, oxidization, paint, graffiti, bird droppings, or anything else that could conceivably be added to a clean surface.

Dirt maps are sometimes a layer in an image file that also includes a clean version of the art. They are kept separate to make modifying either easier to accomplish. When finished, they can be either combined with a color map or exported with an alpha channel as dirt only, to be layered over something else.

When painting a weathered surface, it is helpful to keep in mind that every bit of wear in your map has a highly specific reason behind every color change. An oily object dragged against a wall leaves a smudge. A number of red splotches of rust on concrete match the shape of the bottoms of some tin cans that once rested there. If you do not keep this in mind, but instead think of weathering as a random event, your maps will not contain the kind of detail necessary to make them credible. Just as it is important to understand something of geology before building mountains out of polygons, it is also good to understand something about the nature of how stains and wear come about before attempting to paint them into a map (Figs. 6.18 and 6.19).

Fig. 6.18 In this image, the primary forms of wear are rain streaks on stone and overlapping examples of graffiti. The rain streaks are easily made with a layered dirt map, but the graffiti can be a simple color map without dirt

Fig. 6.19 This image contains a complex pattern of low contrast dirt, exposed bricks under peeling paint, and peeling paint that is best represented as either polygons or normal maps derived from polygons

Part of the reason you need to take great care when texturing the objects in your scene is that you don't want to have textures that fight with your lighting. As described earlier, shadows in maps may not agree with shadows cast by lights in your scene, color temperature of scene lights and maps may be different, and other baked-in effects will cause your texturess to draw attention to them in an unwelcome manner. After you have made your textures and they are clean and accurately represent the information they are meant to contain, it is time to light your scene. Without lights, you won't be able to see anything, but just like textures, any old lights won't do. You'll need to control them very carefully.

Chapter 7
Lighting

Fig. 7.1 Even subjects not ordinarily considered beautiful can be made beautiful with the right lighting, as in this example by Stêphane Moya (Courtesy of Fryrender)

Lighting will determine whether your render is beautiful or not. No matter how well built every other element of your scene is, if your lighting is poor, the quality of the objects in your scene will not be evident. Poor lighting is the easiest way to destroy the good effect of work well done, just as it is the best way to quickly resuscitate even mediocre efforts (Fig. 7.1).

Sometimes the term *photorealism* is used to describe the level of quality expected in a render. What does this mean? A photograph is the equivalent of a render, and, even if the lighting could be described as poor, in a literal sense, the result will always be photographic for that setup. This is because a camera can only produce a photo-real image. Strangely enough, some photographic images are not what is meant by the term "photo real," not because they aren't, but because the term is meant to describe something more specific than just what any camera will record. If it is possible for a photo to fail the test of being "photo real," then clearly, something else is meant by it.

Any object, no matter how fanciful, can be rendered so that it looks real. This is because realism is not a function of models or textures, but lighting and rendering. If a wildly inaccurate model is lit well, it will be a credible 3D object, even if it does not credibly represent the object it is supposed to be. The reason is that, within your scene, as far as the renderer is concerned, it is a real object. Photorealism, then, is the quality of your lighting in a finished render, and the credibility of your scene rests on the accuracy of the objects within it,[1] in combination with the lighting.

The basics of lighting are easily stated, but understanding only comes from practiced observation of how light behaves, both in the real world and within the confines of a CG scene. Real-world lighting is concerned primarily with factors relevant to aesthetic appeal, and virtual lighting is often only meant to imitate real-world lighting. Because it is important that any real-world lighting used as an example is of good quality, this chapter begins with photographic lighting; its goals, methods, and some standards by which its success is judged.

A light source such as the sun, a match, or an incandescent bulb, emits *photons*. These particles travel away from the source at high speed as *rays*. Light from the sun is so distant from their point of origin that its rays are considered parallel. Nearer sources, like a light bulb, discernibly push photons outward at every angle. When an object blocks a photons' path, it is either absorbed or reflected as *bounce light*. Either way, because photons have been blocked, they do not travel through an object to light the other side. This causes shadows to appear. Shadows are not, as they seem to be, a dark color that is cast from an object, but are more like a hole in the lighting that is cast on surrounding objects (Fig. 7.2).

When a photographer lights a scene, he will try to ensure that everything in the scene is clearly lit, even if it is in shadow. This is accomplished by using lights of different intensities in combination with other equipment designed to manipulate light. One of these devices is called a *reflector*. A reflector is a screen that comes in a variety of colors that can be attached to a tripod. It is designed to produce smooth, even *bounce light*. For this reason, its surface is unwrinkled, but has a fine texture that disrupts the direction of reflected light, to remove the hard edge it would otherwise project. These are placed around objects in a scene to intensify, direct, or change the color of bounce light. They work because all things reflect and receive light to some degree. A reflector is not the origin of a photon, but serves to modify and redirect *ambient photons* in a scene.

Bounce light can be used to reflect somewhat dim light into the shadow side of an object, partly illuminating it to make its structure clear. If the reflector has color to it, that color may be used to create contrast with the color of the key light and heighten the structure and depth of the resulting image. Without bounce light, most images would be very flat. With it, they acquire depth (Figs. 7.3 and 7.4).

Depending on your shot, you may want to highlight your subject with a hard outline made of light. This is known as a *rim light* (Fig. 7.5). A rim light is a high intensity light directed at your subject from the sides, top, or back. If angled properly, it will cause a bright highlight to follow the contours of your subject, as if outlined by a glowing brush. The only real trick about using rim lights correctly is to get their intensity and angle right. If you do those two things, they should behave as you expect.

---

[1] When "photo real" is used to describe art before it is rendered, it is meant to describe the credibility of the measurements and textures in the scene. It is improper to use the term in this manner however, because photos, cameras, and renderers all exist independently of an object's absolute dimensions and other visible characteristics.

Fig. 7.2 Blue shadows on snow are a common sight, and a good clue that maybe black shadows are not accurate. Sometimes shadows are so dark that their color is difficult to detect, but it is unlikely to be black. Most shadows have some color associated with them, and the color is related to the color of the light source and the object it falls upon. Shadows can also be highly saturated, contrary to expectation, because there is no light to wash out the color

Fig. 7.3 A reflector illuminates its target and adds its own colorcast. This can be a helpful device to clarify the structure of your subject. In this illustration, the gold reflector card is visible, and casts its color onto objects in the scene

A *fill light* works a bit like a bounce light, but instead of passively reflecting existing light, fill light is created by secondary light sources. Sometimes, to make the light more even, a photographer will put a box around a fill light that has an

Fig. 7.4 This is the same subject as in the previous figure, but here, the reflector is not visible in the scene. It does affect the scene however, and gives the subjects added depth by creating color contrast between polygons based on whether they are facing towards, or away from, the reflector

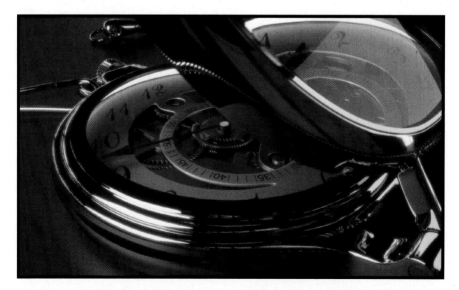

Fig. 7.5 A rim light outlines shadowed portions of the watch in this rendering, unifying all of its components within the same outline (Image by Isaac Mas Torrent, courtesy of Fryrender)

opening on one side covered by a fine white mesh. This disrupts light passing through enough so that, when it emerges on the other side, it is *diffuse* or soft light. This is an effective technique for illuminating a side of your subject indirectly, in an illusion of a higher level of *ambient light* than is ordinarily present.

Light Types

Fig. 7.6 Ambient light defines details on the shadow side of the building in this render, while simultaneously clarifying the structure by strong hue and saturation contrast with those parts of the subject lit with direct light (Image by Jose Manuel Linares, courtesy of Fryrender)

Ambient light is what allows you to see things inside your house during the day, even though no lights are turned on. Sunlight washes over everything because, after direct rays arrive inside through windows, they continue bouncing throughout your house, lighting up even deep corners. Shadows cast by ambient light can be dim and soft, or hard and strong, depending on the intensity of the source. The presence of true ambient light in a scene is very difficult to accurately calculate for a CG rendering, and it is for this reason many cheats have been invented to get around it. Ambient light is so important, that almost every lighting prop is designed to accentuate it in some way (Fig. 7.6).

Spot lights will cast a hard light and shadow in a given direction based on the orientation of the light and the shape of its housing. Spotlights are an excellent means of directing attention towards an element in your scene. With the right modifications, spotlights can cast a variety of different types of light at a very small part of a scene they are aimed at.

Most photographers use a wide variety of devices: umbrellas, reflectors, black mesh light occlusion frames, filters, gels, and just about anything they can think of to change how light affects a scene. All of this equipment is used because whatever natural lighting conditions exist on the set is almost never good enough. This is as true outdoors as it is indoors.

When a cinematographer shoots a building façade at night, he may hire half a dozen cranes to hold huge lights below it, so that it looks like a night scene that just happens to be very clear and aesthetically appealing. One reason extra lights are needed to achieve this effect is that a camera does not see the same thing we see when we look at something. In this sense, a photograph is very unrealistic, unless adjusted with proper lighting.

The first problem any professional photographer encounters when setting up his lighting, is that the image his camera records will not resemble the image he sees with his eyes unless he controls the scene very carefully. The reason for this is that the human brain automatically *white balances* everything it sees, so that white almost always appears to be white, and every other color is automatically balanced so that they appear to be the right color as well. This is necessary because the color of any given light source has such a powerful effect on the colors of everything in its range that they are altered to something else, and that is what the camera sees, unless you use its white balance function.

Visual information passes into our eyes and through our optic nerves in a passive way, just as light passes through a camera lens. Cameras and eyes are somewhat alike in this regard. The optic nerve carries the information to the brain, where it is processed. It is here that discrepancies between a photograph and our own experience of seeing something will occur.

A common experience is to try and take a photograph of a richly luminous landscape at dusk, only to get a photograph of a nearly black foreground, and a beautifully lit sky, or a nearly white sky with a grainy foreground. This happens because the camera doesn't have the same high-quality image-processing powers of your brain, and cannot decide between differing exposure values for the bright sky and darker foreground. Another example of the same phenomenon is an interior photo of something white, but the photo is completely yellow or orange (Fig. 7.9). This is because the automatic white balance function in your brain corrects the colors for you. Because of this, extra lighting is almost always needed to light a scene in such a way that it matches your own experience of seeing things (Fig. 7.7).

Traditionally, *warm colors* are red, yellow, orange, and their derivatives. *Cool colors* are green, blue, violet, and their derivatives. These *color temperature* associations are the opposite of what they should be, because red is actually the coolest visible color temperature, and blue is the hottest. The origin of this error may be that until the modern era, extremely hot blue light could not easily be produced,

Fig. 7.7 A subject like this can be very difficult to photograph properly because the tonal range splits into two distinct, and very different, bands. Our brain can make sense of such a subject, and see a full tonal range in both the light and the dark sections. Likewise, a carefully controlled render can yield a more convincing tonal range than a photo

Fig. 7.8 In this render, a broad tonal range adds clarity and depth to the subject (Image by Erwan Loison, courtesy of Fryrender)

but the red of a common flame was easily found, and the blue of ice may have been a reference for "cool" colors. Regardless of the origin, the temperature of a wavelength determines the color we see (Fig. 7.8).

Below is a rough table of equivalents.

Source	Temperature	Source	Temperature
Flame	1,800 K	Daylight, horizon	5,000 K
Incandescent light	3,000 K	Electronic flash	6,000 K
Studio light	3,400 K	Noon daylight	6,500 K
Moonlight, Xenon lamp	4,100 K	CRT screen	9,300 K

Each of the temperatures listed in the above table corresponds to a specific color, starting with orange, and moving up to blue. At lower temperature levels, color is red, and when it is higher than the highest listed, it becomes ultraviolet.

The colors in this table are fair approximations of the color of light given off by various light sources. You can find more detailed charts elsewhere with minimal effort.

Fig. 7.9 The white stone in this photograph appears to be orange because the photograph has not been white balanced

For a photographer, the most basic goals are these: Structural clarity, mood, and beauty. Achieving these three things has nothing to do with being realistic, but using light to paint the scene in such a way that anyone looking at it will understand any photos made from it. Regardless of the style of the photographer, any professionally

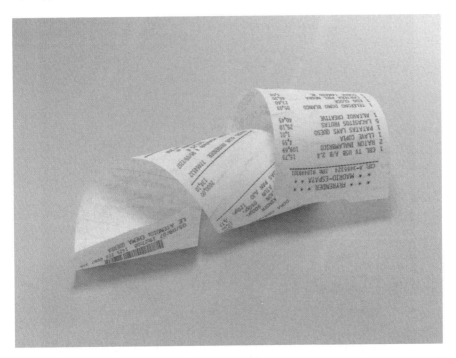

Fig. 7.10 The whites in this render have been beautifully balanced so that the white paper is rendered as white (Image by Henderyut, courtesy of Fryrender)

made photo will be legible, clear, and stylish. These goals are important to the CG artist also, because without them, his work will not demand the kind of attention that a well done work of art always gets (Fig. 7.10).

To "paint" a scene with light, still-life photographers will literally light the different parts of their scene one by one, adding and subtracting light elements as necessary to make the image ever more clear and clean. A *key light*, the light used to set the major color source in a scene, will be placed to light up one side of the still life. A large reflector may be placed opposite the key light, and it will have a tint, to reflect color into the bottom surfaces of the subjects. Other lights will be added to illuminate each side of the still life, and each light will be different from the others, to help define the surface orientation of various parts of each object. An intense rim light might be added above the scene to outline everything with a white halo; this is how lighting works. It is about building color and structure into a scene through the judicious placement and control of light (Fig. 7.11).

After you are comfortable lighting the structure of your subject, you may want to consider mood. It is entirely possible to light the same scene in such a way that with one setup it has one mood, and then change the lights and get a completely different impression. It is precisely because lighting has such a strong effect on a

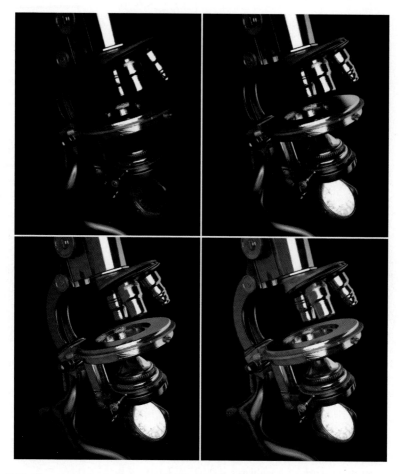

Fig. 7.11 Four stages in rendering a still life: Key light, object specific lights added, rim light added, and a fill light to enrich the shadows (Renders and model by Sebastian Walter)

scene that artists cannot afford to be careless with it. Simply illuminating a scene clearly is not good enough if the render requires some kind of mood, regardless of what that mood might be. It could be anything from techno-cool to playful, sad, dramatic, or romantic. Whatever the mood is, your lighting should accentuate it.

A good source of inspiration for mood lighting can be readily found in feature films, where there is a hundred years of lighting history behind the methods employed by cinematographers and lighting directors to achieve story nuance through lighting. Many video game developers incorporate film-styled lighting into their cut scenes and, sometimes, into real-time rendered scene graphics (Fig. 7.12).

Fig. 7.12 Notice the difference a change in lighting makes? (Image by Jose Manuel Linares, courtesy of Fryrender)

CG Lights

In any given CG scene there are many light sources of various intensities and types. Not all of them are lights, but in one way or another, light comes off them to illuminate something else. The way it works is that photons from an initial light source, a *light emitter*, are projected outwards. These photons travel until they strike something and are either absorbed completely, partly absorbed, or reflected. The reflected light is usually a different color than it was initially, and of lesser intensity, having lost some of its original strength during the process of partial absorption and reflection. This process repeats itself as the photon continues to reflect and be absorbed, until there is nothing left to absorb or reflect. Practically

Fig. 7.13 Well-defined surfaces such as the ones represented in this illustration can only be achieved by lighting the object from all sides. In this case it is achieved with a physically based renderer (Image by Stêphane Moya, courtesy of Fryrender)

speaking, most renderers simply have a cutoff intensity value below which no further calculations are made (Fig. 7.13).

Vector math is used to calculate the intersection of the angle of light and an object's normal. This is done by comparing the sine of the angles on either side of the equation. Changing the value of either the normal vector or the light vector can dramatically affect the result of a render. Changing the light vector is equivalent to changing the direction of a light, which is something easily done with real-world lights. Changing an object's normal can be done for a number of reasons, and cannot be done with real-world objects. This is just one area where CG lighting can be different from real-world lighting. Usually, these differences can be exploited to your advantage, because they provide greater flexibility in your lighting solution than physical lights would give.

Although all lights will cast shadows[2] whenever the path of travel for its photons is blocked, sometimes the shadows are so faint that they are not discernable. It is due to this observation, and the desire to optimize rendering wherever possible,

---

[2]Although it is correct to use the expression "cast shadows," in a literal sense, shadows are not cast at all. What is actually happening is that light is cast against objects, and where an object blocks the path of light, the unaffected area is said to be a "cast shadow."

that CG lights may have their shadows turned off. Lights that do not cast shadows but do project light, can be very useful at providing fill light, or reflected light. What this does is to illuminate surfaces that would otherwise be indistinguishable due to heavy shadow. Because they are already in shadow, there is no need to cast more; conflicting shadows and the fill light can approximate the result of true bounced light. This is a lighting optimization.

Fig. 7.14 This environment from *My Horse and Me* utilizes light maps to allow this scene to render in real time despite complex lighting (Courtesy of W! Games)

CG lights differ from real-world lights in many ways, but the only differences of any import to an artist are related to optimization. The number of photons actually bouncing around in any given environment is so large that it would be physically impossible for any computer to accurately calculate every interaction between every photon and every scene element. Because of this, light calculations are optimized in such a way that a scene may be credibly rendered with a much smaller number of photons, fewer interactions, and various cutoff points beyond which further calculations will not be made. So, to light a scene properly, you must adjust your lights to compensate for the differences between real and optimized CG lights. These adjustments will be of the following types (Fig. 7.14):

- Render type
- Quality settings

The type of renderer used to calculate the final result governs CG lighting solutions. Renderer choice, then, will determine the type of lighting solution you make. The two major types of renderers are rasterizers and ray tracers.

All real-time 3D games presently use rasterizer renderers, though there are some real-time ray tracers currently in production. The primary difference between the way a rasterizer and a ray tracer works is how each projects a 3D scene onto a 2D plane.

A rasterizer projects 3D coordinates against each axis of a 2D plane to determine their location in 2D space. Each location corresponds to a pixel. Lighting calculations performed within the 3D scene are used to determine the colors of any given point in the scene, and these values are projected forward to pixels in the final rendered image.

A ray tracer does the opposite, and projects from each pixel into the 3D scene, and checks for collisions with scene objects or effects. When it does collide, a color value is returned to the screen. If the object it collides with is semi-transparent, the ray continues into the scene until it strikes another object, and its value is used to modify the color of the placeholder pixel generated at the first collision. It continues to do this until it strikes an opaque pixel or reaches a saturation point. The same is true of reflections and refractions. For either of these events, when a ray strikes a surface that is refractive or reflective, a placeholder flag is added to the pixel, and the ray will bounce within the scene, striking other objects that successively modify the value of the placeholder pixel, until a final value is arrived at.

Of the two systems, rasterization is much faster on current game consoles, but when scenes have an extremely large number of triangles, ray tracers become faster. The reason is that performance of a rasterizer decreases rapidly based on the number of triangles in a scene, but with a ray tracer, image size is the most relevant limiting factor. At a certain resolution and triangle count, the two systems perform at about the same frame rate, but ray tracers become faster at higher triangle counts. Of the two, ray tracing tends to generate much higher-quality solutions. One of the reasons for this is that certain calculations that are difficult to make accurately with a rasterization render, like determining whether either of two polygons is overlapping when they are both very close together, can be done more accurately with a ray tracer. This is why ray tracers are associated with such things as reflections, refractions, and clean shadows, but rasterizers require a number of faked solutions to arrive at similar results.

Radiosity is a type of ray-traced rendering that creates its own bounce light by calculating a fairly high number of photon/object bounce interactions. Radiosity renders are time consuming to make, but they can also be very convincing. A popular method of lighting a scene uses a radiosity calculation to produce *light maps*, which are applied to scene objects that are then rendered in real time with a rasterizer. With this type of solution, after the lighting is calculated for the first frame, subsequent frame render times are very fast because the light maps are used instead of new calculations. This solution does not work for scenes that are lit with animated lights or animated objects that are meant to interact with lighting.

The impact on lighting of renderer type is quite strong. Here are some of the limitations of a raster engine:

Dynamic raster only:

- No global illumination/radiosity
- No soft shadows
- No real-time reflections
- No real-time refractions
- Fill lights of various types can be used to imitate global illumination and radiosity

Dynamic raster plus baked lighting:

- All lighting effects may be processed off-line by a ray tracer and added to texture or light maps
  ○ Limited to static light solutions. If lights move in the scene, or their values change, light maps will not be recalculated to match
- Shadow maps may be pre-calculated

Raster rendering, then, is more limited than ray tracing, apart from the significant speed bonus achieved at smaller scene sizes.

Quality Settings

Quality settings determine the accuracy, type, and number of calculations made for your render. These are very useful when making test renders, to keep time spent during iterations to a minimum. For your first renders, you may only need to check key light color and illumination levels. For that, you don't need anti-aliasing or shadows, so you can turn them off. Likewise, resolution doesn't have to be high, texture maps may be turned off, number of reflection rays can be zero, and many other settings may be adjusted to speed up render times and give you the opportunity to make more iterations of your lighting solution.

The highest quality settings can be unrenderable, so your goal as an artist is to find a balance between practicality and quality. There are many ways to modify your settings and scene elements to give you exactly what you want with a highly efficient render time.

Lighting is the most important part of any render, but amateurs and students too often put it last on their list of priorities and accomplish only the destruction of whatever else they have made. For the best results, keep lighting in mind from the very beginning of your project. Some artists will set up either basic lighting as a first step, or will make a separate low-resolution stage file to test lighting solutions. Whether you plan for it in the beginning, or simply make a serious effort at the end of a project, if you are sensitive to what good lighting is and make the effort to put that quality into your file, your work will be dramatically improved and taken more seriously by your audience.

Chapter 8
Project, Grading, and Conclusion

Fig. 8.1 Cathedral, by Mark Knoop

3D3
Project 1
Environment

Overview

The goal of this project is to create a polygonal stage (Fig. 8.1). It must include a minimum of one architectural element and terrain. Both must be built to the same level of resolution. This means that surface variations, light poles, sewer grates, and all other articles normally found embedded in, or attached to, terrain will be included in the file. All files must be fully prepared to receive both *normal maps* and *tile sets*. In most cases, this will require two UV sets and model subdivision to accommodate tile sets. Please do not confuse *tile sets* with *tiling*.

A. Paquette, *Computer Graphics for Artists II: Environments and Characters,*   123
© Springer-Verlag London Limited 2009

The finished model will be low resolution, but will have a high-resolution architectural façade on a hidden layer, to create normal maps. Do not think of this as an architectural model with some land attached. This project is about making both *together* as seamlessly as possible. No matter how well one or the other is built, if one does not match the resolution or quality of the other, the project is incomplete.

Fig. 8.2 In this example by Ruard Veerman, the lack of regularity in paving stone layout adds welcome variety to the scene

Fig. 8.3 The tiling paving stone patterns in this image are able to follow the contour of the surfaces they are mapped to because each map is mapped to a single quad and each quad's UV are mapped independently of each other (Image from a model by Robert Joosten)

A note on terrain: Terrain is very complex, much more so than most students imagine. Even in supposedly flat countries, like the Netherlands, it is not flat. If your terrain for this project is flat, it will in most cases be a critical mistake. Before you build your terrain, please go outside and look at all the height differences in the ground around you. No matter where you are, you will find a large amount of variety. This information must be included in your model (Figs. 8.2–8.4).

Fig. 8.4 Although this is a beautifully made model of a cathedral, it needs context, in the form of surrounding terrain, props, and other decoration, to be finished (Courtesy Laurens van den Heijkant)

Supplies/materials required

1. Drawings of subject
2. (Optional) digital camera

Instructions

1. Find/create lot plan for your building.
2. Create contour map for terrain your building will rest upon.
3. Build terrain object, all building foundations, and street dressing.
4. Build architectural subjects:
   (a) High resolution for normal maps
   (b) Low resolution for rendering
      (i) Be very careful to set it up properly for tile sets!
5. Add landscaping.
6. Add UVs for all elements and apply as many reference maps as required:
   (a) "REFERENCE MAPS" for this project must contain a schematic layout of all structural details, to show exact tiling values.
7. Add lighting.
   (a) The word, "lighting" refers to finished naturalistic lighting. Lights will be referred to as either (1) work lights or (2) render lights. Work lights will be expected on all projects, render lights, when requested. This project requires both. Do not imitate night lighting for this project. Full day lighting is required. Please keep work and render lights on separate layers, and name them.
8. Check model for errors against polygon checklist and fix all errors.
9. Deliver an archived file containing the following:
   (a) Two reference images, jpg format, no bigger than 800 × 600
   (b) One render of scene using render lights only
   (c) Geometry file containing:
      (i) High-resolution model
      (ii) Low-resolution model

Rules

1. Finished model is fully polygonal. Nurbs may be used as intermediate objects or for high-resolution model.
2. Alpha maps are optional
   (a) If used, they must be included in final file and may not exceed 512 × 512 resolution.
3. Scale is 100:1

4. Resolution notes:
   (a) Poly budget for full scene, exclusive of high-resolution façade for normal mapping, may not exceed 100,000 triangles
   (b) High-resolution façade may not exceed 100,000 triangles
   (c) Resolution and poly budgets are not the same thing. A building with 1,000 triangles can be the same resolution as a building with 1,00,000 triangles, if it doesn't require any more triangles to represent its parts. The difference is in the amount of detail in either building. Unlike a human, which always has the same number of limbs, and resolution changes that primarily serve to increase the level of curve detail, architecture and terrain will not always have the same number of parts, and so the minimum needed triangles to represent those parts will differ. For this reason, no guidance beyond this will be given in writing.
5. Penetration allowed for optimization purposes only
6. Naming convention for intermediate hand-ins:
   (a) lastnameFirstnameProjectname.rar/zip
7. For normal map UV set, all portions of all objects in scene (except duplicated sections) will occupy *unique texture space*
   (a) This means that either or both of the following is true:
      (i) Each part has a unique texture assigned to it (no shared shaders unless duplicate object)
      (ii) Each part has unique, non-overlapping UVs
8. For tile sets, each "tile" must completely fill legal UV space, from 0–1.

Expectations

1. Likeness is mandatory. Failure to achieve this goal will result in a failing grade, regardless of any other factor.
2. High-resolution model will be constructed with enough detail to be seamlessly composited with a photographic element.
3. Low-resolution model will be reduced to minimum necessary to comfortably accommodate normal maps, or render using color maps only without crippling loss of quality.
4. No technical errors will be present in this model.

Delivery schedule

This schedule is intended for use by students to improve their ability to determine whether their work will be sufficient or not, and as an aid in scheduling the progress of their project.

1. Contour map and terrain
    (a) Contour map is complete
    (b) Terrain is complete
        (i) Foundation for building and any other land-clearing required for object
            is included
2. Low resolution model
    (a) All objects are represented
        (i) This does not mean "all detail parts", but all parts intended for retention
            in the low resolution model.
    (b) Model must be solid, without gaps
3. High-resolution building; major structures only
    (a) All terrain, walls, roof, chimneys and other major details are present
    (b) All moving objects (windows, doors, etc.) are present
    (c) Errors are allowed
4. High-resolution building; details
    (a) All major details have been built. This may include: bricks, roofing tiles,
        moldings, sculptured elements, mullions, staircase decorations, etc.
        (i) "Major" is defined as: Details likely to be noticed. No obvious gaps or
            missing parts. All parts required as a base or attachment point for another
            surface are present, i.e.: If a clock is attached by a brace to a wall, then either
            (1) wall only, or (2) wall and brace are preferable to (3) wall and clock
5. UVs
    (a) UVs must be projected for all parts
        (i) UVs must be edited into legal 0–1 UV space
6. Lighting
    (a) Lighting is present in model
    (b) All surfaces are illuminated from all angles

If built properly, the finished model will be:

- Efficient enough to render quickly
- Complete
- Interesting

Depending on the layout of your stage, you may want to add a seamless 360°
background matte. If you do, your key lighting colors and intensities should match
whatever lighting is present in the image.

Ten-point grading criteria:

1. Likeness: No object receives a passing grade that is not a good likeness. No
   object receives higher than an 8 if it is not an excellent likeness.
2. Detail: Level of detail must be consistent throughout model. If architecture,
   terrain, and set dressing have conflicting levels of detail, grade cannot be higher
   than an 8.
3. Complexity: This refers exclusively to the number of real-world parts contained
   in the set, not how they are broken into polygons. Therefore, a Gothic cathedral

has a greater complexity than almost any other kind of building and has a higher complexity ranking. Only complex subjects are eligible for a 9 or 10 grade.

4. Geometry checklist: A perfect model will have no errors of the types described on the clean geometry checklist. A small number of careless errors are allowed within passing grades, but if the number is large, the project cannot pass. A large number of errors will affect 1% of the scene geometry or more and will be of five or more types. If the errors affect more than 1% of the scene, the file cannot receive a grade higher than a 3.

5. Tile sets: Tile sets are worth a total possible deduction of 3 points, regardless of other factors, if they contain mistakes.

6. UVs: Worth a total possible deduction of 2 points, regardless of other factors. Problems with UVs will be poor projection, distortion, poor layout, inefficient layout, or contrary to requirements for tile sets.

7. Lighting: A maximum of one point deduction. Deciding factors are clarity and render efficiency.

8. Poly count: Any model that exceeds poly count limits may not receive a grade higher than an 8, and then only if it is built well. If the poly count interferes noticeably with rendering, grade cannot exceed a 6.

9. Triangle pattern: If the triangle pattern is clean, it will not draw attention to itself because it will closely follow the structure of the subject. If it does draw attention to itself, it can be cause for a deduction. Only in extreme cases, such as when it seriously detracts from the visual coherence of the subject, should the full 2-point deduction be taken.

Despite the wide range of subjects that may be submitted for this project, most projects that receive a certain grade will possess common attributes. Below are examples of grades given to various projects, and the attributes that are most responsible for the grade awarded.

(10) No technical errors, excellent likeness, complex subject, interesting set dressing, consistent level of detail. Texture maps are simple, clean, and split into correct layers. Tile sets are cleanly laid out with minimum additional geometry to accommodate texture maps. UVs are tightly packed, well aligned, and projected without any distortion. Lighting is appealing and model is efficient for quick renders (based on complexity of model, actual render time may vary).

(9) Same as for 10, but may contain a maximum of one example of a technical error. Model may be so detailed that render is inefficient or impossible. In that case, grade is recognition for detail, effort, and observation skills, but penalized for poor renderability.

(8) Stage is a complex subject, an excellent likeness, with interesting set dressing. Some inconsistency between level of detail in architecture and terrain may exist. Technical errors may be present, but not in great quantity. There should be no more than three types of errors, and very few examples of each. Scene will render, but may be slow.

(8)   Stage is not a complex subject, but is executed perfectly, as in a 10 grade for a complex subject. Alternatively, it may be complex, but incomplete, or missing UVs in many places.

(7.5) Inconsistent levels of detail exist within a complex subject, some checklist errors are present, and render time is not efficient. Serious problems exist with either UVs or tile sets. Likeness is good, not excellent.

(7.5) Most factors are the same as for item 9, but a simple subject.

(7)   Some likeness errors, inconsistent detail, inefficient render, some checklist errors (usually naming, grouping, transforms present in model, and n-gons), but a good likeness.

(7)   Same as for complex subject with a grade of 8, but not a complex subject

(6)   Complexity of subject is irrelevant at this grade. Likeness is good, but model contains either five types of checklist error or more, or contains numerous examples of a few errors. "Numerous" is defined here as a total of 15 or more examples in total. Model is inefficient, has exceeded poly count, and probably will not render.

(6)   Incomplete. Some parts of the project may be executed very well and have an excellent or very good likeness, but other parts are either missing entirely, or are unfinished.

(5)   Failing grade. This model is not a good likeness, but is recognizable. Triangulation pattern is probably sloppy. Checklist errors are easily found. Naming and grouping is either incorrect or not done at all. UVs have not been assigned, or are edited so badly that they cannot be used.

(4)   Poor likeness, simple subject, incomplete, and checklist errors are easy to find.

(3)   Extremely poor likeness, simple object, large number of checklist errors, incomplete, and all objects present are missing almost all details.

(2)   Not a serious effort. A file with this grade will have only a few hours of work put into it. Most elements are missing; errors may or may not be present.

(1)   The only positive thing to say about a file that achieves this grade is that it was handed in.

(0)   Not handed in or plagiarized in part or whole.

Clean Geometry Checklist

1. File naming convention must be followed: lastnameFirstnameProjectname. extension For example: paquetteAndrewCathedral.rar
2. File must be compressed and saved in an archive file
3. File must contain 3D file, refmap and reference image file (to compare with model for likeness)
4. All objects named
5. All objects grouped
6. All grouping hierarchies correct
7. All layers named
8. No unused layers

9. All construction geometry deleted
10. All null nodes deleted
11. Appropriate poly count (not too low to catch important detail, not too high for game engine)
12. No coincident vertices within the same polyset
13. No gaps in geometry, all objects are solid
14. No spikes
15. No bow-tie faces
16. No smoothing errors
17. No floating faces
18. No separated faces
19. Self-penetration not allowed
20. Object to object penetration not allowed
21. Object must be centered on 0,0,0, with its bottommost point at $Y = 0$
22. Pivots for all parts and groups should be positioned correctly
23. Non-planar quads must be made planar or triangulated by hand
24. No n-gons
25. No distorted geometry
26. No distorted UVs
27. No wrong-way normals
28. No misaligned textures
29. No isolated vertices
30. All extrusion-related unmotivated gaps must be sealed
31. Aspect ratio for all triangles and quads should be as close to 1.0 as possible. This does not mean that other aspect ratios are illegal, but that they are not ideal. Penalties my apply for polygons that exceed AR 6.0 or are below AR .167
32. Triangulation patterns should be well-ordered, neat, and follow shortest-edge rule wherever possible
33. Lamina faces are illegal
34. Coincident faces within the same polyset are illegal
35. Coincident faces between separate polysets are allowed
36. Duplicate edges are illegal
37. Holes are illegal
38. Non-manifold geometry is not allowed (for this project. In other circumstances, it may be allowed. In this case, it is not allowed because of the solid part requirement.)
39. All vertices must contribute to surface or texture border definition
40. Ragged edge shapes are not ideal. Borders must follow target border shape
41. Locked normals are illegal
42. Reference map path must refer to image in same directory as object file
43. Reference map must be correctly attached
44. Zero edge-length faces are illegal

Conclusion, Part One

Environments are not just buildings slapped down on flat surfaces with a couple of textures thrown in. Nor are they always a bunch of endlessly repeated boxes with brick and window textures plastered all over their faces. A properly built environment will, in an optimized form, successfully translate as much detail as possible from the target environment into the CG environment. To do this, an artist must be aware of the kind of detail he must be sensitive to; he must have strong observation skills, and must be prepared for whatever technical challenges he will face while executing the project.

After reading this section of the book and putting that information to practical use in the exercise, if you received a 7 or above by the criteria given here, you should be well prepared for most of the problems any professional can expect to encounter on this type of project. If you earned a 10, congratulations! You have matched a professional standard.

3D4/Anatomy for Characters

Part II
Introduction

Character design and construction will result in a convincing character only if easily observed details of human or animal anatomy are used as a foundation. This is true of cartoon characters like the dog Scooby-Doo, and realistic characters like the Tonton beasts from *Star Wars, the Empire Strikes Back*. When artists ignore anatomical structure, their audience notices the errors because human audiences are very sensitive to this type of detail. To understand characters, then, you must first understand anatomy.

Artists who work with traditional materials study *superficial anatomy*, to acquaint themselves with all superficial anatomical features visible without dissection. They do not need to study deep anatomy, because deep anatomy is largely invisible on the surface and does not affect an artist's ability to either recognize anatomical details from a live model, or create a drawing without one. CG artists, on the other hand, do benefit from an understanding of non-superficial details. This is because the way a character animates, or rather, the way it moves, is governed completely by close interaction between surface and subsurface anatomy. Certain motions are completely impossible without deeply buried muscles. Animators should be aware of how these work to better inform their animations, even if they never animate a model that actually has every muscle built into it.

Anatomical information is not theoretical and it does not vary according to aesthetic whim. Anatomy is a science based on many careful observations made over centuries by thousands of individuals. These observations are condensed here over several chapters, with the aim of providing any artist with a ready reference for this information. Later chapters deal with variations encountered in character design and character building for efficient rendering and animation. If you learn this material well, it will serve you for the rest of your career as an artist.

The illustrations for this section of the book are a collaborative effort by several students and me. Special thanks go to Robert Joosten, who did the majority of the CG modeling and texturing; and Perry Leijten and Sebastian Mollet, who helped with labeling many of the illustrations. Below is a full credit list:

Primary low-resolution skeleton model: Robert Joosten, Perry Leijten, Sebastian Mollet

High-resolution skull model: Robert Joosten and Andrew Paquette

High-resolution muscle model and textures (nurbs): Robert Joosten

High-resolution digitized foot bones: Mark Knoop and Andrew Paquette

High-resolution digitized hand bones: Andrew Paquette and Robert Joosten

Renders: Andrew Paquette

Chapter 9
Anatomy

Fig. 9.1 Bones, tendons, and muscles of the lower arm and hand. Model and render courtesy of Sebastian Walter

The human body is designed to move and can be understood within the context of mechanical engineering. The human body, and the body of any biological entity, is at its most basic level a very complex and well-engineered machine (Fig. 9.1). All human characters are made of the same number of mechanical parts. They have a head, chest, pelvis, two arms with hands at the end, and two legs with feet at the end. Because the number of parts does not vary, it is possible to create a prototype character with generic characteristics, and use it as a base model for later characters, thus simplifying and making more efficient subsequent iterations of the modeling process. The aim of this chapter is to provide you with enough information to make such a prototype, so that you will know exactly what you are doing whenever you work with a character model in the future. The material presented here is primarily specific to human anatomy, but is generically applicable to any animal with a tetrapod body plan. This includes birds, lizards, mammals, and some cetaceans.

Body Plans

A body plan is a kind of schematic layout of how an animal's parts are arranged. The number of limbs, body segments, and symmetry of a creature are all part of its body plan. Four-limbed vertebrates are all tetrapods (*quadrupeds* in Latin), and thus, include humans. *Cetaceans* (or whales) have a body plan that resembles that of a tetrapod apart from lacking pelvis, legs, and feet. Their facial structure is compressed and tilted upwards to accommodate breathing, but otherwise retains most of the structure familiar from other mammals (Fig. 9.2).

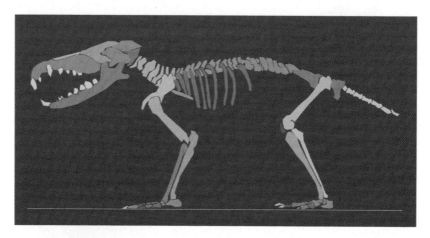

Fig. 9.2 This skeleton of a prehistoric giant groundhog is topologically homotopic with a human skeleton, and that of other land-based mammals. It is a tetrapod, meaning it has four feet. Although humans can be described as bipedal, or two-footed, our body plan is the same as this groundhog, with our arms being identical in arrangement and purpose as the forelimbs of this animal and all other tetrapods

Architects have to remember terms that specify certain architectural elements of a building. Quoining, roofing, joists, and plumbing are all terms an architect must know the name and function of, as well as other information relevant to each term. The character artist must likewise know many things about any character he wishes to build, but for a character artist, there is a major difference between the type of information he needs to remember and the information an architect must use. For an architect, although each part of a house, as described with a category name, like "foundation," will always function the same way, it can take a variety of shapes and be made out of a variety of different materials. In combination with other parts of a building, the topological network of various things will vary from structure to structure. This is not true of a character model. Character models always have the same topology, the same parts, and even the same basic shapes. The biggest difference between elements in any two characters is the *proportions* of the parts, but not the topology or shape (Fig. 9.3).

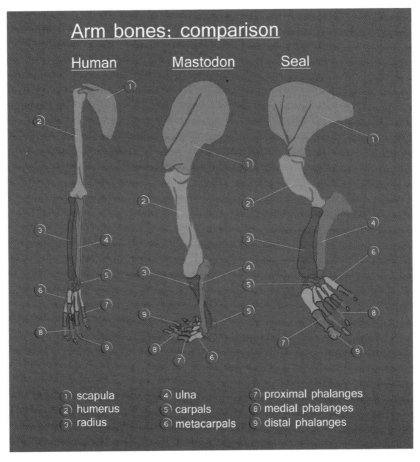

Fig. 9.3 The relative size and shape of the different bones in any group of mammalian species, their arrangement, purpose, and topology remain identical across species.

Because character topology does not vary, it can be memorized and reused. For the artist, this is a worthwhile exercise, because it provides greater freedom when working on a character model. Imagine a group of stuffed animals on a bed. Now imagine a thin opaque sheet draped over them. Imagine now that you must model that sheet exactly, without error. Without being able to lift up the sheet to see the stuffed animals underneath, it would be less easy to measure the drapery over them, because you will lack solid reference points to compare your observations to. Now imagine the stuffed animals moving around underneath the sheet, and how its shape would change. The same situation is the biggest problem any character artist has to overcome.

Homotopic Mammalian Topology

The superficial appearance of a human body is in great part governed by how skin drapes over muscle, which is in turn bound tightly across bone and organs. Without knowing the shape and relationship of these various hidden parts, it is very difficult to check your work on the skin. Some artists may be such keen observers that they don't need to know subsurface anatomy in order to correctly measure the skin attached to it, but this is an unusual artist. For most, knowledge of anatomy helps distinguish the various details of a figure more easily, and results in a more accurate model. Even for artists who are capable of accurately measuring shapes without reference to subsurface anatomy, knowledge of anatomy will enhance the speed of their efforts because measurements can be fixed to known anatomical reference points instead of randomly selected prominences that change depending on posture and lighting.

Mechanical Properties

An interesting fact about skeletal anatomy is that no muscle is attached on either end to the same bone. This is because such a muscle would have no mechanical utility. Even if it was flexible, and the ligament that attached it to either end was flexible as well, no amount of flexing or extending would result in any skeletal movement. Instead, muscles attach to two or more bones (Fig. 9.4), so that *flexion* and *extension* result in skeletal movement. Both are accomplished by contraction of various muscles, and the movement of actin against myosin accomplishes this. All muscles and all bones, indeed all parts of any creature's anatomy, fulfill specific mechanical purposes. This is just one of the reasons that a lack of anatomical knowledge often results in mistakes that destroy the credibility of a model. If an artist puts an extra bulge on a creature in imitation of a muscle, but in a location that has no discernable mechanical reason for being there, it is more likely to be interpreted as a tumor than a muscle for the simple reason that most humans are very sensitive to these differences and will know intuitively that it is wrong.

Here, then, are the things you will need to know in order to make a credible character:

1. Body plan (most often, tetrapod)
2. Bones: names, shapes, position in body plan
3. Muscles: names, shapes, position in body plan
   (a) *Origin*: the place on the fixed bone of a joint that a muscle is attached to
   (b) *Insertion*: the place on the freely moving bone of a joint that a muscle is attached to.

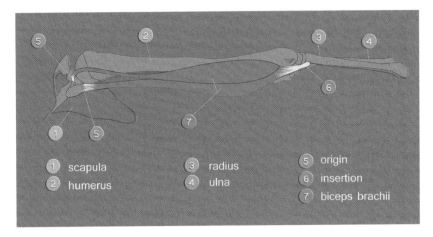

Fig. 9.4 Origins and insertion of the biceps brachii muscle

Navigation Terms

Anatomical terms used to describe the various parts of a body follow a few rules. Understanding these rules makes it easier to remember the names of the parts, as well as where they belong in the body plan. The first part of many of these names[1] tells you the location of the part relative to the rest of the body.

(a) Medial, medialis, or internal = Center
(b) Lateral, lateralis, external, or externus = Outside, or away from center
(c) Anterior, frontal, or ventral = Front
(d) Posterior or dorsal = Back
(e) Proximal = Closer to the root of the limb than another part
(f) Distal = Farther from the root of the limb than another part
(g) Superior = Above another part
(h) Inferior = Below another part

Muscle Types

Anatomical names frequently contain references to what a muscle does. Here are the most common types:

(i) Extensor
  • A muscle that, when contracted, causes extension, or the opening of a joint. In the elbow joint, this would happen if the hand started in a position near

---

[1] Latin names will be used in this book

the shoulder, and then through extension, the lower arm was rotated away from the shoulder to its fullest extent.

(j) Flexor
- A muscle that, when contracted, causes the angle formed by bones on either side of a joint to decrease. In the elbow joint, *flexion* occurs when the arm starts from a fully extended position and the hand is brought to the shoulder by contracting the elbow joint. Flexors oppose the action of extensors, and are frequently found grouped on the opposite side of the same bone.

(k) Abductor
- A muscle that pulls a bone away from the center of the body, like when raising an arm or leg to the side.

(l) Adductor
- A muscle that pulls a bone towards the center of the body, and opposes the action of an abductor.

(m) Rotator
- A spinal muscle that connects any two to three vertebrae in succession and causes rotation.

(n) Pronator
- A muscle that causes *pronation*. Pronation is when the hand or foot is rotated away from its natural *anatomical pose* to face anteriorly instead of posteriorly.

(o) Supinator
- A muscle that rotates the hand or foot back to its natural anatomical pose, by performing the opposite action of a pronator.

Species Shape Variations

There are three types of muscles: smooth muscle, cardiac muscle, and skeletal muscle. Cardiac muscle is only found in the heart and is an involuntary muscle. Smooth muscle is also involuntary, and may be found within organ walls. Skeletal muscle is a voluntary muscle, and is ordinarily what is meant when the word "muscle" is used. Skeletal muscle is attached to the skeleton, and is used to make it move. This is the kind of muscle we are primarily concerned with. Apart from special cases, like medical visualization, or unusual vfx work, as in the feature film *Hollow Man*, where smooth muscle and cardiac muscle were exposed, you are unlikely to encounter them in most projects.

A model of a human figure, where a perfectly straight line spanning the distance between origin and insertion represents every muscle, would have a silhouette that resembles a fully rounded figure to a remarkable degree. The *belly* of any muscle adds some volume to it, and is responsible for the numerous rounded shapes we are accustomed to seeing in any figure, but the primary shape comes from the correct connection between origin and insertion points. For a CG artist, this is extremely important to know. The credibility of your model will to a great extent rest upon

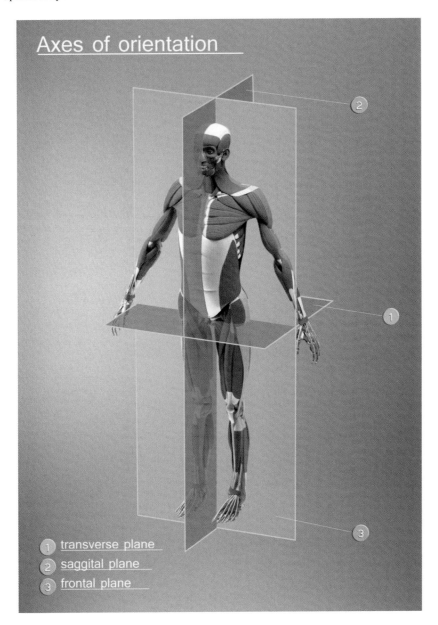

Fig. 9.5 A figure in the anatomical pose, divided by the three major reference planes

how well you have located the origin and insertion points, and how well you have built and positioned the bones they are dependent on (Figs. 9.5 and 9.6).

A model built around an incorrect skeleton, or with improperly positioned origin and insertion points, may come out somewhat disfigured, or like some other kind

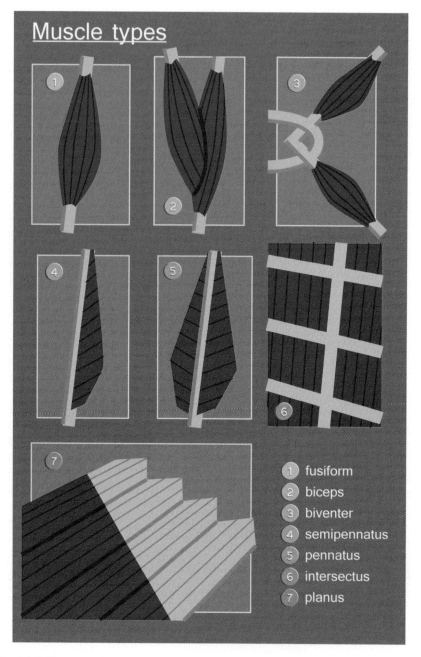

Fig. 9.6 Different types of muscle fibre growth patterns

of mammal. Most mammals either have a set of bones and muscles that is identical to those of a human in number and purpose, or very nearly so. The names of the bones and muscles are retained throughout many animal species for the simple reason that the bones are there to accomplish the same mechanical purpose and are located in the same position in the body plan. The differences between the body of a human and any other mammal can be summarized as (Fig. 9.7):

1. Proportion. A seal has an articulated arm with the same bones and muscles as a human, all the way down to the carpals and metacarpal bones of the hand, but their proportions relative to each other is a great deal different. The humerus is not long and thin as in a human, but short and stout. The same is true of the radius and ulna, which are so fat that it is hard to imagine them rotating around each other, yet owing to their shape, they do. In a horse, deer, elk, or other similar creature, the skeleton may look less similar to a human's at first, because it is not immediately evident that, due to the extreme shortness of the lower arm and lower leg bones, the bones just beneath them are elongated metacarpal, or finger, bones.
2. Shape. The sternum of a bird looks very little like a human sternum. In comparison, it looks like a boat's keel and a human sternum resembles a wooden ruler with a couple of bite-shaped chunks missing. Despite the obvious shape differences, the two bones are similar in other respects. They are located in the same position in the body plan, ribs and clavicles are attached to both, and they share the same name. Other bones, like the pelvis, vary in shape as well, but contain all of the same grooves and slots, to accommodate the same muscles, nerves, and other anatomical parts, as in any other tetrapod.
3. Number. Some animals have more of a certain kind of bone than others. The places this is most evident is in the digits and spine. Some mammals have three, four, or five fingers and toes. This is the only variation in the number of digits. In the spine, the difference in number of vertebrae is most evident in the cervical vertebrae, where each additional bone provides greater flexibility. Hence, birds often have a very large number of cervical vertebrae in comparison to a human, and are able to turn their head completely around in a three hundred and sixty degree arc. On the other end of the spine, animals with tails have more vertebrae to allow mobility of the tail.

The important point is that the study of human anatomy will inform you a great deal about the anatomy of other creatures as well. Every bone and muscle mentioned in this volume has a counterpart of similar shape and body plan position, with the same or similar insertion and origins, in the anatomy of other animals. Knowing this, you will also be able to create your own creatures that are credible because they share recognizable anatomical characteristics with animals that are familiar to you and your audience.

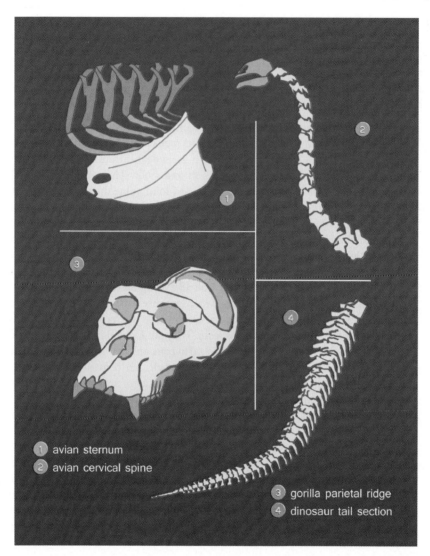

Fig. 9.7 Although skeletal topologies are similar across species, there are variations, most notably in shape and number of vertebrae. Here, the differences between the human parietal bones, which join at a tangent to each other, and those of a gorilla, which join to form a pronounced midline crest, are typical shape variations within land-based species. Avian species have many fused bones, as in the thoracic cage shown here They also have a major change in the shape of their sternum, called a "keel," which allows for the attachment of the very large muscles needed to power flight. In the example of the cervical vertebrae of a bird and the tail of a dinosaur, notice that both have many more vertebrae in both sections than a human, but that the vertebrae fulfill the same function and are similar in shape to the corresponding vertebrae of a human

Chapter 10
The Skeleton/Axial

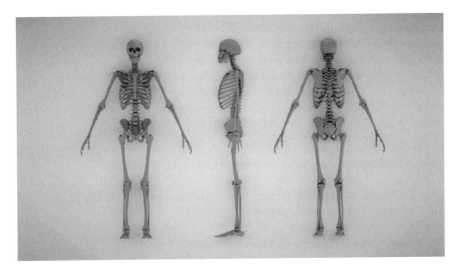

Fig. 10.1 The human skeleton in anterior, lateral, and posterior views

The skeleton allows locomotion, protects vital organs, and provides support for every part of the human body. The external shape of a character is more closely governed by the shape and alignment of its skeleton than any other structural feature. Therefore, if you are to understand why a character looks the way it does and how it moves, you must start with the skeleton (Fig. 10.1).

The skeleton is classified into two different groups. The *axial skeleton* is made up of all bones that cross the medial line of the body (Fig. 10.5). This includes the spine, ribcage, and head. Bones of the limbs and hip make up the *appendicular skeleton*. The axial skeleton is the primary support structure of the body, while the appendicular skeleton provides mobility. Within each group, there are bone series. These bones are numbered for identification. Numbered bones are found in the spine, fingers, and toes.

A. Paquette, *Computer Graphics for Artists II: Environments and Characters,*
© Springer-Verlag London Limited 2009

Bone Feature Types

Each bone has a highly specific shape. Unlike the cartoon versions of bones we are all familiar with, real bones are covered with dents, pits, holes, blades, bumps, and other surface detail. Together, these details give bones a weathered look, as if they are the product of damage due to a succession of minor impacts over the years of a bones' life. This is not the case. Instead, every one of these details exists, and has its specific shape, for an important mechanical purpose. Rough patches on bones are frequently attachment sites for ligaments. Holes in some facial bones allow nerves to pass from one side to the other. A groove in the top of the humerus gives passage and extra support to one head of the *biceps brachii* muscle, which passes over it before connecting to the *scapula*. The twist found in both the ulna and radius provides greater torque to muscles attached to them, enhancing the strength of any effort made by muscles attached to them. When building a skeleton, then, it is a good idea to pay careful attention to these details. If you get them wrong, you will not only make it inaccurate in the medical sense, but you may unintentionally shift the position of a muscle's attachment point, and that would change the shape of the character you are building. There are anatomical names to describe these features. Here is a list of the most commonly used words (Figs. 10.2–10.4):

- *Process*
    - A protuberance, usually a long one, extending from a bone.
- *Fossa*
    - The Latin word for ditch, used to describe a concavity, usually large in area relative to the bone it is part of.
- *Foramen*
    - A hole, usually penetrating from one side of a bone to the other. These allow nerves and veins to pass through or into bones.

Fig. 10.2 Anatomical features: process, foramen, and fossa

- *Suture*
    - A boundary between bones, across which a fibrous joint is formed

- *Tuberosity*
  - A site for the attachment of muscle, rounded in shape

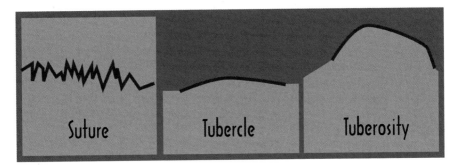

Fig. 10.3 Anatomical features: suture, tubercle, and tuberosity

- *Tubercle*
  - A site for attachment of muscle, smaller than a tuberosity, usually rough in texture
- *Condyle*
  - A process, usually occurring in a fused pair, as in the base of the humerus and femur bones. An attachment point for muscles.
- *Epicondyle*
  - A smaller version of a condyle, usually located near a pair of condyles, or on them
- *Ramus*
  - An elongated, flat process; a branch
- Styloid
  - A long pointed protuberance, shaped something like a spike.

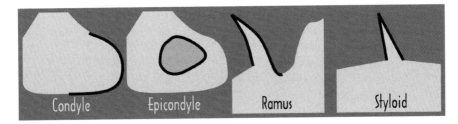

Fig. 10.4 Anatomical features: condyle, epicondyle, ramus, and styloid

- *Transverse*
  - To cross
- *Articular*
  - Related to movement of a joint
- Margo
  - A boundary with another bone
- Sulcus
  - A shallow trench
- Incisura
  - A notch

The Axial Skeleton

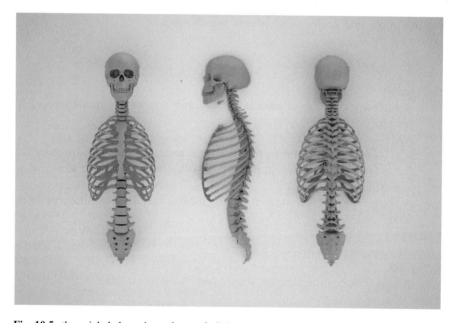

Fig. 10.5 the axial skeleton is made up of all the bones belonging to the spine, thoracic cage, and skull. Anterior, lateral, and posterior views

Skull

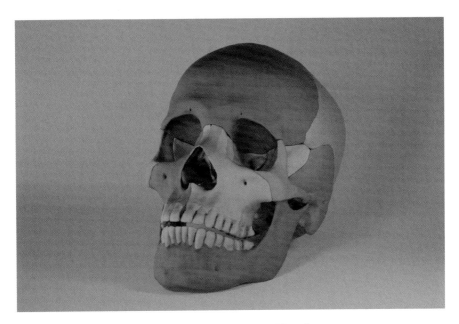

Fig. 10.6 The skull is made up of 22 separate bones plus 32 teeth

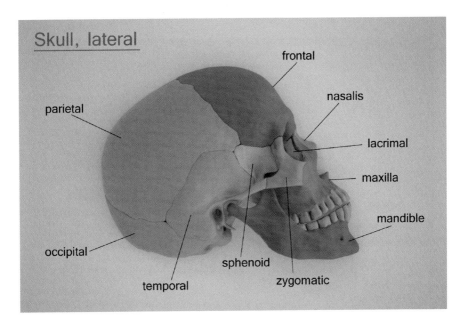

Fig. 10.7 Externally visible bones of the skull, lateral view

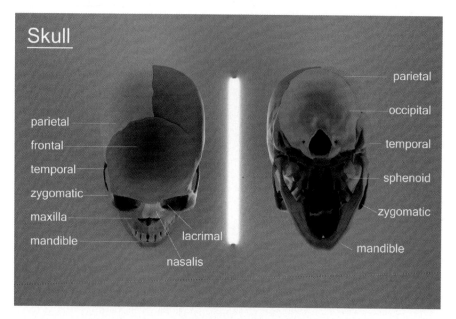

Fig. 10.8   Superior and inferior views of the skull

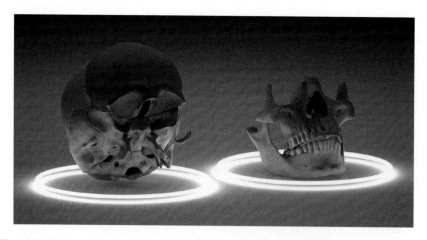

Fig. 10.9   The cranial bones, seen separate from facial bones and mandible, anterior view

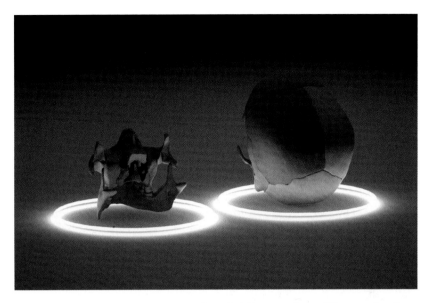

Fig. 10.10 The cranial bones, seen separate from facial bones and mandible, posterior view

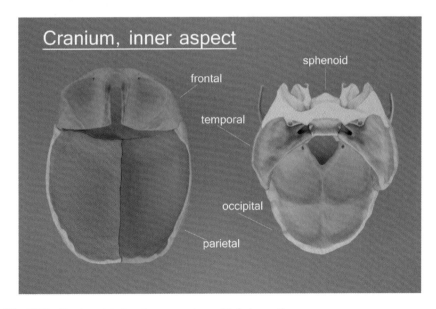

Fig. 10.11 Cranium, interior views, superior and inferior sections

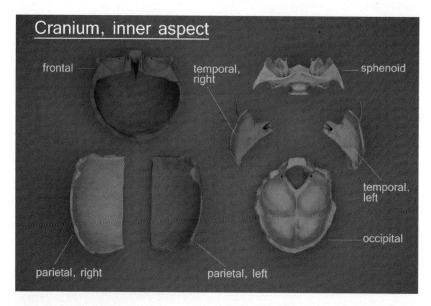

Fig. 10.12   Cranium, exploded view

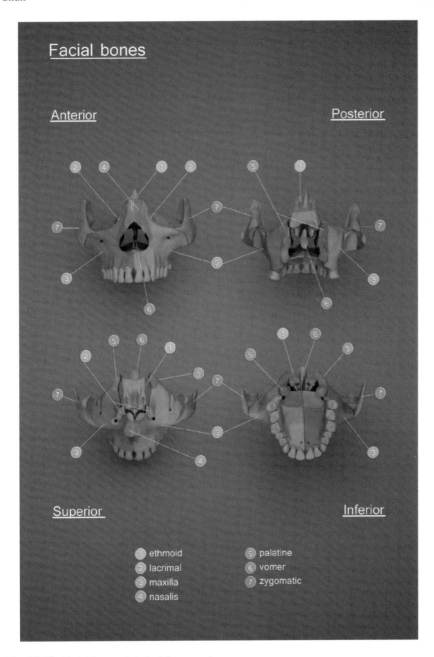

Fig. 10.13 Facial bones, detached from cranium

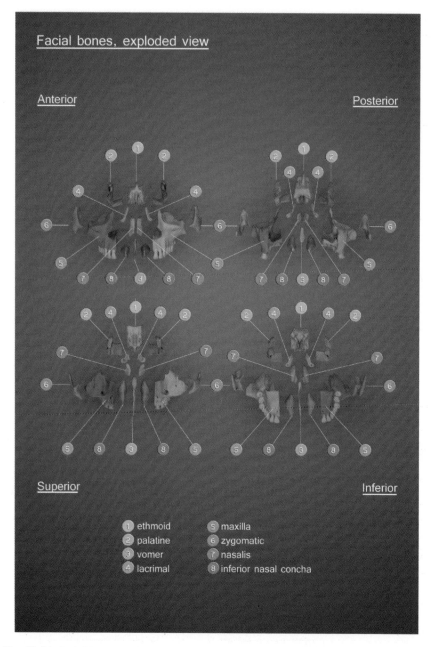

Fig. 10.14 Facial bones, exploded view

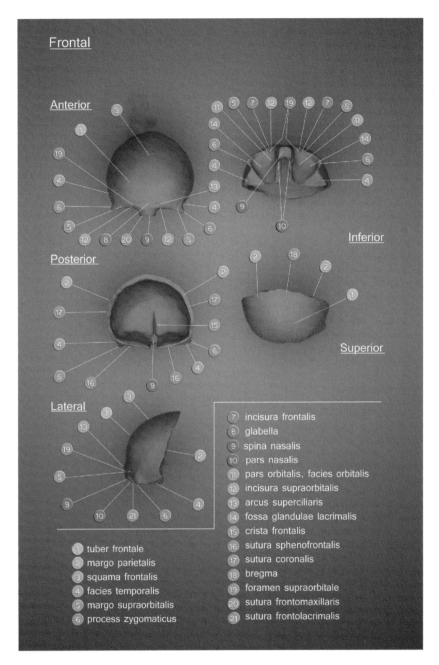

Fig. 10.15 Views, frontal bone

Frontal

Anterior

Posterior

Inferior

Superior

Lateral

7 incisura frontalis
8 glabella
9 spina nasalis
10 pars nasalis
11 pars orbitalis, facies orbitalis
12 incisura supraorbitalis
13 arcus superciliaris
14 fossa glandulae lacrimalis
15 crista frontalis
16 sutura sphenofrontalis
17 sutura coronalis
18 bregma
19 foramen supraorbitale
20 sutura frontomaxillaris
21 sutura frontolacrimalis

1 tuber frontale
2 margo parietalis
3 squama frontalis
4 facies temporalis
5 margo supraorbitalis
6 process zygomaticus

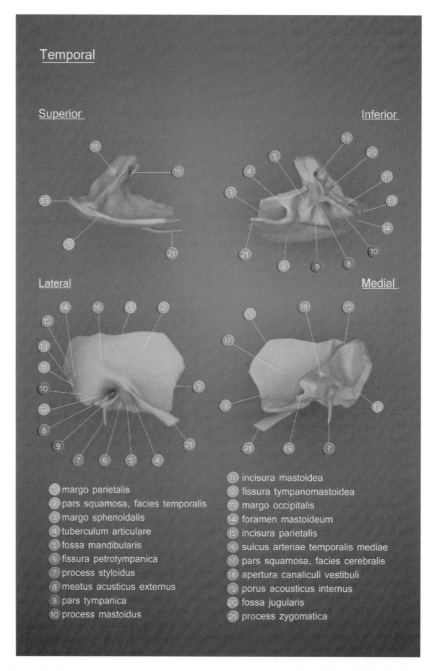

Temporal

Superior   Inferior

Lateral   Medial

1 margo parietalis
2 pars squamosa, facies temporalis
3 margo sphenoidalis
4 tuberculum articulare
5 fossa mandibularis
6 fissura petrotympanica
7 process styloidus
8 meatus acusticus externus
9 pars tympanica
10 process mastoidus

11 incisura mastoidea
12 fissura tympanomastoidea
13 margo occipitalis
14 foramen mastoideum
15 incisura parietalis
16 sulcus arteriae temporalis mediae
17 pars squamosa, facies cerebralis
18 apertura canaliculi vestibuli
19 porus acousticus internus
20 fossa jugularis
21 process zygomatica

Fig. 10.16   Views, Temporal bone

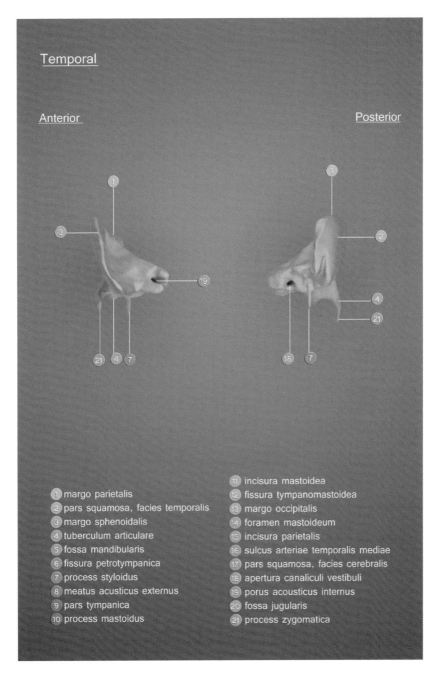

Temporal

Anterior   Posterior

1 margo parietalis
2 pars squamosa, facies temporalis
3 margo sphenoidalis
4 tuberculum articulare
5 fossa mandibularis
6 fissura petrotympanica
7 process styloidus
8 meatus acusticus externus
9 pars tympanica
10 process mastoidus

11 incisura mastoidea
12 fissura tympanomastoidea
13 margo occipitalis
14 foramen mastoideum
15 incisura parietalis
16 sulcus arteriae temporalis mediae
17 pars squamosa, facies cerebralis
18 apertura canaliculi vestibuli
19 porus acousticus internus
20 fossa jugularis
21 process zygomatica

Fig. 10.17   Views, temporal bone (cont'd)

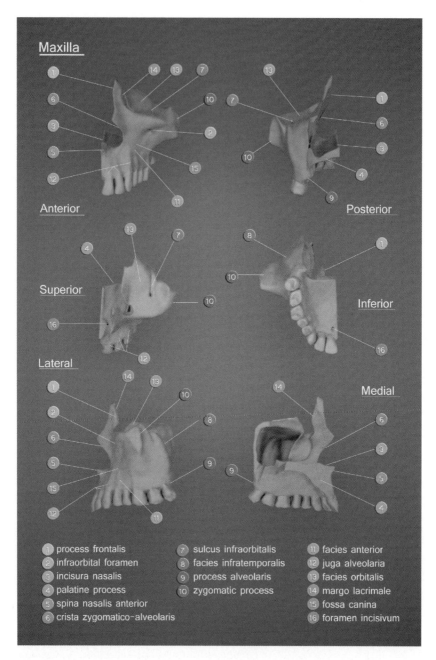

Fig. 10.18   Views, maxilla bone

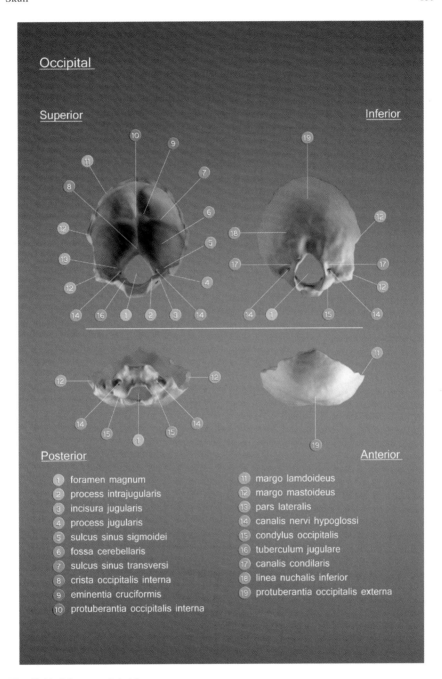

Occipital

Superior **Inferior**

Posterior **Anterior**

1. foramen magnum
2. process intrajugularis
3. incisura jugularis
4. process jugularis
5. sulcus sinus sigmoidei
6. fossa cerebellaris
7. sulcus sinus transversi
8. crista occipitalis interna
9. eminentia cruciformis
10. protuberantia occipitalis interna

11. margo lamdoideus
12. margo mastoideus
13. pars lateralis
14. canalis nervi hypoglossi
15. condylus occipitalis
16. tuberculum jugulare
17. canalis condilaris
18. linea nuchalis inferior
19. protuberantia occipitalis externa

Fig. 10.19 Views, occipital bone

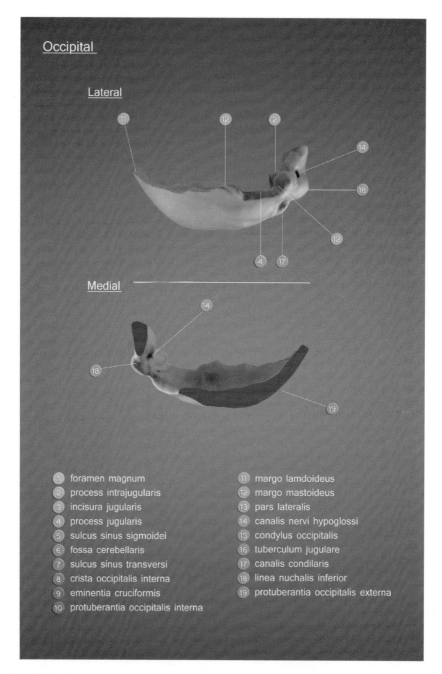

Occipital

Lateral

Medial

1 foramen magnum
2 process intrajugularis
3 incisura jugularis
4 process jugularis
5 sulcus sinus sigmoidei
6 fossa cerebellaris
7 sulcus sinus transversi
8 crista occipitalis interna
9 eminentia cruciformis
10 protuberantia occipitalis interna
11 margo lamdoideus
12 margo mastoideus
13 pars lateralis
14 canalis nervi hypoglossi
15 condylus occipitalis
16 tuberculum jugulare
17 canalis condilaris
18 linea nuchalis inferior
19 protuberantia occipitalis externa

Fig. 10.20   Views, occipital bone (cont'd)

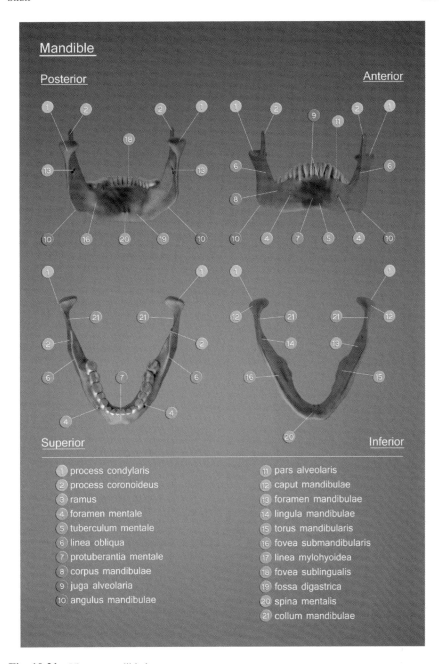

Fig. 10.21   Views, mandible bone

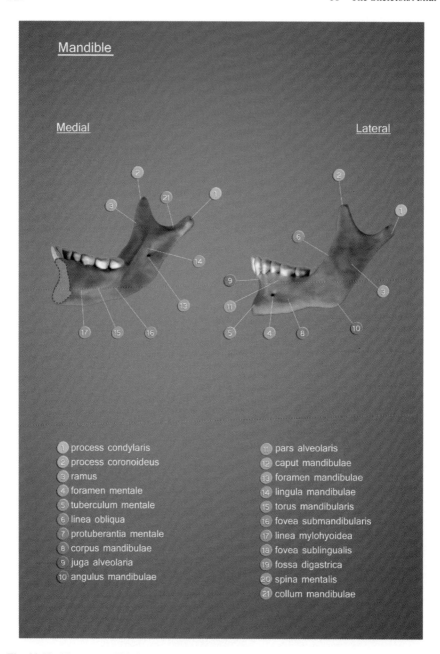

Mandible

Medial   **Lateral**

1 process condylaris	11 pars alveolaris
2 process coronoideus	12 caput mandibulae
3 ramus	13 foramen mandibulae
4 foramen mentale	14 lingula mandibulae
5 tuberculum mentale	15 torus mandibularis
6 linea obliqua	16 fovea submandibularis
7 protuberantia mentale	17 linea mylohyoidea
8 corpus mandibulae	18 fovea sublingualis
9 juga alveolaria	19 fossa digastrica
10 angulus mandibulae	20 spina mentalis
	21 collum mandibulae

Fig. 10.22   Views, mandible bone (cont'd)

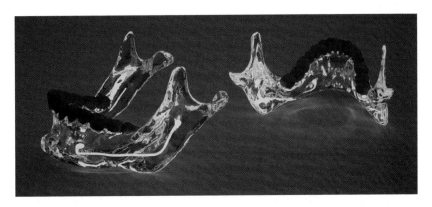

Fig. 10.23 Mandible with nerve channel highlighted in light blue

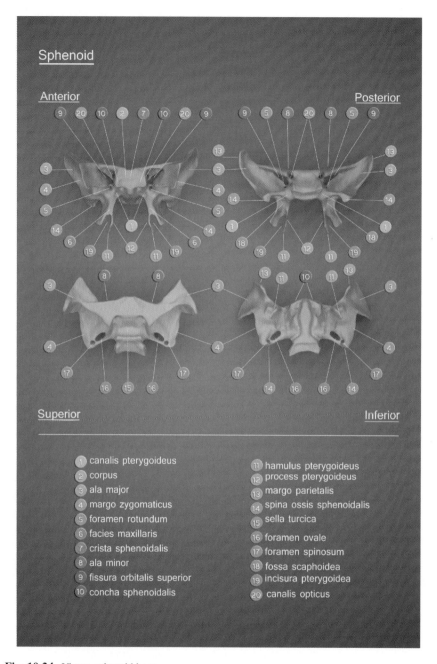

Fig. 10.24 Views, sphenoid bone

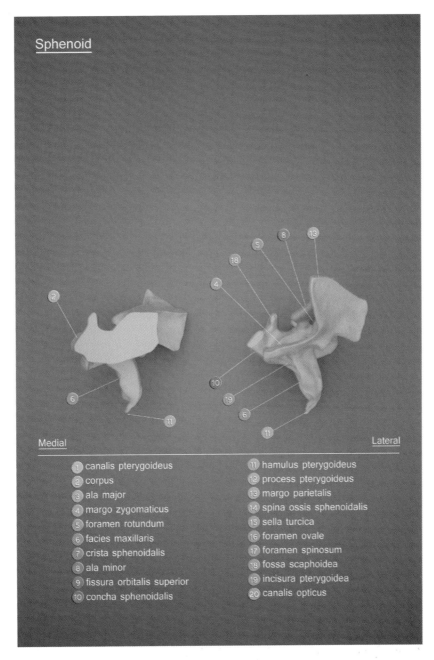

Sphenoid

Medial   Lateral

1 canalis pterygoideus   11 hamulus pterygoideus
2 corpus   12 process pterygoideus
3 ala major   13 margo parietalis
4 margo zygomaticus   14 spina ossis sphenoidalis
5 foramen rotundum   15 sella turcica
6 facies maxillaris   16 foramen ovale
7 crista sphenoidalis   17 foramen spinosum
8 ala minor   18 fossa scaphoidea
9 fissura orbitalis superior   19 incisura pterygoidea
10 concha sphenoidalis   20 canalis opticus

Fig. 10.25   Views, sphenoid bone (cont'd)

Spine

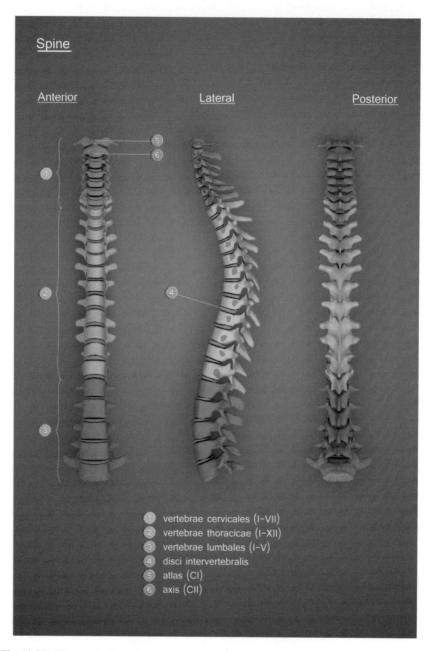

Fig. 10.26   Views, spinal vertebrae

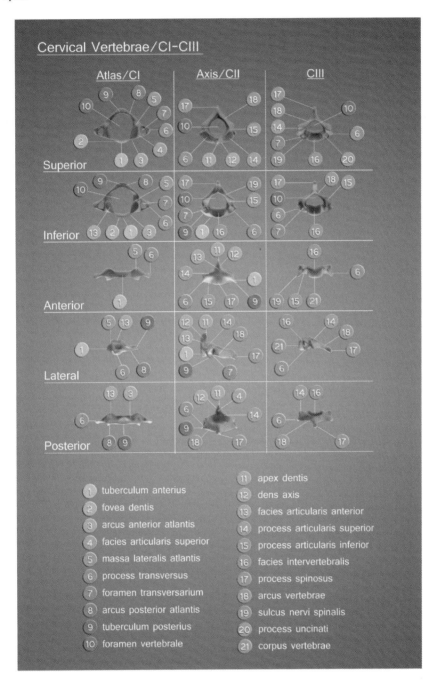

Fig. 10.27   Views, cervical vertebrae/CI-CIII

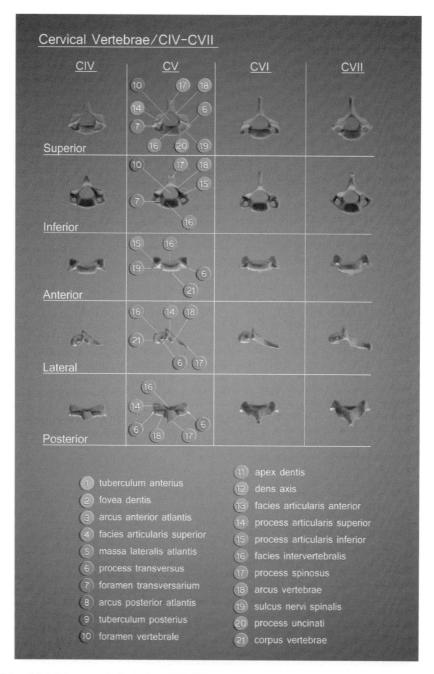

Cervical Vertebrae/CIV–CVII

CIV	CV	CVI	CVII
Superior			
Inferior			
Anterior			
Lateral			
Posterior			

1   tuberculum anterius
2   fovea dentis
3   arcus anterior atlantis
4   facies articularis superior
5   massa lateralis atlantis
6   process transversus
7   foramen transversarium
8   arcus posterior atlantis
9   tuberculum posterius
10 foramen vertebrale

11 apex dentis
12 dens axis
13 facies articularis anterior
14 process articularis superior
15 process articularis inferior
16 facies intervertebralis
17 process spinosus
18 arcus vertebrae
19 sulcus nervi spinalis
20 process uncinati
21 corpus vertebrae

Fig. 10.28   Views, cervical vertebrae/CIV-CVII

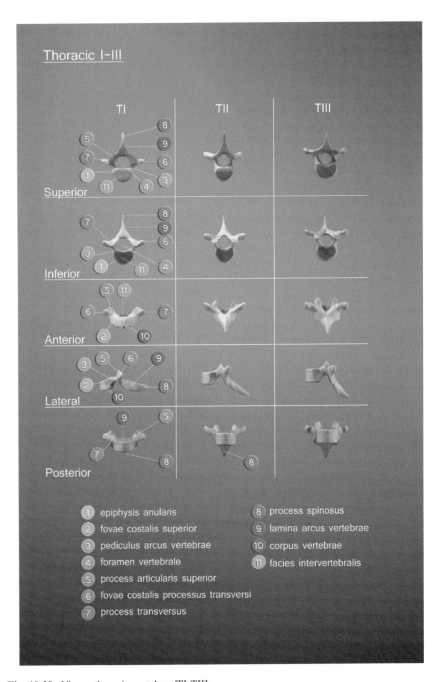

Fig. 10.29 Views, thoracic vertebrae/TI-TIII

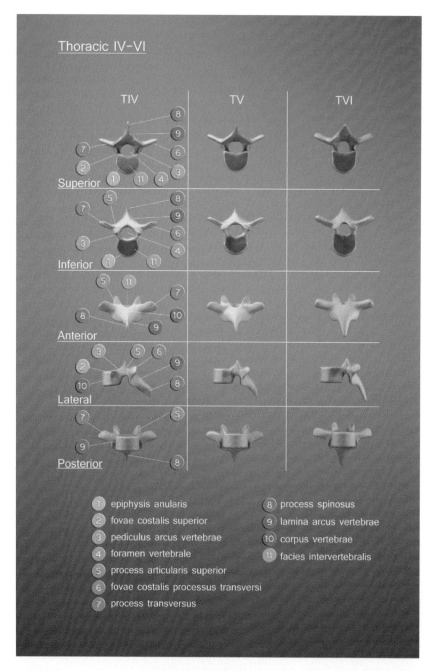

Fig. 10.30   Views, thoracic vertebrae/TIV-TVI

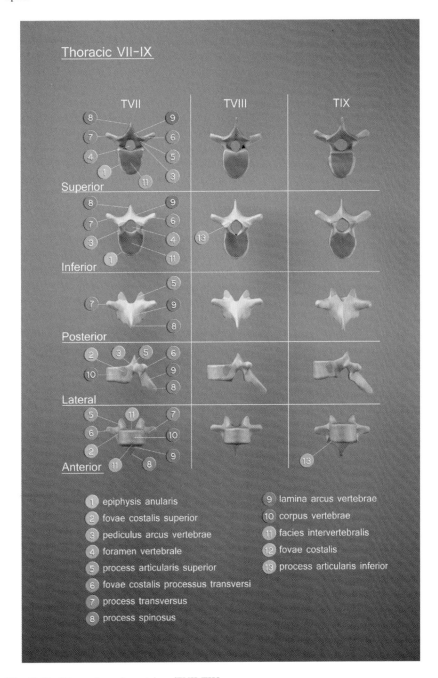

Fig. 10.31 Views, thoracic vertebrae/TVII-TIX

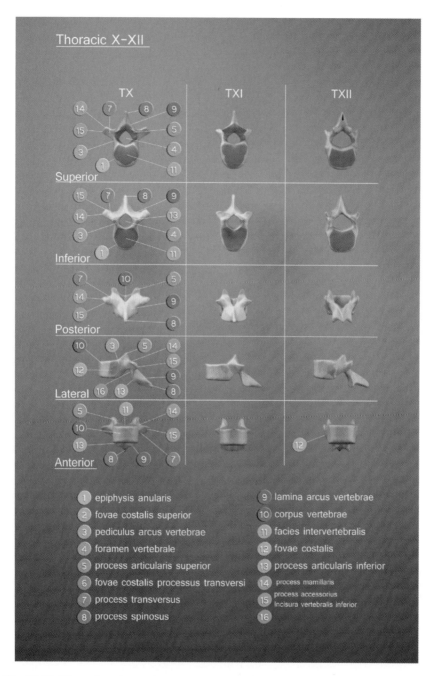

Fig. 10.32   Views, thoracic vertebrae/TX-TXII

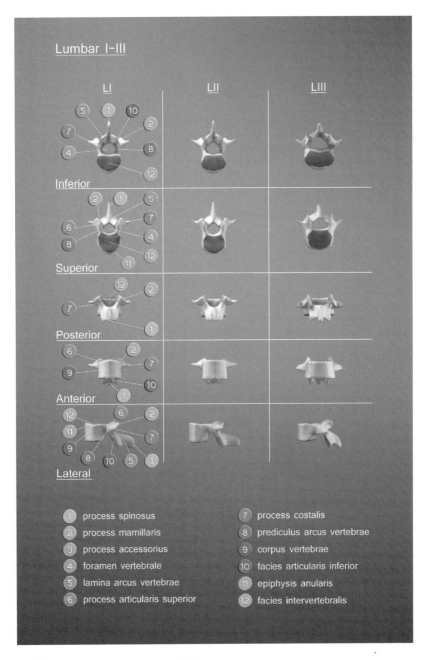

Fig. 10.33 Views, lumbar vertebrae/LI-LIII

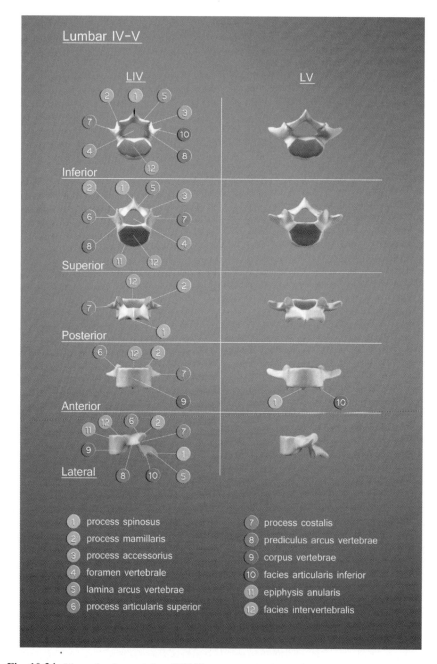

Fig. 10.34   Views, lumbar vertebrae/LIV-V

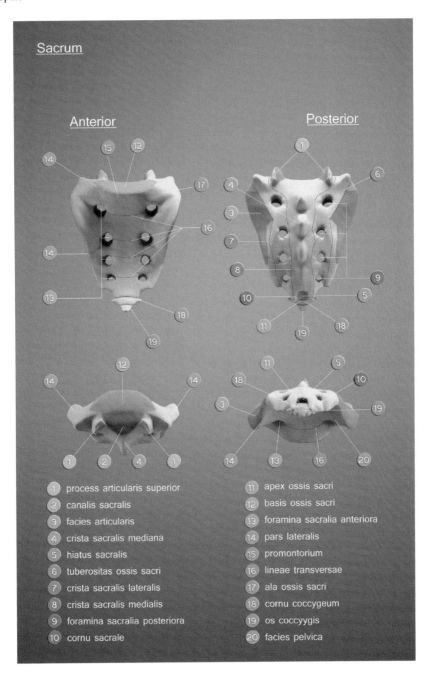

Fig. 10.35 Views, sacrum

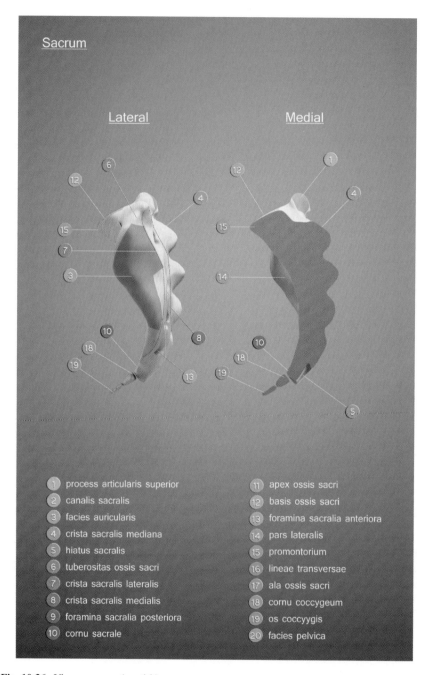

Sacrum

Lateral

Medial

1. process articularis superior
2. canalis sacralis
3. facies auricularis
4. crista sacralis mediana
5. hiatus sacralis
6. tuberositas ossis sacri
7. crista sacralis lateralis
8. crista sacralis medialis
9. foramina sacralia posteriora
10. cornu sacrale

11. apex ossis sacri
12. basis ossis sacri
13. foramina sacralia anteriora
14. pars lateralis
15. promontorium
16. lineae transversae
17. ala ossis sacri
18. cornu coccygeum
19. os coccyygis
20. facies pelvica

Fig. 10.36 Views, sacrum (cont'd.)

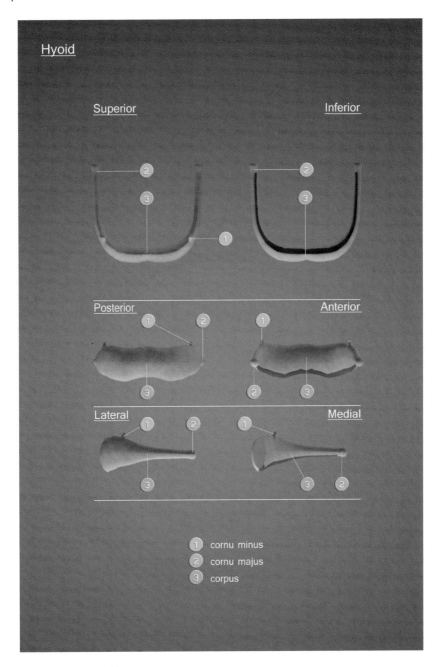

Fig. 10.37 Views, hyoid

Thoracic Cage

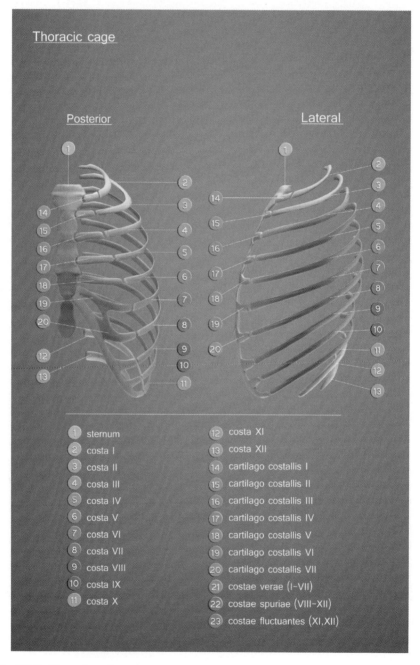

Fig. 10.38 Views, thoracic cage

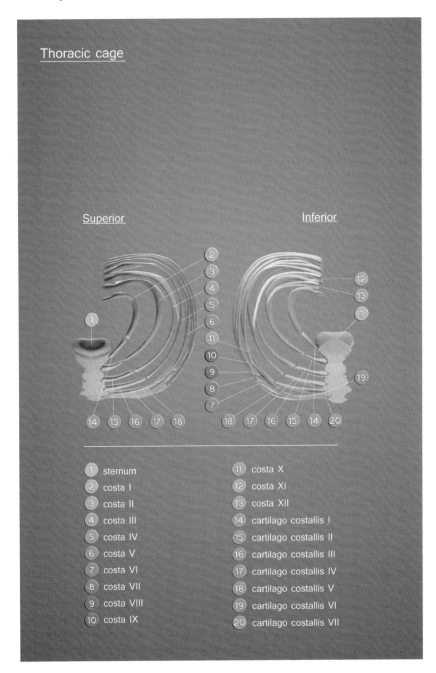

Fig. 10.39 Views, thoracic cage (cont'd.)

Chapter 11
Appendicular Skeleton

General

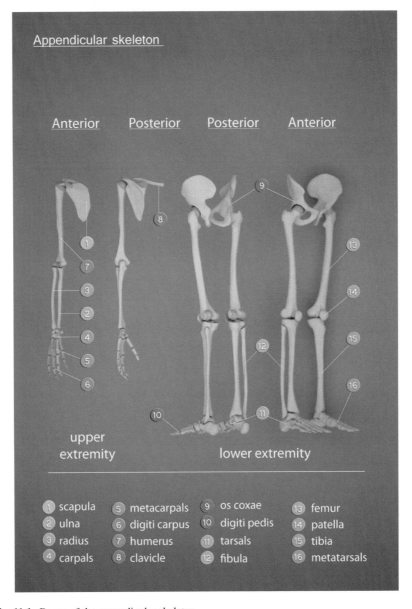

Fig. 11.1 Bones of the appendicular skeleton

A. Paquette, *Computer Graphics for Artists II: Environments and Characters,*
© Springer-Verlag London Limited 2009

Pectoral Girdle

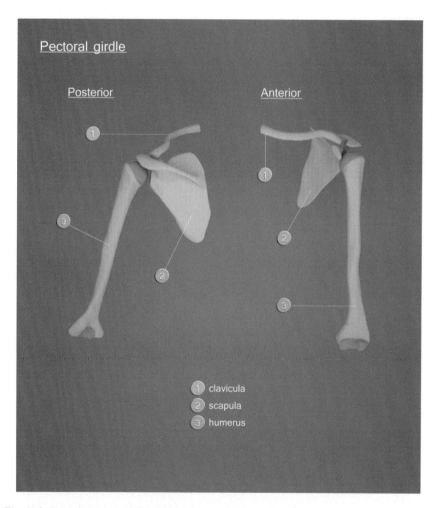

Fig. 11.2 Bones of the pectoral girdle

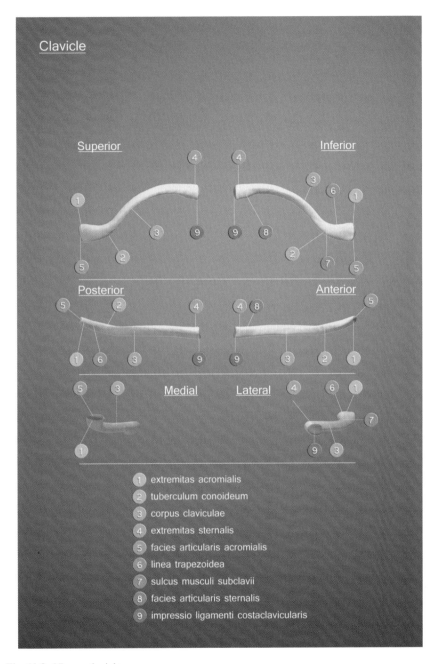

Fig. 11.3 Views, clavicle

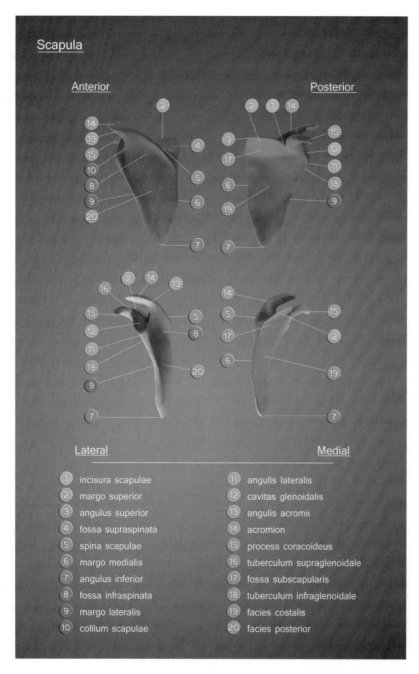

Fig. 11.4 Views, scapula

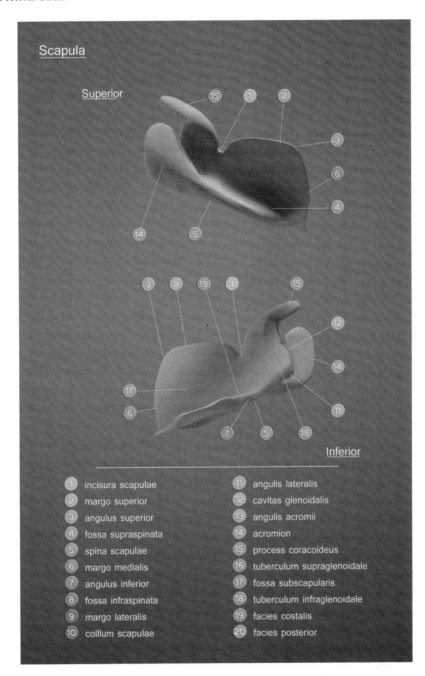

Fig. 11.5 Views, scapula (cont'd.)

Arm

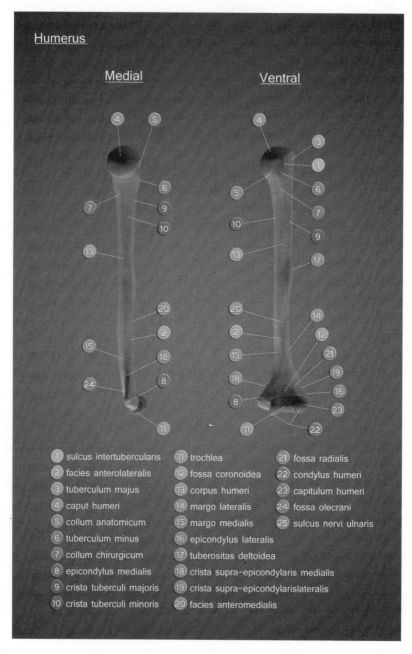

Fig. 11.6 Views, humerus

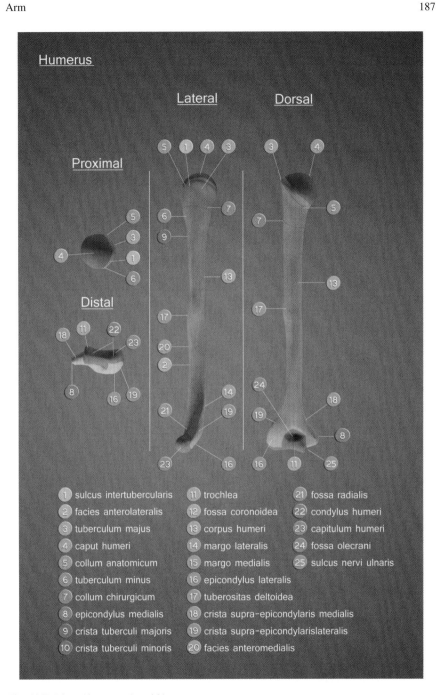

Fig. 11.7 Views, humerus (cont'd.)

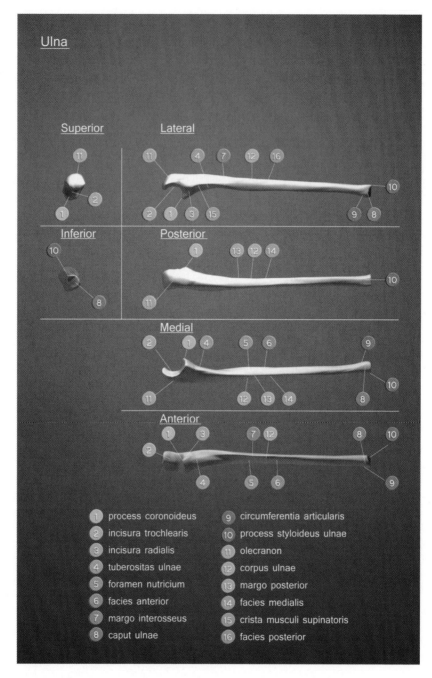

Fig. 11.8 Views, ulna

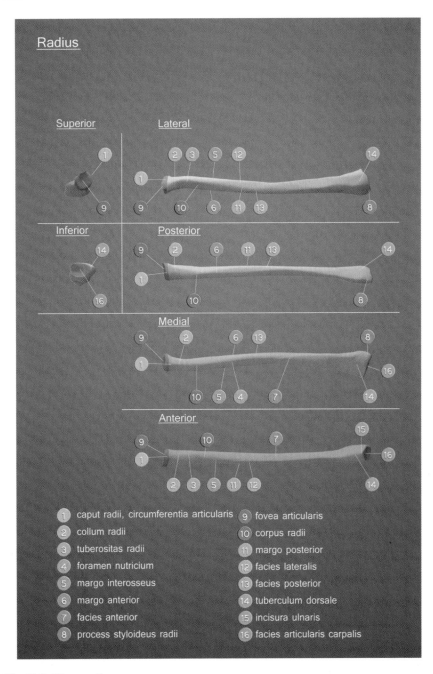

Fig. 11.9 Views, radius

Hand

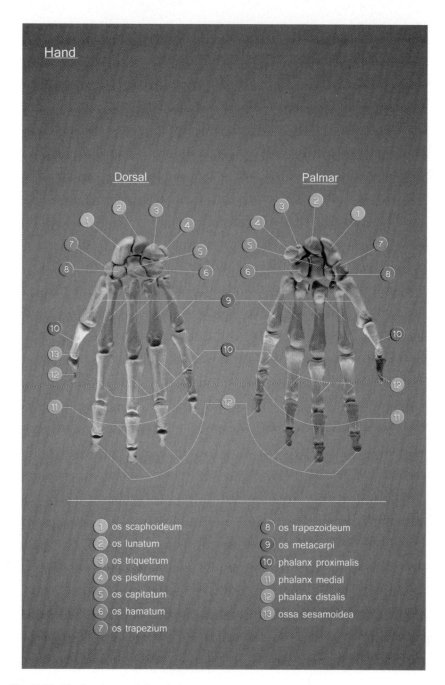

Fig. 11.10 Hand, palmar and dorsal views

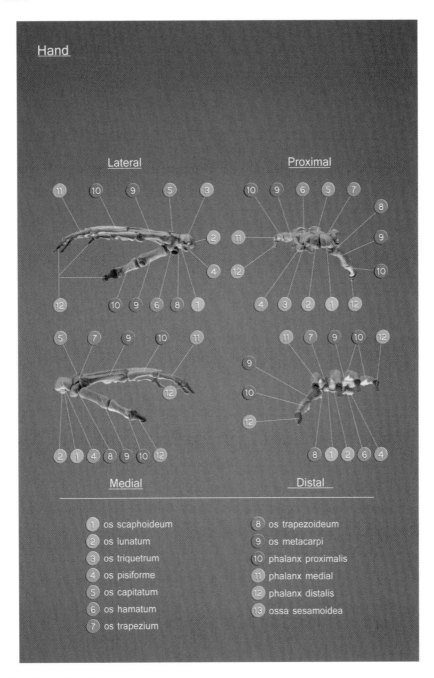

Fig. 11.11 Views, hand

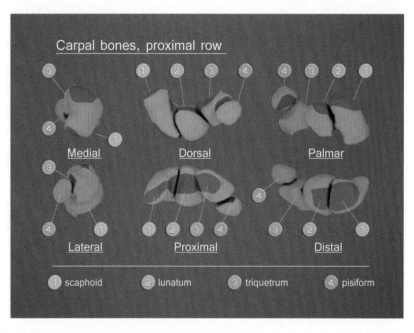

Fig. 11.12   Views, bones of the wrist, proximal row

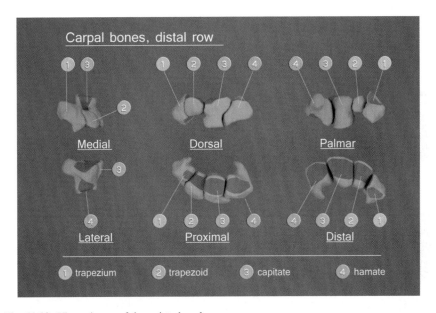

Fig. 11.13 Views, bones of the wrist, dorsal row

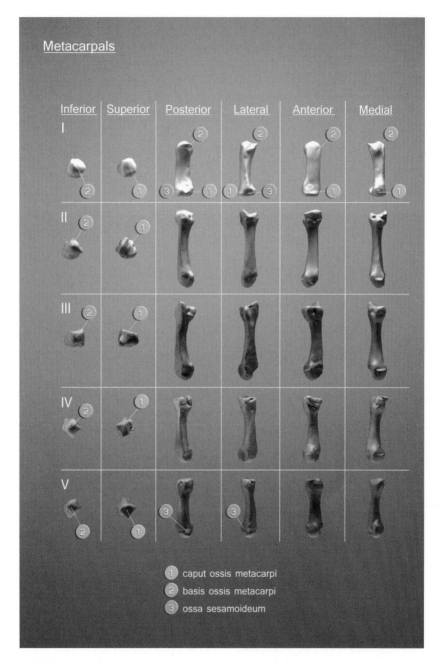

Fig. 11.14   Views, metacarpal bones

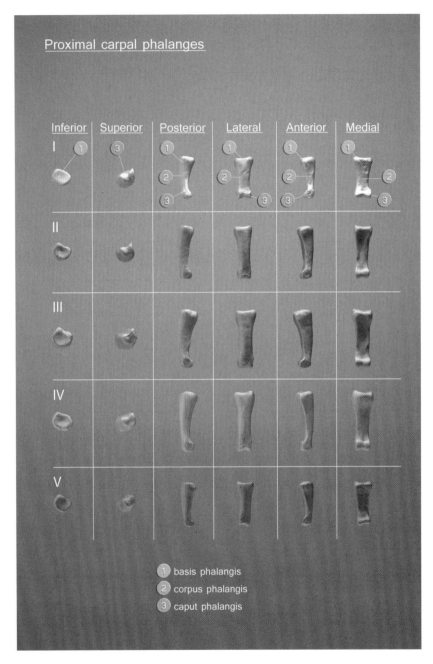

Fig. 11.15 Views, proximal carpal phalanges

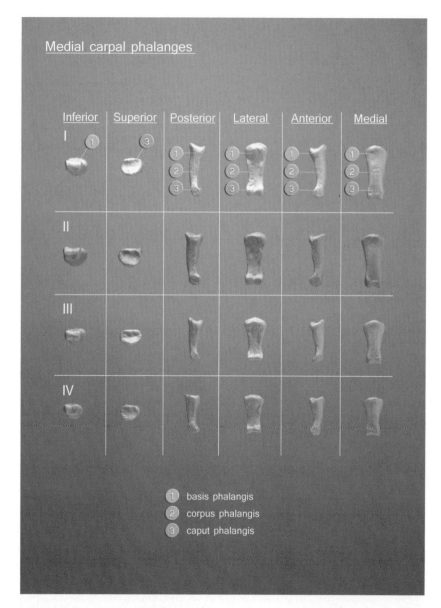

Fig. 11.16 Views, medial carpal phalanges

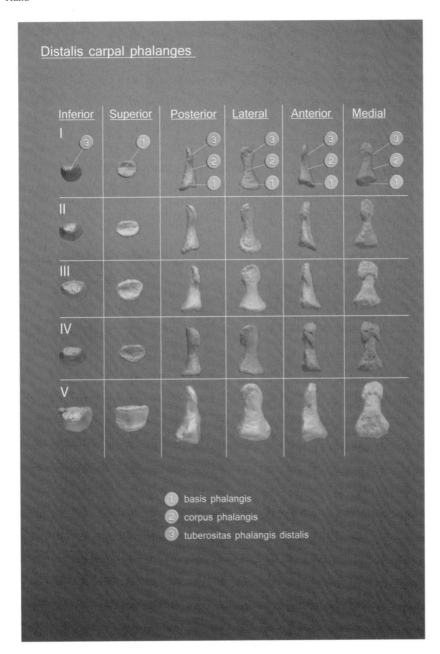

Fig. 11.17 Views, distalis carpal phalanges

Hip

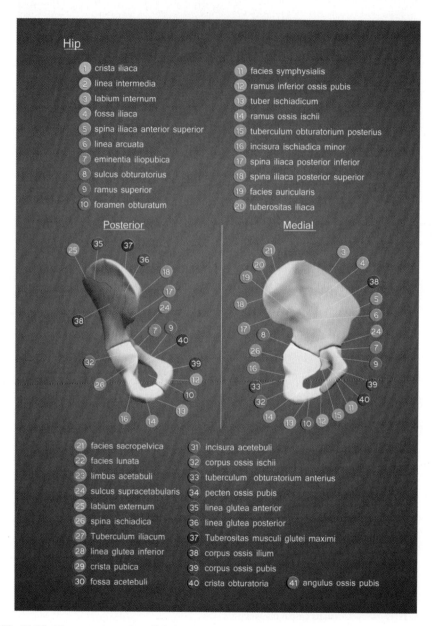

Hip

1 crista iliaca
2 linea intermedia
3 labium internum
4 fossa iliaca
5 spina iliaca anterior superior
6 linea arcuata
7 eminentia iliopubica
8 sulcus obturatorius
9 ramus superior
10 foramen obturatum

11 facies symphysialis
12 ramus inferior ossis pubis
13 tuber ischiadicum
14 ramus ossis ischii
15 tuberculum obturatorium posterius
16 incisura ischiadica minor
17 spina iliaca posterior inferior
18 spina iliaca posterior superior
19 facies auricularis
20 tuberositas iliaca

Posterior   **Medial**

21 facies sacropelvica
22 facies lunata
23 limbus acetabuli
24 sulcus supracetabularis
25 labium externum
26 spina ischiadica
27 Tuberculum iliacum
28 linea glutea inferior
29 crista pubica
30 fossa acetabuli

31 incisura acetebuli
32 corpus ossis ischii
33 tuberculum obturatorium anterius
34 pecten ossis pubis
35 linea glutea anterior
36 linea glutea posterior
37 Tuberositas musculi glutei maximi
38 corpus ossis ilium
39 corpus ossis pubis
40 crista obturatoria   41 angulus ossis pubis

Fig. 11.18 Hip, posterior and medial views

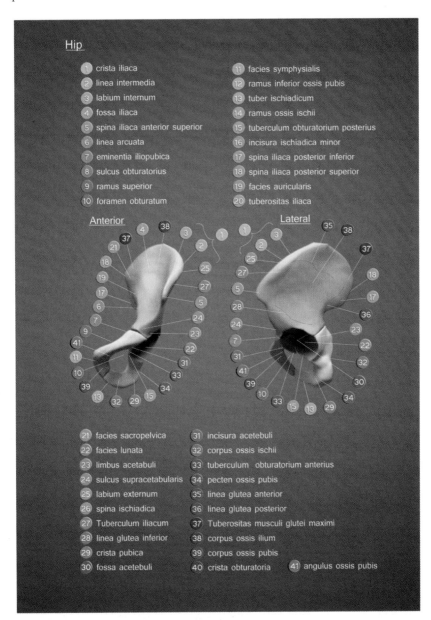

Fig. 11.19 Hip, anterior and lateral views

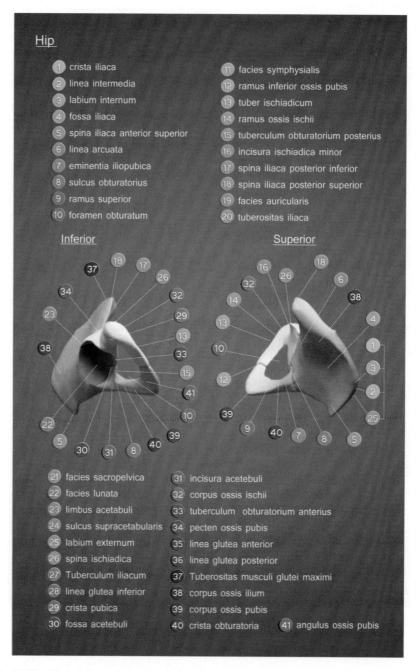

Hip

1 crista iliaca
2 linea intermedia
3 labium internum
4 fossa iliaca
5 spina iliaca anterior superior
6 linea arcuata
7 eminentia iliopubica
8 sulcus obturatorius
9 ramus superior
10 foramen obturatum

11 facies symphysialis
12 ramus inferior ossis pubis
13 tuber ischiadicum
14 ramus ossis ischii
15 tuberculum obturatorium posterius
16 incisura ischiadica minor
17 spina iliaca posterior inferior
18 spina iliaca posterior superior
19 facies auricularis
20 tuberositas iliaca

Inferior   Superior

21 facies sacropelvica
22 facies lunata
23 limbus acetabuli
24 sulcus supracetabularis
25 labium externum
26 spina ischiadica
27 Tuberculum iliacum
28 linea glutea inferior
29 crista pubica
30 fossa acetebuli

31 incisura acetebuli
32 corpus ossis ischii
33 tuberculum obturatorium anterius
34 pecten ossis pubis
35 linea glutea anterior
36 linea glutea posterior
37 Tuberositas musculi glutei maximi
38 corpus ossis ilium
39 corpus ossis pubis
40 crista obturatoria   41 angulus ossis pubis

Fig. 11.20 Hip, inferior and superior views

Leg

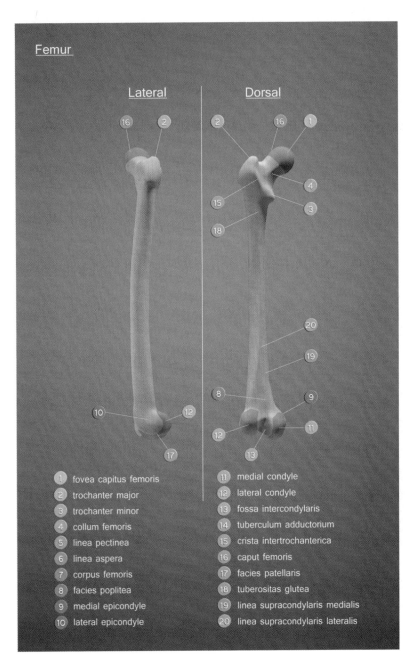

Fig. 11.21 Views, femur

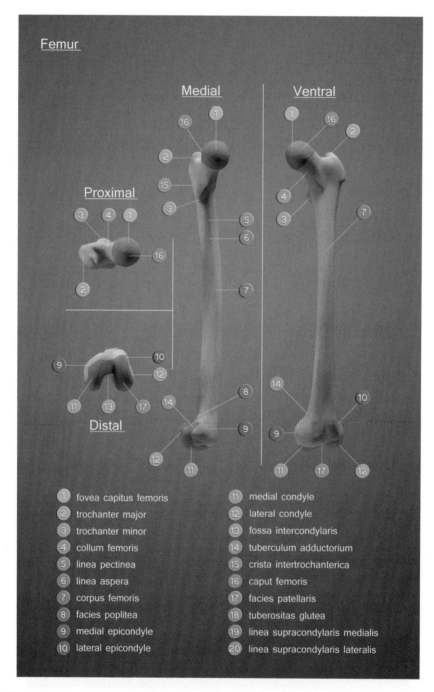

Fig. 11.22   Views, femur (cont'd.)

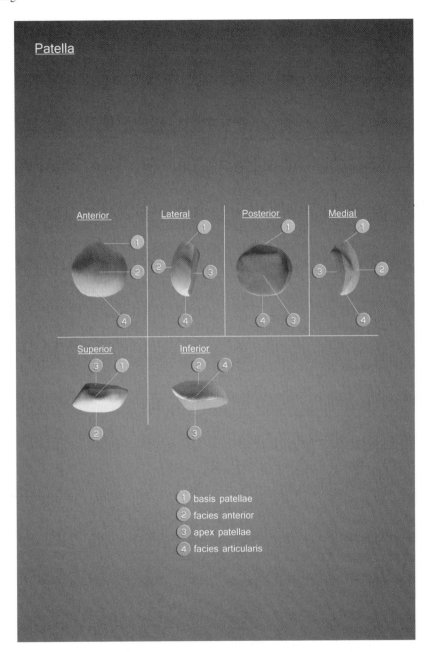

Fig. 11.23 Views, patella

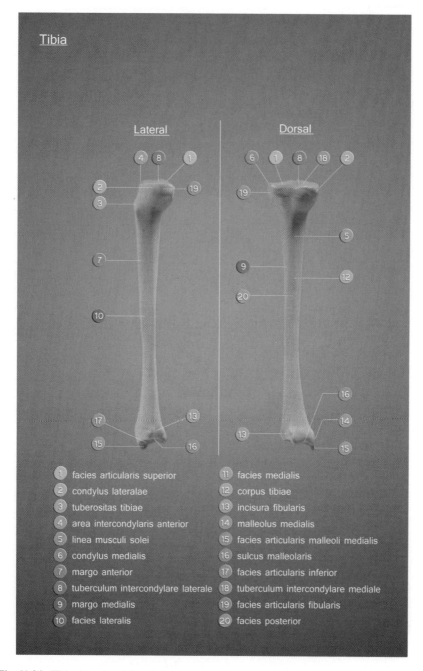

Fig. 11.24 Tibia, lateral and dorsal views

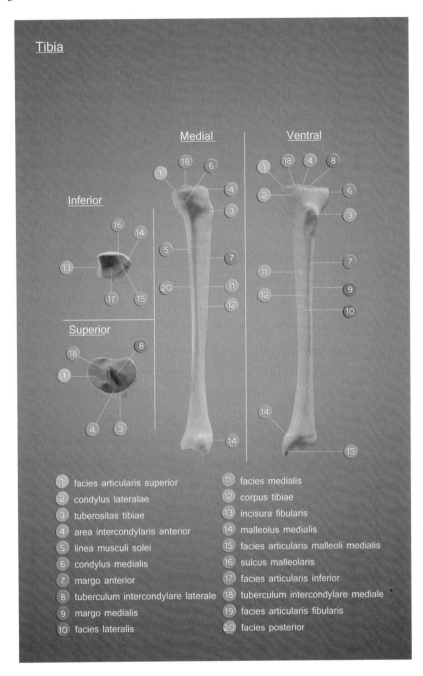

Tibia

Medial   Ventral

Inferior

Superior

1 facies articularis superior
2 condylus lateralae
3 tuberositas tibiae
4 area intercondylaris anterior
5 linea musculi solei
6 condylus medialis
7 margo anterior
8 tuberculum intercondylare laterale
9 margo medialis
10 facies lateralis
11 facies medialis
12 corpus tibiae
13 incisura fibularis
14 malleolus medialis
15 facies articularis malleoli medialis
16 sulcus malleolaris
17 facies articularis inferior
18 tuberculum intercondylare mediale
19 facies articularis fibularis
20 facies posterior

Fig. 11.25 Views, tibia (cont'd.)

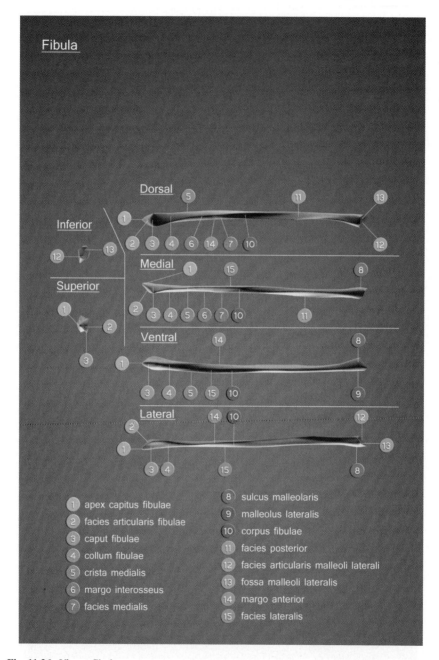

Fig. 11.26 Views, fibula

Foot

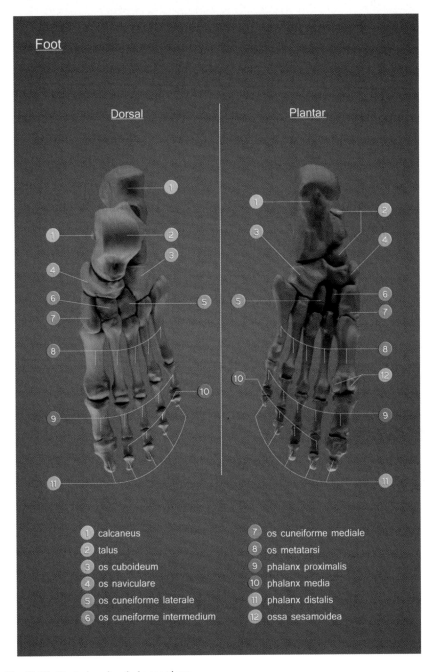

Fig. 11.27 Foot, dorsal and plantar views

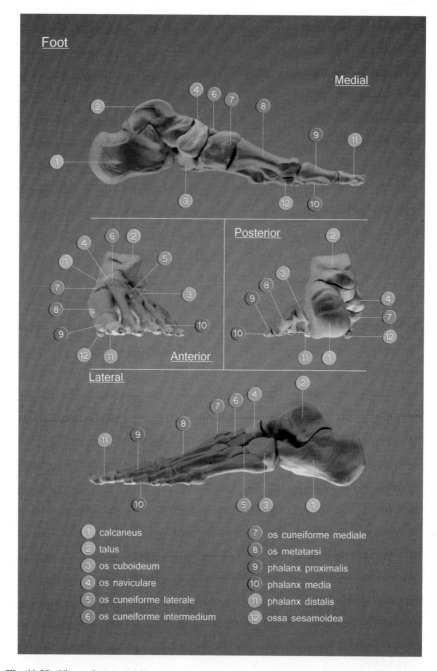

Fig. 11.28   Views, foot (cont'd.)

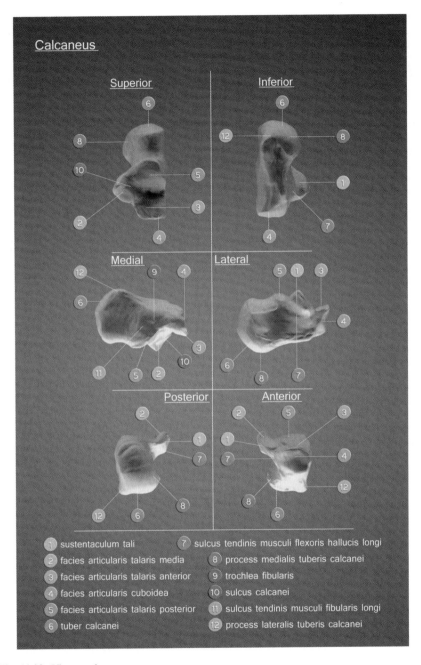

Fig. 11.29 Views, calcaneus

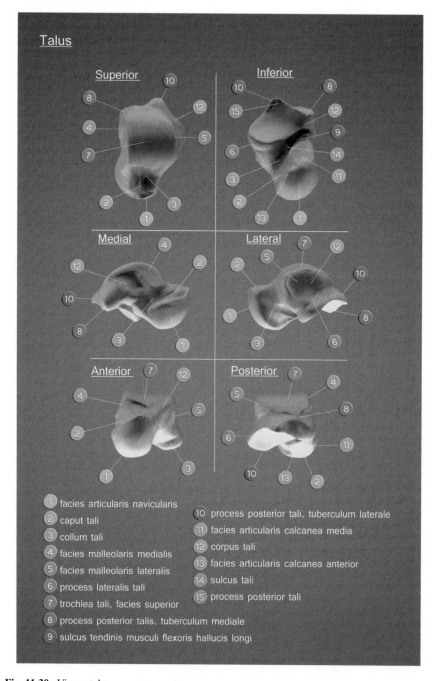

Fig. 11.30 Views, talus

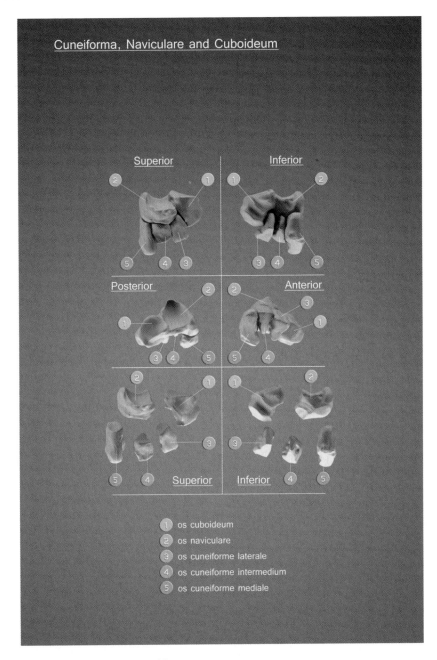

Fig. 11.31 Exploded views, tarsal bones

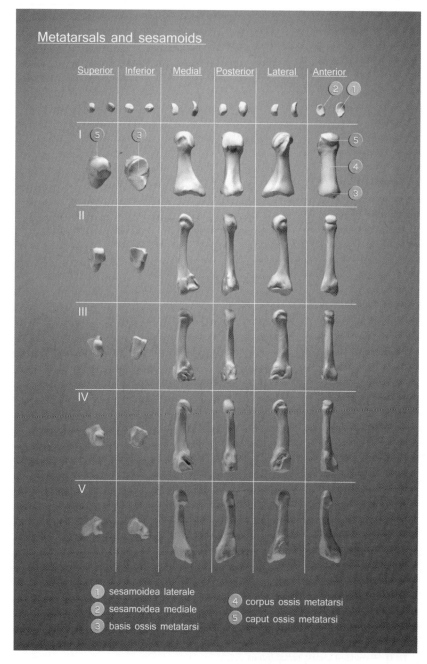

Fig. 11.32 Views, metatarsals and sesamoids

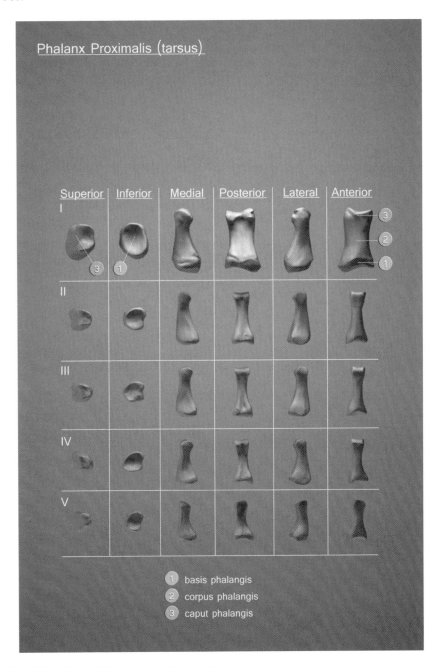

Fig. 11.33 Views, phalanx proximalis (tarsus)

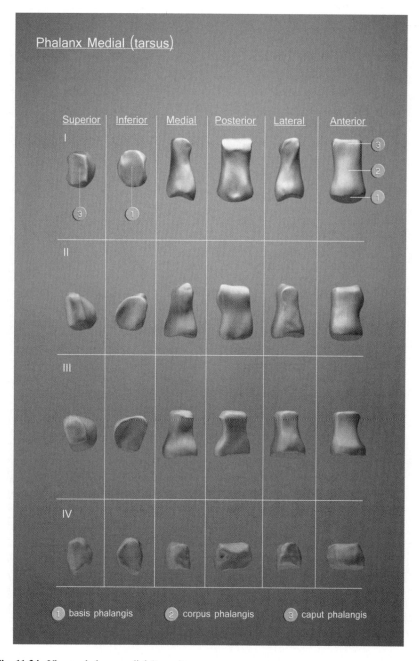

Fig. 11.34 Views, phalanx medial (tarsus)

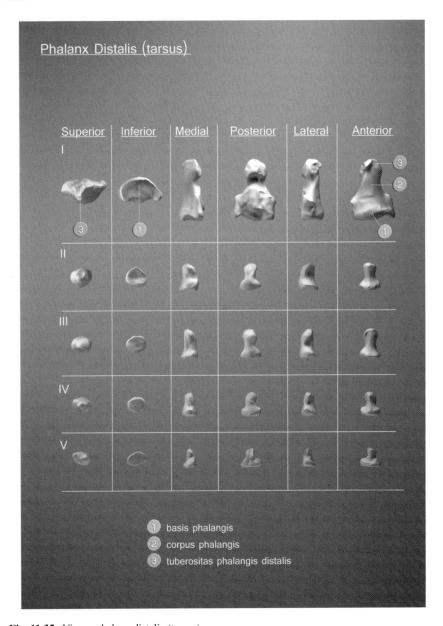

Fig. 11.35 Views, phalanx distalis (tarsus)

Chapter 12
Musculature

General

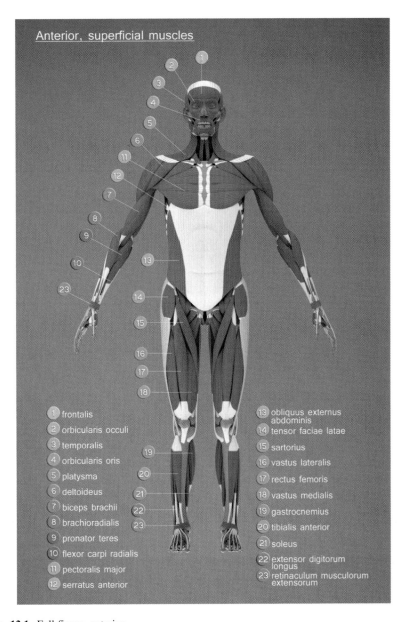

Anterior, superficial muscles

1 frontalis
2 orbicularis occuli
3 temporalis
4 orbicularis oris
5 platysma
6 deltoideus
7 biceps brachii
8 brachioradialis
9 pronator teres
10 flexor carpi radialis
11 pectoralis major
12 serratus anterior
13 obliquus externus abdominis
14 tensor faciae latae
15 sartorius
16 vastus lateralis
17 rectus femoris
18 vastus medialis
19 gastrocnemius
20 tibialis anterior
21 soleus
22 extensor digitorum longus
23 retinaculum musculorum extensorum

Fig. 12.1 Full figure, anterior

Skeletons are tightly bound by hundreds of muscles, most of which are fairly thin relative to their surface area. They appear to be thicker than they are because of the many muscles and other anatomical features that lie beneath them in dozens of criss-crossing layers. To understand how these muscles act on the skeleton and on each other is to understand how the human body is articulated, and its outward appearance. The most important factors in determining both these things are the attachment points for each muscle, the shape of the bone it is attached to, and the shape of any other structure that might deform the muscle (Figs. 12.1–12.28).

Muscle attachments are called *origins* and *insertions*. The origin of a muscle is the location on the fixed bone of a joint where the fibers of a muscle's tendon join with the surface of that bone. The insertion of a muscle is where a muscle's tendon joins with the free bone of a joint. For example, the biceps brachii muscle has two origins, one for each head of the two sections of the muscle, at different parts of the scapula. The scapula in this case is the fixed joint. On the other end, the muscle narrows to a tendon, which has an insertion at the head of the radius bone. The radius bone is the free bone, because it is moved when the bicep is flexed, while the scapula remains in place.

Depending on which source you use, the human body has anywhere from 639 named skeletal muscles to about 850. The principal disagreement about the number of muscles is the classification of what constitutes an independent muscle worthy of a separate name, and what should be considered a part of another, larger muscle. The other source of discrepancy, though to a much smaller degree, is variations from body to body that blur the distinction between muscles that can be considered distinct and those that cannot. Either way, there are a lot of muscles to keep track of. For the CG artist, it would be an unusual project that requires all 639 named muscles to be built. More likely, if all the muscles are built independently, the number required would be around 75 unique muscles, copied to both halves of the body, for a total of slightly less than 150 muscles.[1] These muscles are the *superficial muscles* of the body. All the other muscles are deep muscles. Those that contribute to skeletal articulation to any important degree will be described in this book, but many will be left out because they are either too small, like some muscles of the inner ear, or they do not significantly affect the movement of the skeleton or the superficial appearance of the body.

Skeletal movement is caused when the fiber of a muscle, or more commonly, a group of muscles, contracts. This happens when a signal is sent from the peripheral nervous system to the muscle, prompting an interaction between myosin and actin that results in muscle fiber contraction. This is the only way independent skeletal movement is effected. This means that every motion of the body is accomplished by the shortening of a muscle or group of muscles, usually in a linear fashion.

Any movement of the skeleton that appears to be circular or in some other way nonlinear is caused by a coordinated series of contractions involving several muscles, such as in the eye or the hip.

---

[1] Some muscles do not appear in pairs across the median line, like the mentalis in the face.

Smooth muscle, or muscle attached to organs, will not be described in any detail here, apart from mentioning that it is this muscle type that allows, for instance, the walls of an organ to compress in order to shift the position of its contents. However, there is one matter of importance to discuss in reference to the axial skeleton and organs. Most organs are well protected by the thoracic cage and skull. For this reason, they do not contribute to the outward appearance of the body, and apart from providing the motivating force, for instance, through the action of the heart, they do not affect the motion of the body to any significant degree. An exception is the organs of the abdomen. These do contribute to the outward appearance of the body, and for that reason will be described briefly at the end of the chapter.

A mistake some artists make when creating anatomical models, is to pack the various parts loosely rather than tightly. This is very much like the infamous "alien autopsy" video, where a man dressed like a doctor cuts open a cadaver of unusual proportions and then proceeds to remove what appear to be organs, as if they were articles from a lunch box! In any mammalian system, the various parts are so well protected by sheaths of bone, ligaments, and overlapping muscle that it takes a great deal of effort to extract anything, let alone allowing a person to reach in and grab organ after organ as if they were simply plugged into a wall socket. In your modeling effort, remember this, because failure to keep it in mind can result in the grotesque exaggeration of the distance between bone and the epidermis at any given location, and thus, the likeness of your model will be affected adversely.

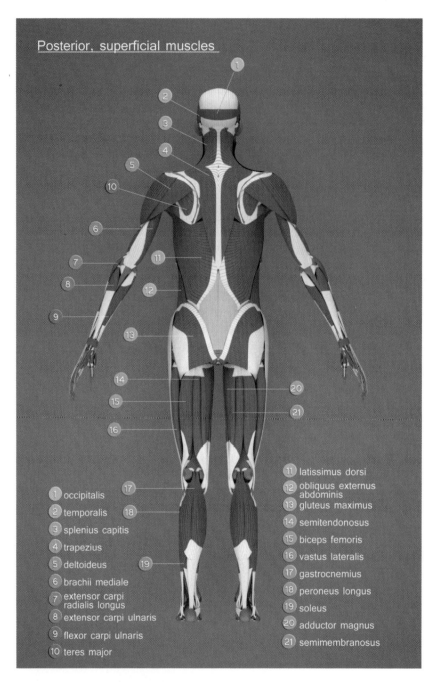

Posterior, superficial muscles

1 occipitalis
2 temporalis
3 splenius capitis
4 trapezius
5 deltoideus
6 brachii mediale
7 extensor carpi radialis longus
8 extensor carpi ulnaris
9 flexor carpi ulnaris
10 teres major
11 latissimus dorsi
12 obliquus externus abdominis
13 gluteus maximus
14 semitendonosus
15 biceps femoris
16 vastus lateralis
17 gastrocnemius
18 peroneus longus
19 soleus
20 adductor magnus
21 semimembranosus

Fig. 12.2 Full figure, posterior view

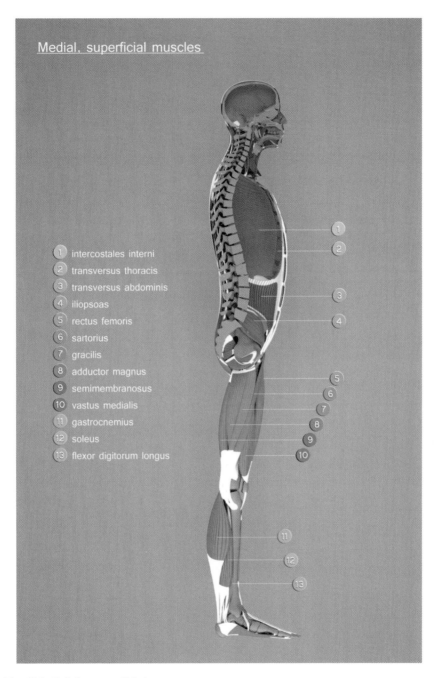

Medial, superficial muscles

1. intercostales interni
2. transversus thoracis
3. transversus abdominis
4. iliopsoas
5. rectus femoris
6. sartorius
7. gracilis
8. adductor magnus
9. semimembranosus
10. vastus medialis
11. gastrocnemius
12. soleus
13. flexor digitorum longus

Fig. 12.3 Full figure, medial view

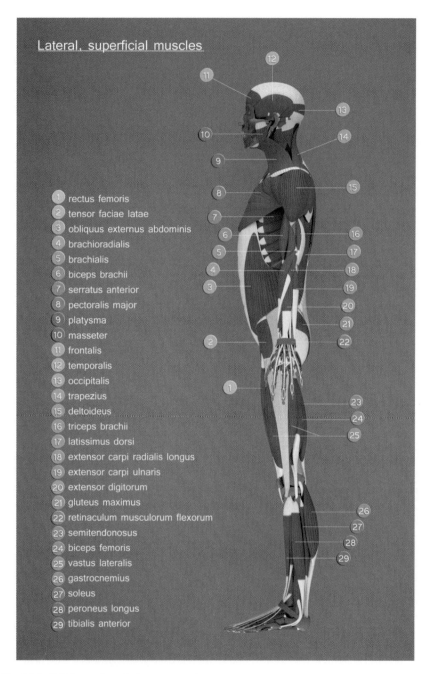

Lateral, superficial muscles

1 rectus femoris
2 tensor faciae latae
3 obliquus externus abdominis
4 brachioradialis
5 brachialis
6 biceps brachii
7 serratus anterior
8 pectoralis major
9 platysma
10 masseter
11 frontalis
12 temporalis
13 occipitalis
14 trapezius
15 deltoideus
16 triceps brachii
17 latissimus dorsi
18 extensor carpi radialis longus
19 extensor carpi ulnaris
20 extensor digitorum
21 gluteus maximus
22 retinaculum musculorum flexorum
23 semitendonosus
24 biceps femoris
25 vastus lateralis
26 gastrocnemius
27 soleus
28 peroneus longus
29 tibialis anterior

Fig. 12.4   Full figure, lateral view

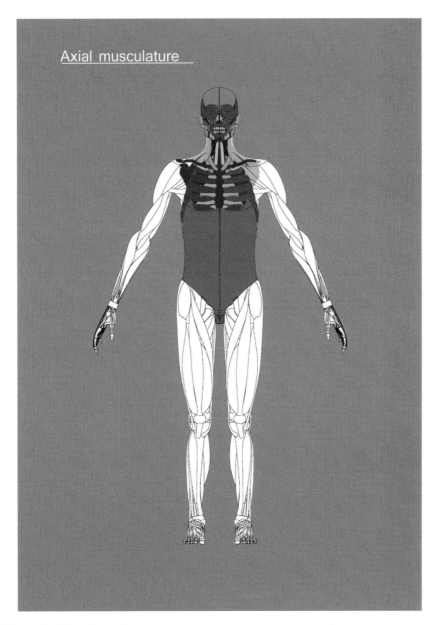

Fig. 12.5 Schematic, axial musculature

Torso

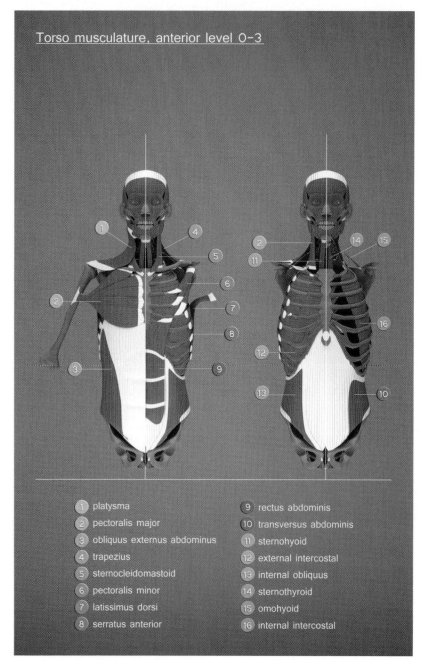

Fig. 12.6 Torso, anterior view, levels 0–3

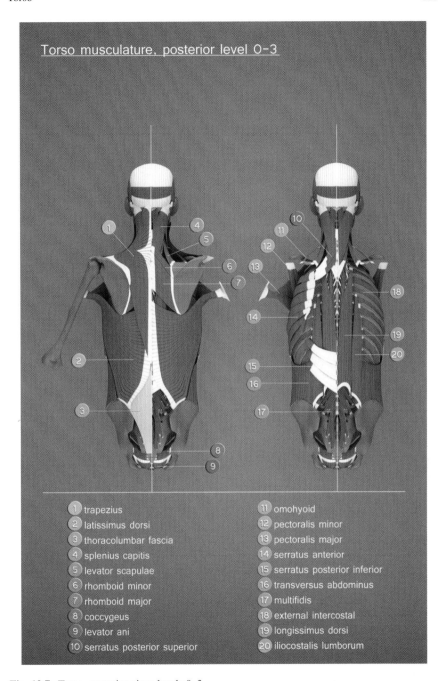

Fig. 12.7 Torso, posterior view, levels 0–3

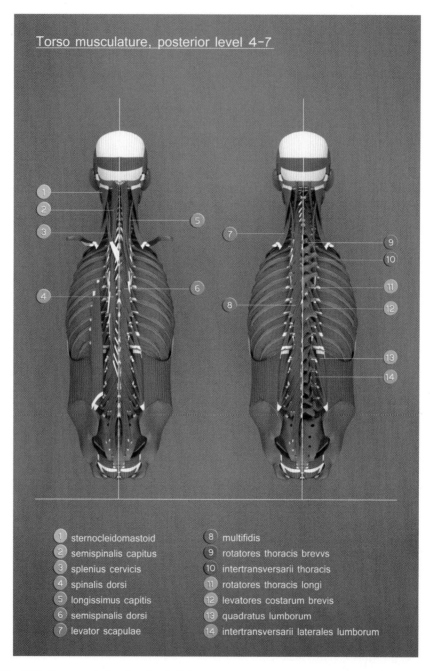

Torso musculature, posterior level 4-7

1 sternocleidomastoid
2 semispinalis capitus
3 splenius cervicis
4 spinalis dorsi
5 longissimus capitis
6 semispinalis dorsi
7 levator scapulae
8 multifidis
9 rotatores thoracis brevvs
10 intertransversarii thoracis
11 rotatores thoracis longi
12 levatores costarum brevis
13 quadratus lumborum
14 intertransversarii laterales lumborum

Fig. 12.8 Torso, posterior view, levels 4–7

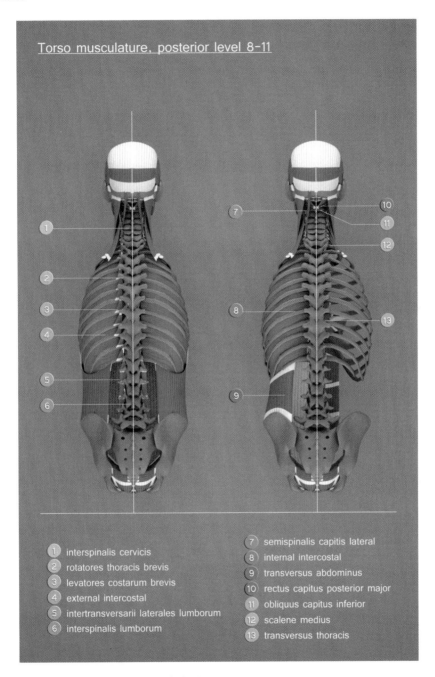

Fig. 12.9 Torso, posterior view, levels 8–11

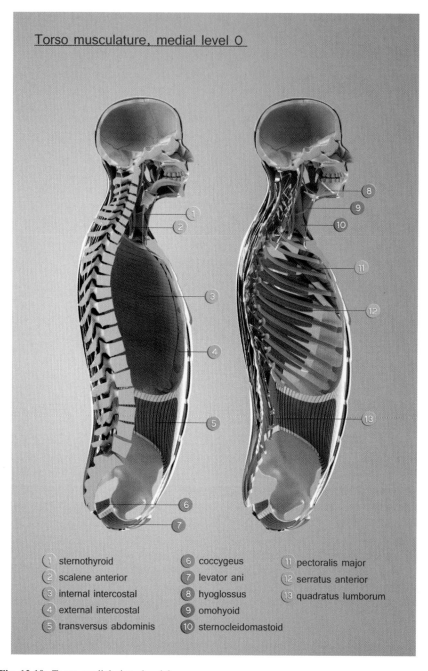

Torso musculature, medial level 0

1 sternothyroid
2 scalene anterior
3 internal intercostal
4 external intercostal
5 transversus abdominis
6 coccygeus
7 levator ani
8 hyoglossus
9 omohyoid
10 sternocleidomastoid
11 pectoralis major
12 serratus anterior
13 quadratus lumborum

Fig. 12.10   Torso, medial view, level 0

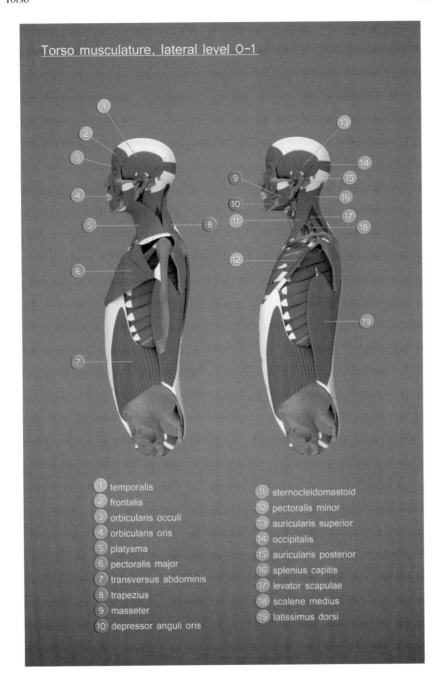

Fig. 12.11   Torso, lateral view, levels 0–1

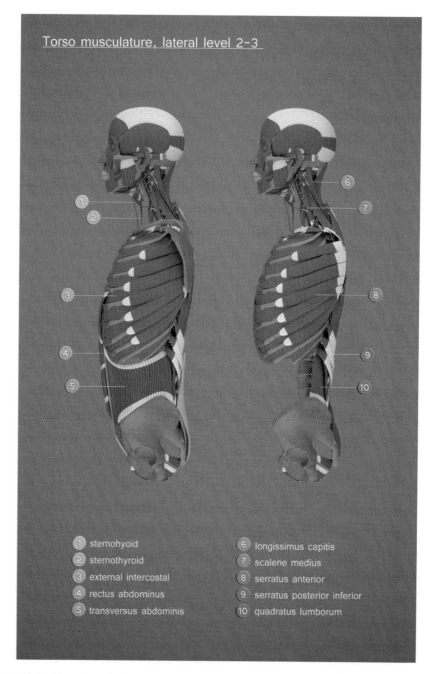

Fig. 12.12 Torso, lateral view, levels 2–3

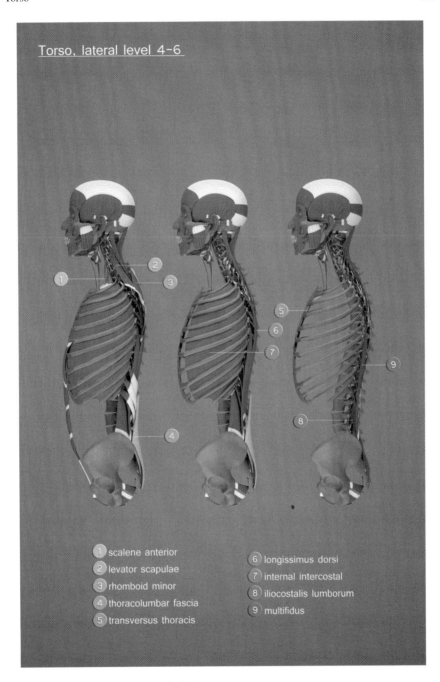

Fig. 12.13 Torso, lateral view, levels 4–6

Head

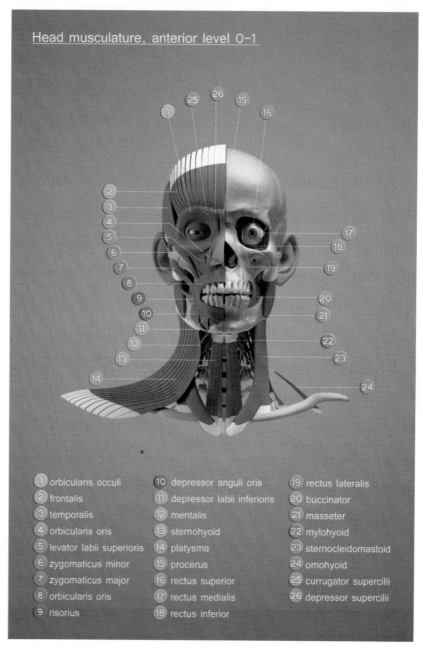

Fig. 12.14 Head, anterior view, levels 0–1

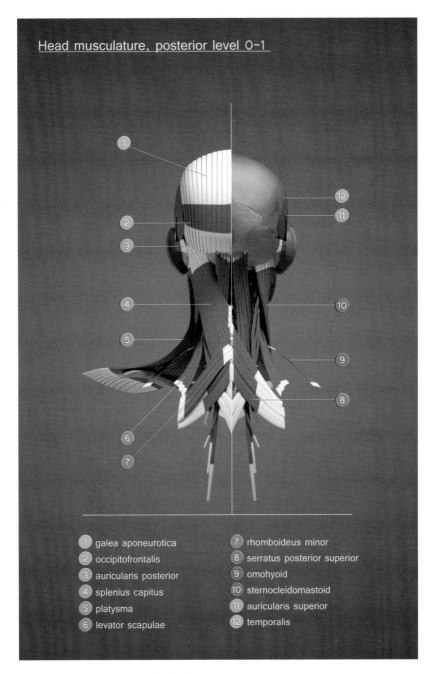

Fig. 12.15 Head, posterior view, levels 0–1

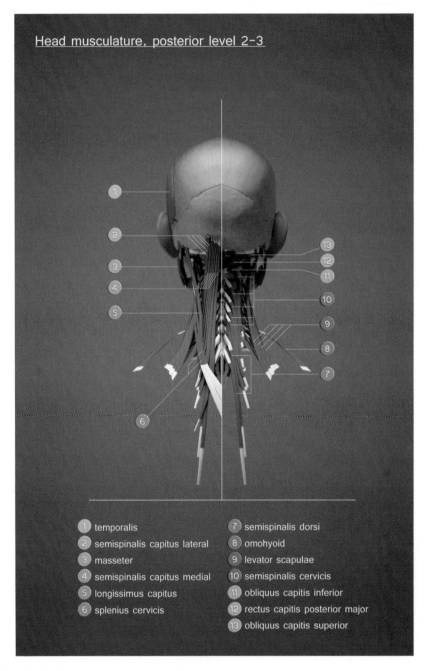

Fig. 12.16 Head, posterior view, levels 2–3

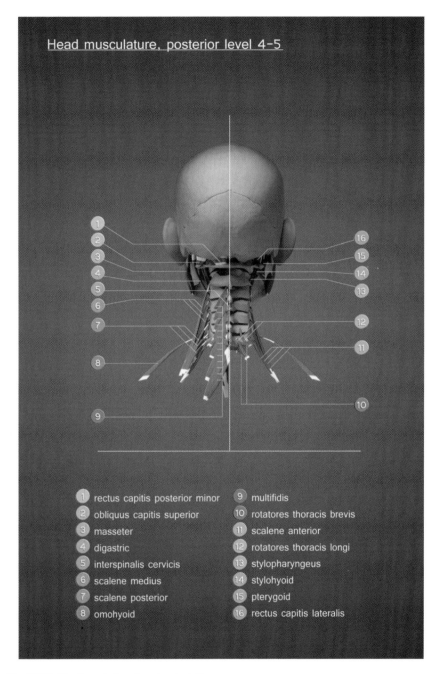

Fig. 12.17 Head, posterior view, levels 4–5

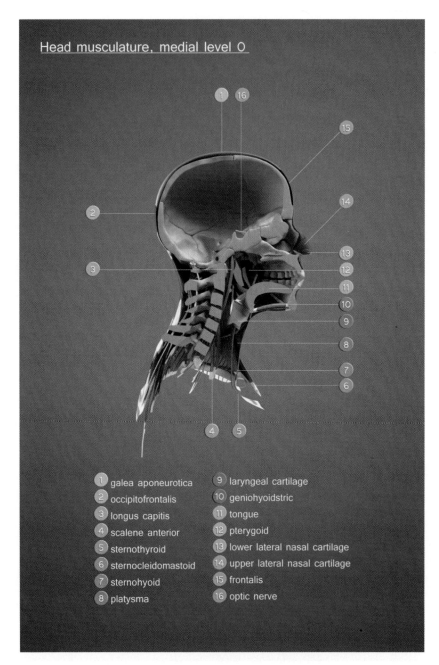

Head musculature, medial level 0

1 galea aponeurotica   9 laryngeal cartilage
2 occipitofrontalis   10 geniohyoidstric
3 longus capitis   11 tongue
4 scalene anterior   12 pterygoid
5 sternothyroid   13 lower lateral nasal cartilage
6 sternocleidomastoid   14 upper lateral nasal cartilage
7 sternohyoid   15 frontalis
8 platysma   16 optic nerve

Fig. 12.18 Head, medial view, level 0

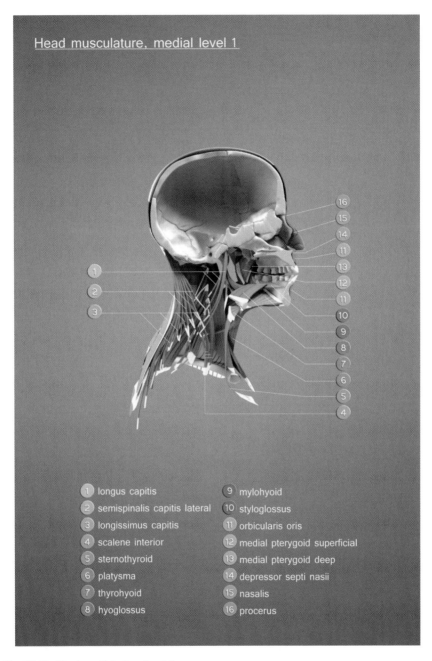

Fig. 12.19 Head, medial view, level 1

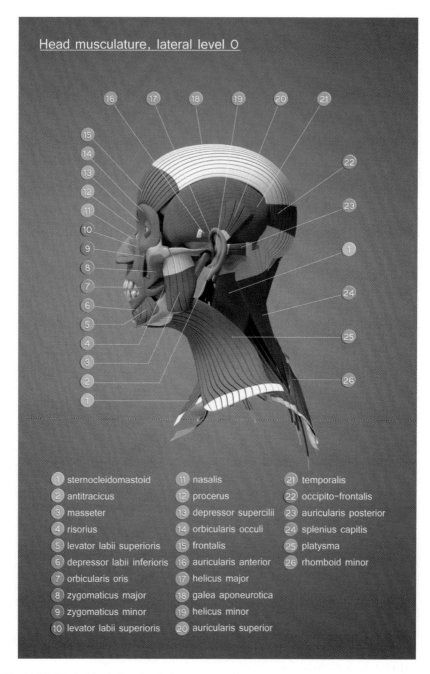

Fig. 12.20 Head, lateral view, levels 0

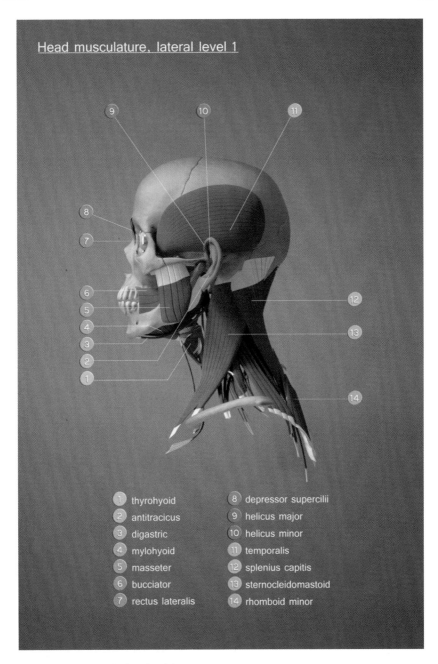

Head musculature, lateral level 1

1	thyrohyoid	8	depressor supercilii
2	antitracicus	9	helicus major
3	digastric	10	helicus minor
4	mylohyoid	11	temporalis
5	masseter	12	splenius capitis
6	bucciator	13	sternocleidomastoid
7	rectus lateralis	14	rhomboid minor

Fig. 12.21 Head, lateral view, level 1

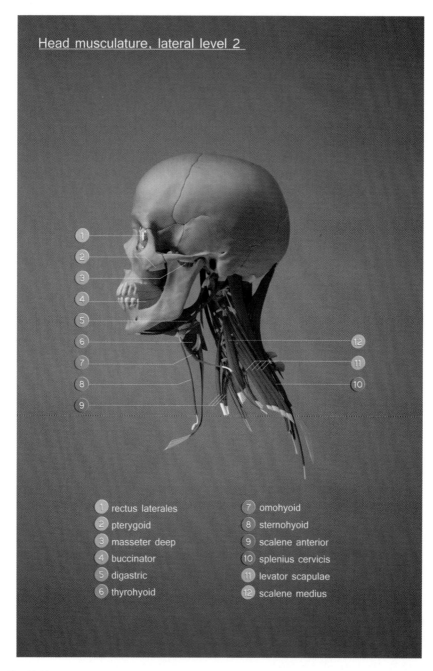

Fig. 12.22 Head, lateral view, level 2

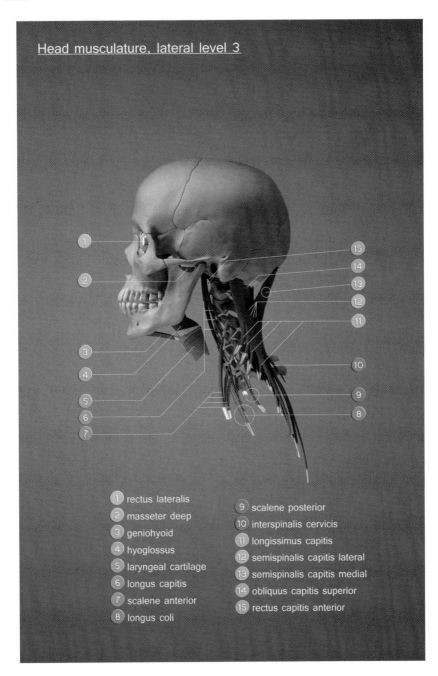

Fig. 12.23 Head, lateral view, levels 3

Eye

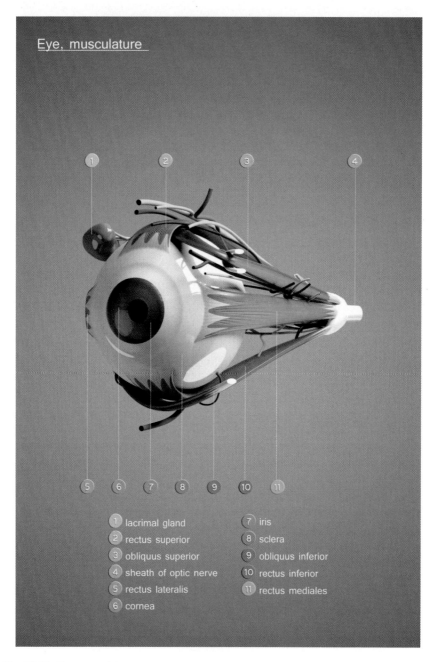

Fig. 12.24 Eye, musculature

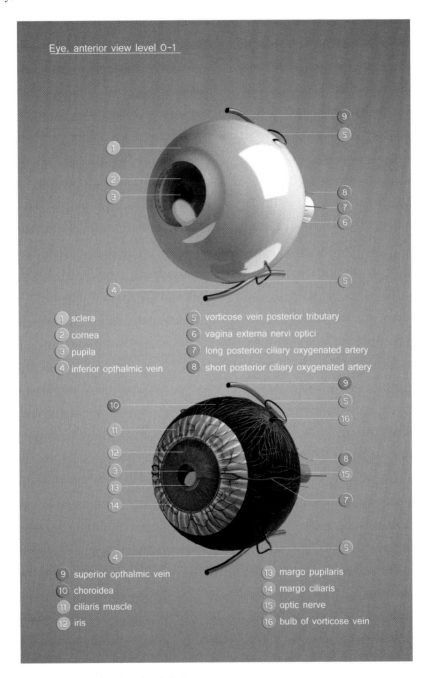

Fig. 12.25 Eye, anterior view, levels 0–1

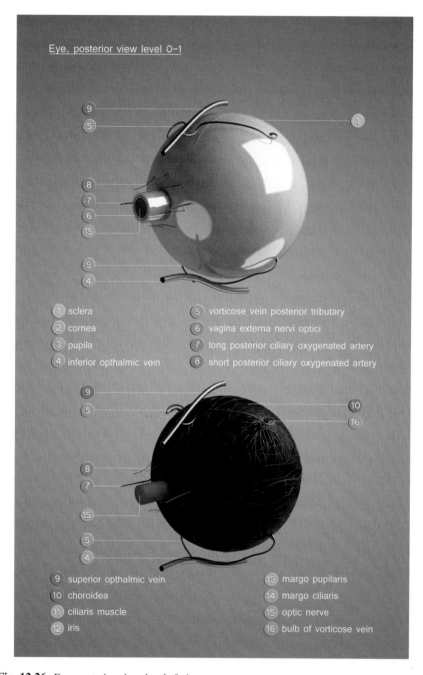

Fig. 12.26 Eye, posterior view, levels 0–1

Chapter 13
Musculature (Continued)

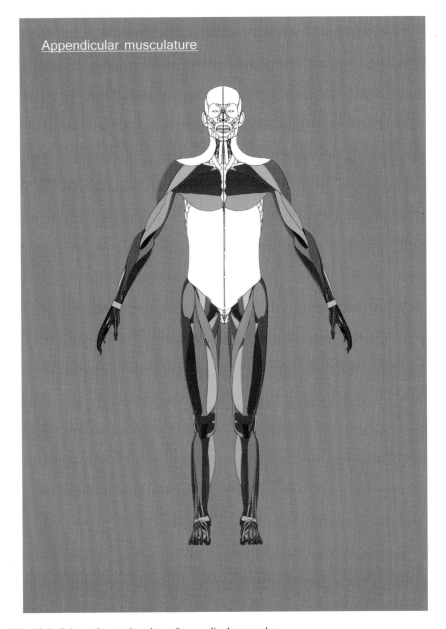

Fig. 13.1 Schematic anterior view of appendicular muscles

A. Paquette, *Computer Graphics for Artists II: Environments and Characters,*
© Springer-Verlag London Limited 2009

General

The superficial muscles of the arm and leg are well known, at least by outward appearance. Their mechanical function, however, is not clear because their attachments remain hidden. The latissimus dorsi, for instance, is a very large muscle whose origin is found in the posterior thoracic cage. Its action is made by the bone it actually moves, the humerus in the arm. It is sometimes classified as a back muscle, yet it actually contributes very little, if anything, to the movement of the back. It moves the upper arm, just as the most prominent chest muscle, the pectoralis major.

The iliopsoas, unlike the latissimus dorsi or pectoralis major, is a muscle that is not even visible on the surface, but has a very strong mechanical effect on the upper leg, thanks to its insertion at the neck of the femur. If you were to see this muscle within the body, you would see that its origin is not very far from that of the latissimus dorsi, but because it is differently inserted, it is a deep leg muscle instead of a superficial arm muscle.

Knowing how these muscles work is crucial to understanding how to rig a character for animation, and how to shape it for its rest pose.

The following diagrams are designed to illustrate as clearly as possible the appearance, function, origin, and insertion of each of the muscles of the appendicular skeleton (Figs. 13.1–13.41)

Arm

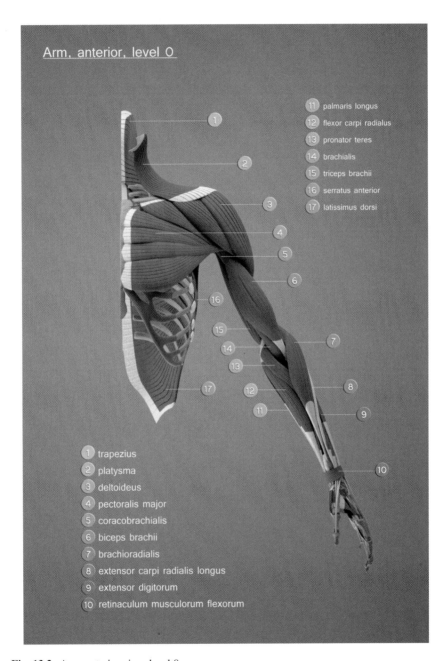

Fig. 13.2 Arm, anterior view, level 0

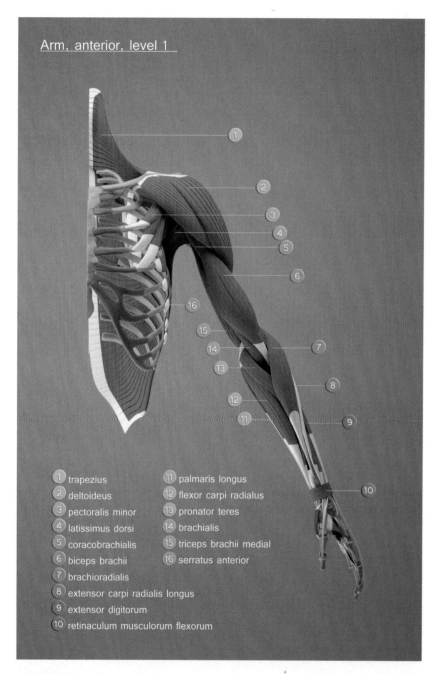

Arm, anterior, level 1

1 trapezius
2 deltoideus
3 pectoralis minor
4 latissimus dorsi
5 coracobrachialis
6 biceps brachii
7 brachioradialis
8 extensor carpi radialis longus
9 extensor digitorum
10 retinaculum musculorum flexorum
11 palmaris longus
12 flexor carpi radialus
13 pronator teres
14 brachialis
15 triceps brachii medial
16 serratus anterior

Fig. 13.3   Arm, anterior view, level 1

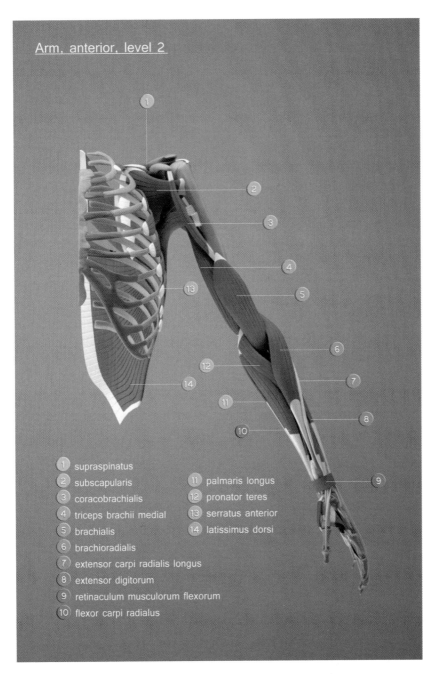

Arm, anterior, level 2

1 supraspinatus
2 subscapularis
3 coracobrachialis
4 triceps brachii medial
5 brachialis
6 brachioradialis
7 extensor carpi radialis longus
8 extensor digitorum
9 retinaculum musculorum flexorum
10 flexor carpi radialus

11 palmaris longus
12 pronator teres
13 serratus anterior
14 latissimus dorsi

Fig. 13.4 Arm, anterior view, level 2

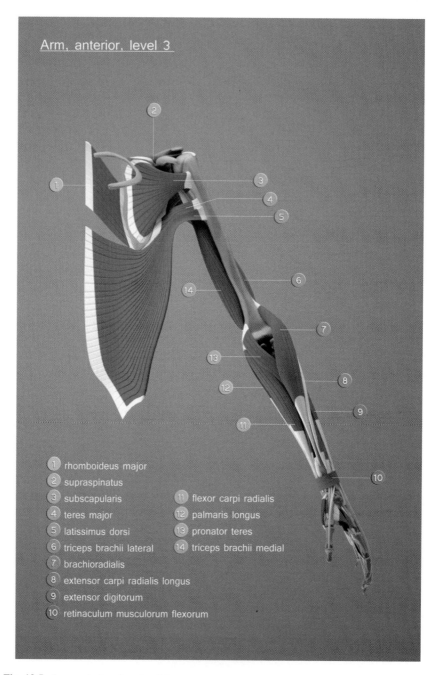

Arm, anterior, level 3

1 rhomboideus major
2 supraspinatus
3 subscapularis   11 flexor carpi radialis
4 teres major   12 palmaris longus
5 latissimus dorsi   13 pronator teres
6 triceps brachii lateral 14 triceps brachii medial
7 brachioradialis
8 extensor carpi radialis longus
9 extensor digitorum
10 retinaculum musculorum flexorum

Fig. 13.5 Arm, anterior view, level 3

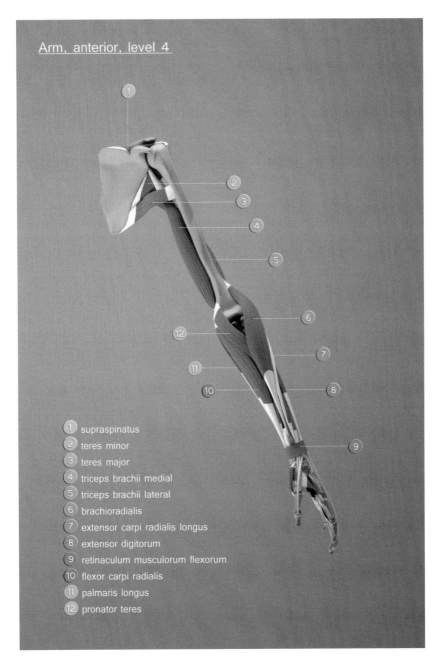

Arm, anterior, level 4

1 supraspinatus
2 teres minor
3 teres major
4 triceps brachii medial
5 triceps brachii lateral
6 brachioradialis
7 extensor carpi radialis longus
8 extensor digitorum
9 retinaculum musculorum flexorum
10 flexor carpi radialis
11 palmaris longus
12 pronator teres

Fig. 13.6 Arm, anterior view, level 4

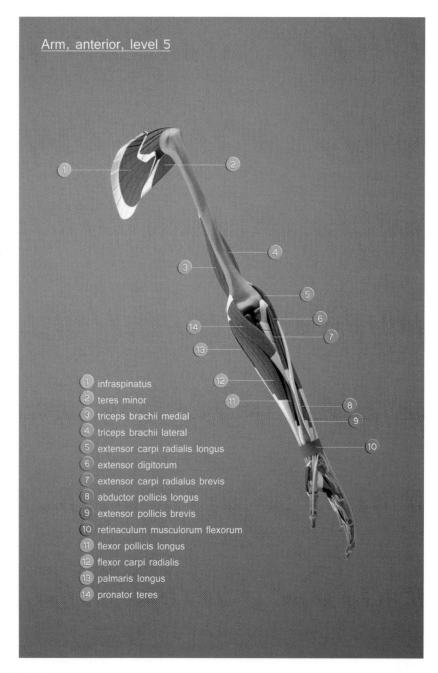

Arm, anterior, level 5

1 infraspinatus
2 teres minor
3 triceps brachii medial
4 triceps brachii lateral
5 extensor carpi radialis longus
6 extensor digitorum
7 extensor carpi radialus brevis
8 abductor pollicis longus
9 extensor pollicis brevis
10 retinaculum musculorum flexorum
11 flexor pollicis longus
12 flexor carpi radialis
13 palmaris longus
14 pronator teres

Fig. 13.7 Arm, anterior view, level 5

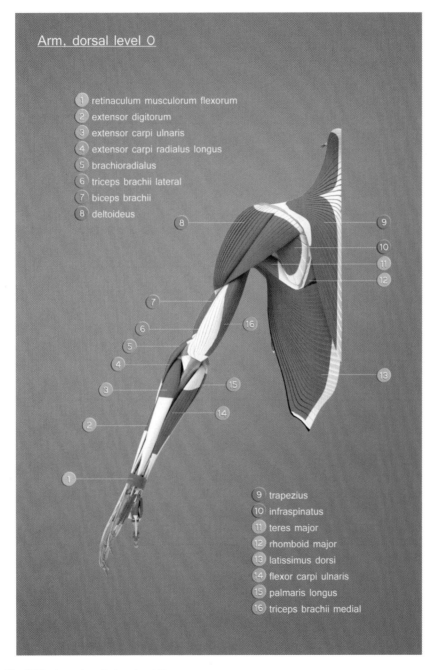

Arm, dorsal level 0

1 retinaculum musculorum flexorum
2 extensor digitorum
3 extensor carpi ulnaris
4 extensor carpi radialus longus
5 brachioradialus
6 triceps brachii lateral
7 biceps brachii
8 deltoideus

9 trapezius
10 infraspinatus
11 teres major
12 rhomboid major
13 latissimus dorsi
14 flexor carpi ulnaris
15 palmaris longus
16 triceps brachii medial

Fig. 13.8 Arm, dorsal view, level 0

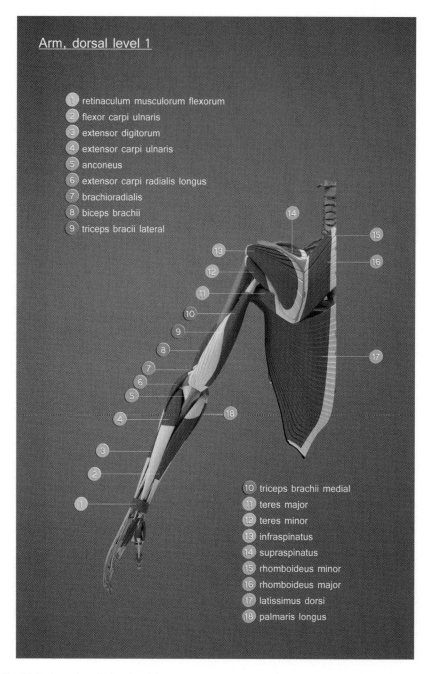

Arm, dorsal level 1

1 retinaculum musculorum flexorum
2 flexor carpi ulnaris
3 extensor digitorum
4 extensor carpi ulnaris
5 anconeus
6 extensor carpi radialis longus
7 brachioradialis
8 biceps brachii
9 triceps bracii lateral

10 triceps brachii medial
11 teres major
12 teres minor
13 infraspinatus
14 supraspinatus
15 rhomboideus minor
16 rhomboideus major
17 latissimus dorsi
18 palmaris longus

Fig. 13.9 Arm, dorsal view, level 1

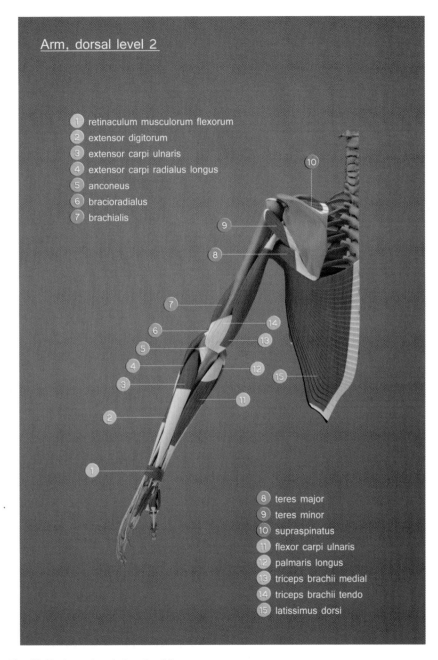

Arm, dorsal level 2

1 retinaculum musculorum flexorum
2 extensor digitorum
3 extensor carpi ulnaris
4 extensor carpi radialus longus
5 anconeus
6 bracioradialus
7 brachialis

8 teres major
9 teres minor
10 supraspinatus
11 flexor carpi ulnaris
12 palmaris longus
13 triceps brachii medial
14 triceps brachii tendo
15 latissimus dorsi

Fig. 13.10 Arm, dorsal view, level 2

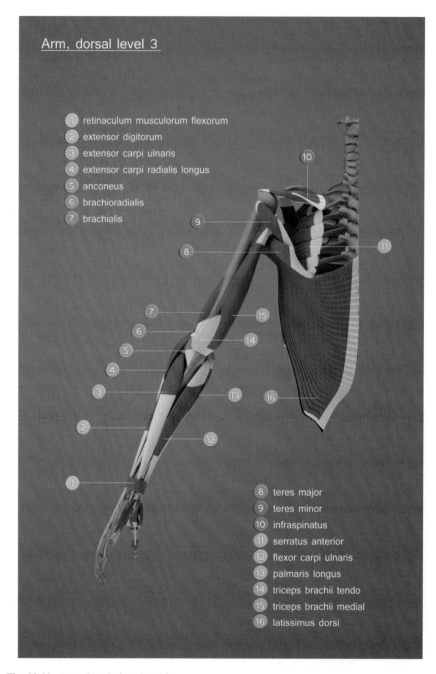

Arm, dorsal level 3

1 retinaculum musculorum flexorum
2 extensor digitorum
3 extensor carpi ulnaris
4 extensor carpi radialis longus
5 anconeus
6 brachioradialis
7 brachialis

8 teres major
9 teres minor
10 infraspinatus
11 serratus anterior
12 flexor carpi ulnaris
13 palmaris longus
14 triceps brachii tendo
15 triceps brachii medial
16 latissimus dorsi

Fig. 13.11   Arm, dorsal view, level 3

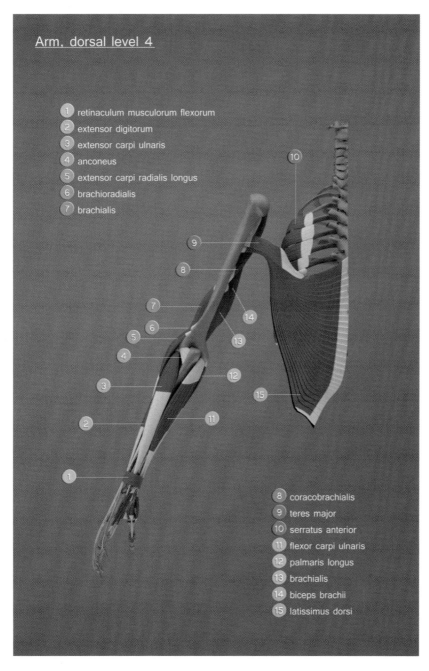

Fig. 13.12 Arm, dorsal view, level 4

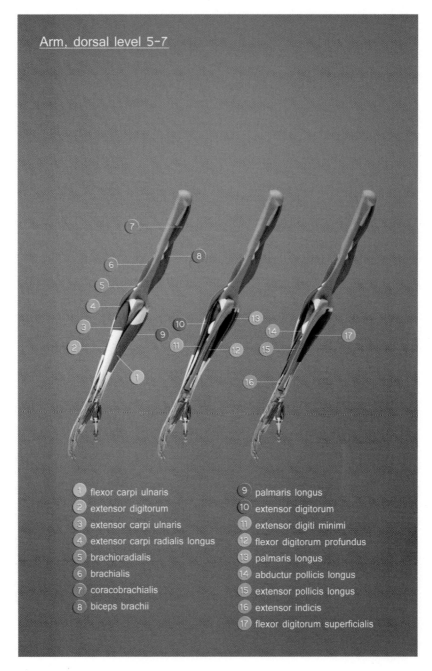

Fig. 13.13   Arm, dorsal view, level 5–7

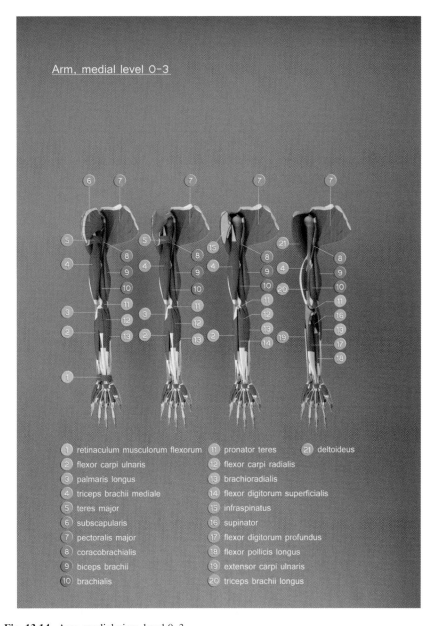

Arm, medial level 0-3

1 retinaculum musculorum flexorum	11 pronator teres	21 deltoideus
2 flexor carpi ulnaris	12 flexor carpi radialis	
3 palmaris longus	13 brachioradialis	
4 triceps brachii mediale	14 flexor digitorum superficialis	
5 teres major	15 infraspinatus	
6 subscapularis	16 supinator	
7 pectoralis major	17 flexor digitorum profundus	
8 coracobrachialis	18 flexor pollicis longus	
9 biceps brachii	19 extensor carpi ulnaris	
10 brachialis	20 triceps brachii longus	

Fig. 13.14 Arm, medial view, level 0–3

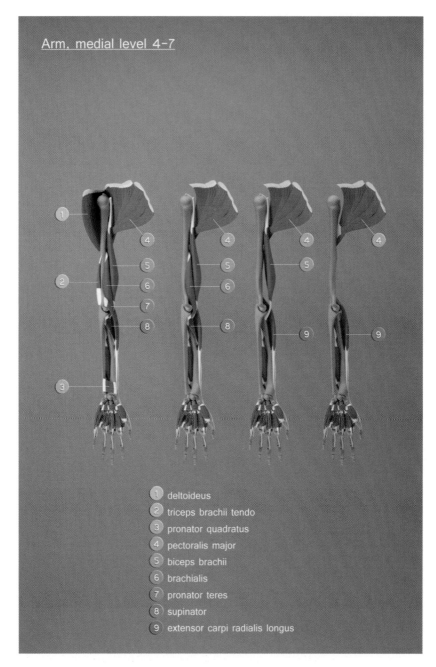

Fig. 13.15 Arm, medial view, level 4–7

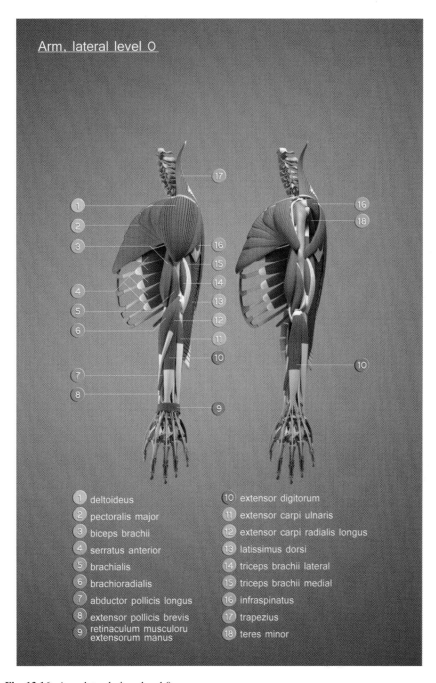

Fig. 13.16 Arm, lateral view, level 0

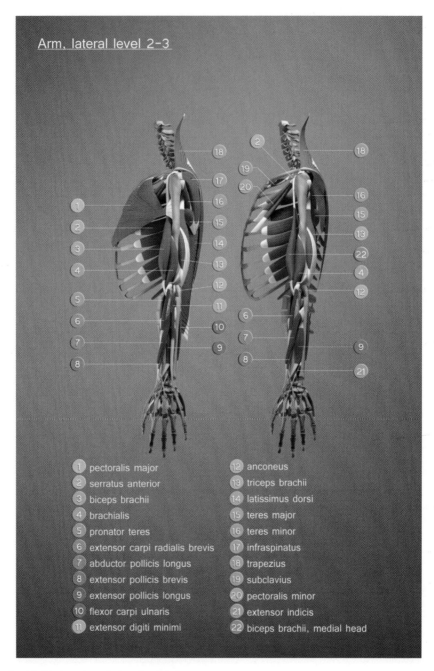

Arm, lateral level 2-3

1. pectoralis major
2. serratus anterior
3. biceps brachii
4. brachialis
5. pronator teres
6. extensor carpi radialis brevis
7. abductor pollicis longus
8. extensor pollicis brevis
9. extensor pollicis longus
10. flexor carpi ulnaris
11. extensor digiti minimi
12. anconeus
13. triceps brachii
14. latissimus dorsi
15. teres major
16. teres minor
17. infraspinatus
18. trapezius
19. subclavius
20. pectoralis minor
21. extensor indicis
22. biceps brachii, medial head

Fig. 13.17 Arm, lateral view, level 2–3

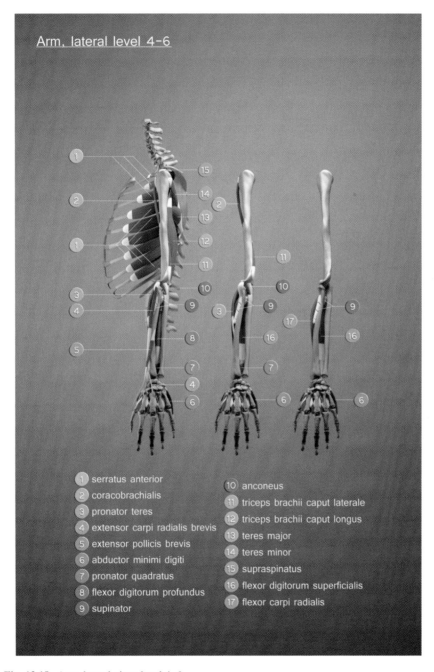

Arm, lateral level 4-6

1 serratus anterior
2 coracobrachialis
3 pronator teres
4 extensor carpi radialis brevis
5 extensor pollicis brevis
6 abductor minimi digiti
7 pronator quadratus
8 flexor digitorum profundus
9 supinator

10 anconeus
11 triceps brachii caput laterale
12 triceps brachii caput longus
13 teres major
14 teres minor
15 supraspinatus
16 flexor digitorum superficialis
17 flexor carpi radialis

Fig. 13.18 Arm, lateral view, level 4–6

Hand

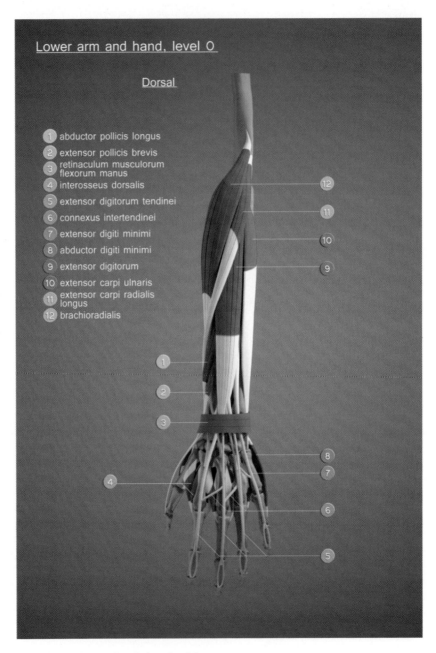

Fig. 13.19 Lower arm, dorsal view, level 0

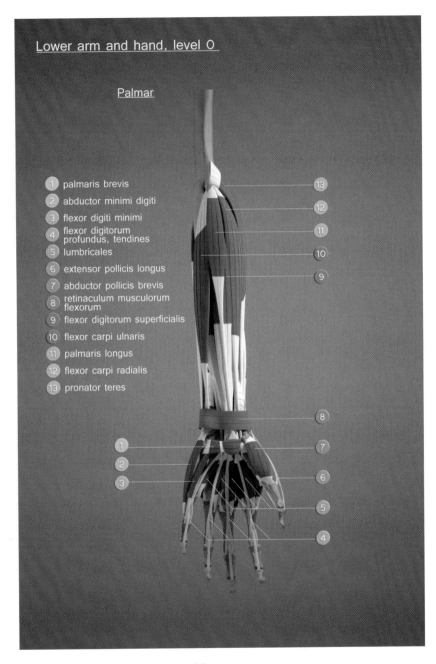

Fig. 13.20 Lower arm, palmar view, level 0

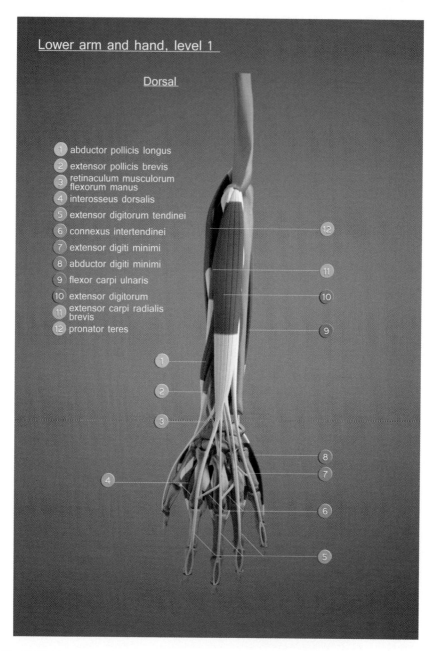

Fig. 13.21 Lower arm, dorsal view, level 1

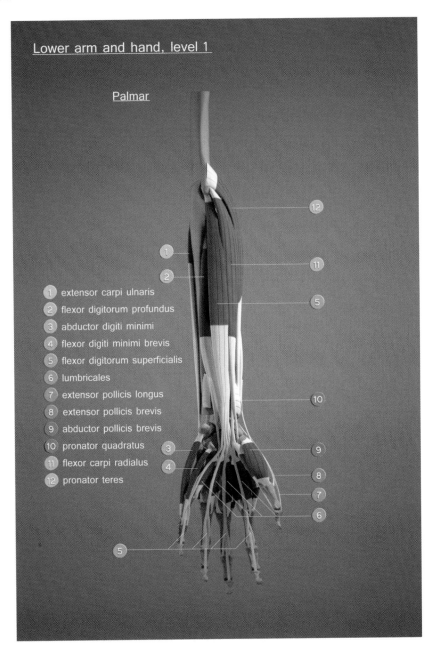

Lower arm and hand, level 1

Palmar

1 extensor carpi ulnaris
2 flexor digitorum profundus
3 abductor digiti minimi
4 flexor digiti minimi brevis
5 flexor digitorum superficialis
6 lumbricales
7 extensor pollicis longus
8 extensor pollicis brevis
9 abductor pollicis brevis
10 pronator quadratus
11 flexor carpi radialus
12 pronator teres

Fig. 13.22 Lower arm, palmar view, level 1

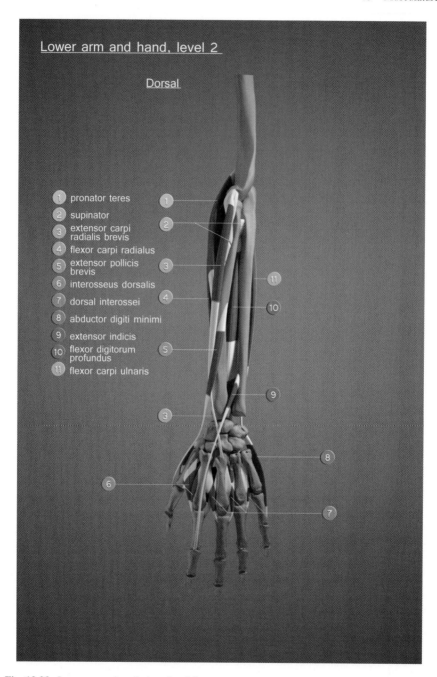

Fig. 13.23 Lower arm, dorsal view, level 2

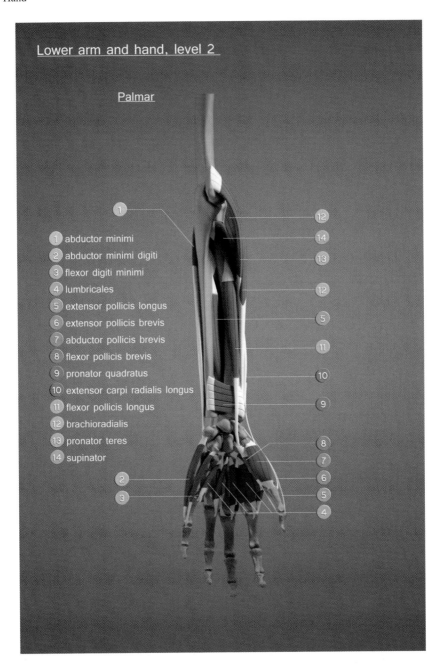

Lower arm and hand, level 2

Palmar

1. abductor minimi
2. abductor minimi digiti
3. flexor digiti minimi
4. lumbricales
5. extensor pollicis longus
6. extensor pollicis brevis
7. abductor pollicis brevis
8. flexor pollicis brevis
9. pronator quadratus
10. extensor carpi radialis longus
11. flexor pollicis longus
12. brachioradialis
13. pronator teres
14. supinator

Fig. 13.24 Lower arm, palmar view, level 2

Leg

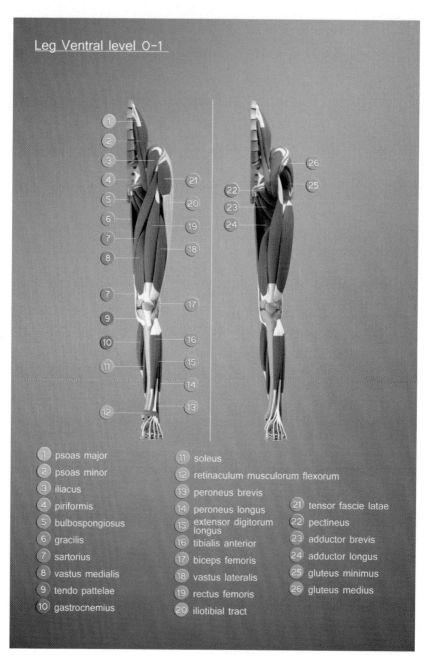

Leg Ventral level 0–1

1 psoas major
2 psoas minor
3 iliacus
4 piriformis
5 bulbospongiosus
6 gracilis
7 sartorius
8 vastus medialis
9 tendo pattelae
10 gastrocnemius
11 soleus
12 retinaculum musculorum flexorum
13 peroneus brevis
14 peroneus longus
15 extensor digitorum longus
16 tibialis anterior
17 biceps femoris
18 vastus lateralis
19 rectus femoris
20 iliotibial tract
21 tensor fascie latae
22 pectineus
23 adductor brevis
24 adductor longus
25 gluteus minimus
26 gluteus medius

Fig. 13.25 Leg, ventral view, level 0–1

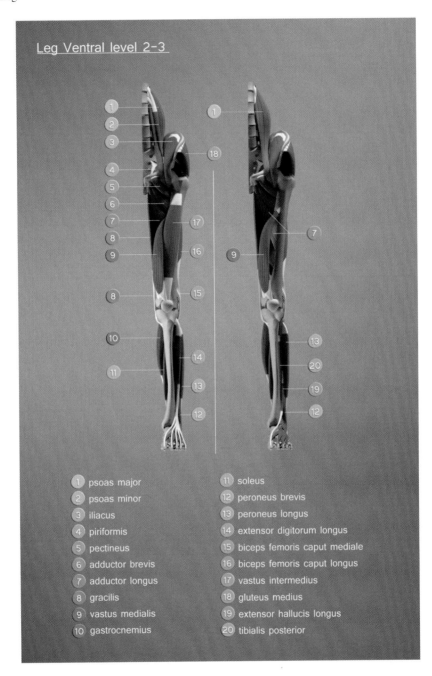

Fig. 13.26 Leg, ventral view, level 2–3

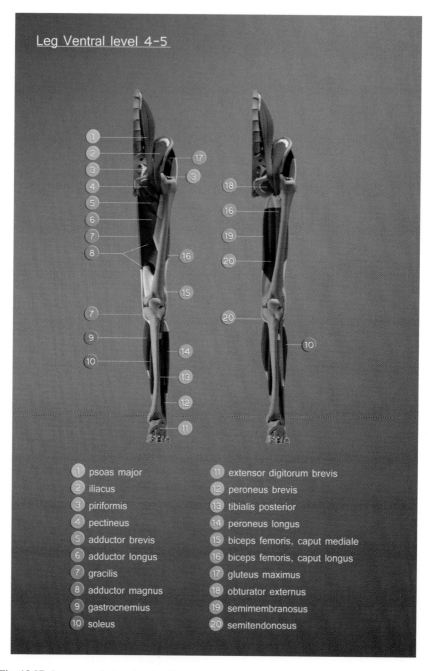

Fig. 13.27 Leg, ventral view, level 4–5

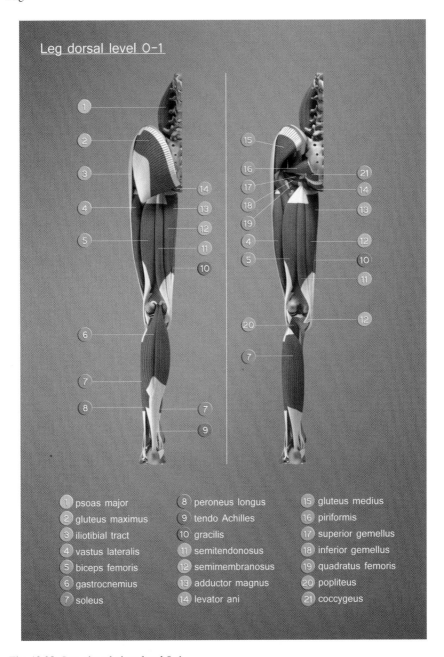

Leg dorsal level 0-1

1 psoas major	8 peroneus longus	15 gluteus medius
2 gluteus maximus	9 tendo Achilles	16 piriformis
3 iliotibial tract	10 gracilis	17 superior gemellus
4 vastus lateralis	11 semitendonosus	18 inferior gemellus
5 biceps femoris	12 semimembranosus	19 quadratus femoris
6 gastrocnemius	13 adductor magnus	20 popliteus
7 soleus	14 levator ani	21 coccygeus

Fig. 13.28 Leg, dorsal view, level 0–1

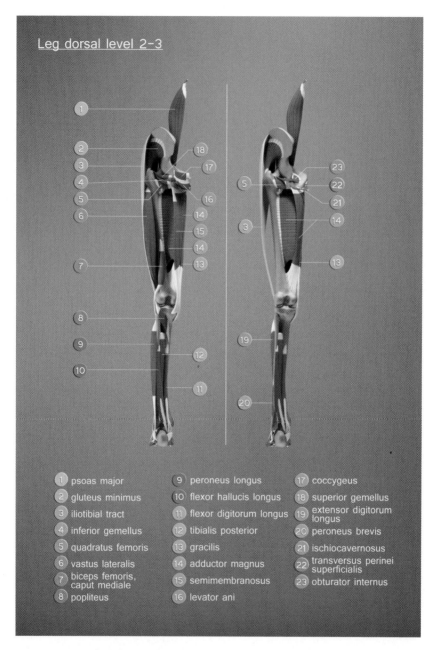

Leg dorsal level 2–3

1 psoas major	9 peroneus longus	17 coccygeus
2 gluteus minimus	10 flexor hallucis longus	18 superior gemellus
3 iliotibial tract	11 flexor digitorum longus	19 extensor digitorum longus
4 inferior gemellus	12 tibialis posterior	20 peroneus brevis
5 quadratus femoris	13 gracilis	21 ischiocavernosus
6 vastus lateralis	14 adductor magnus	22 transversus perinei superficialis
7 biceps femoris, caput mediale	15 semimembranosus	23 obturator internus
8 popliteus	16 levator ani	

Fig. 13.29 Leg, dorsal view, level 2–3

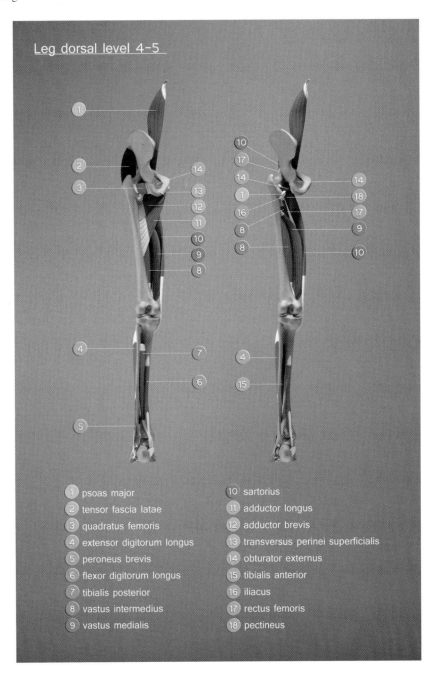

Fig. 13.30 Leg, dorsal view, level 4–5

Leg dorsal level 4-5

1. psoas major
2. tensor fascia latae
3. quadratus femoris
4. extensor digitorum longus
5. peroneus brevis
6. flexor digitorum longus
7. tibialis posterior
8. vastus intermedius
9. vastus medialis
10. sartorius
11. adductor longus
12. adductor brevis
13. transversus perinei superficialis
14. obturator externus
15. tibialis anterior
16. iliacus
17. rectus femoris
18. pectineus

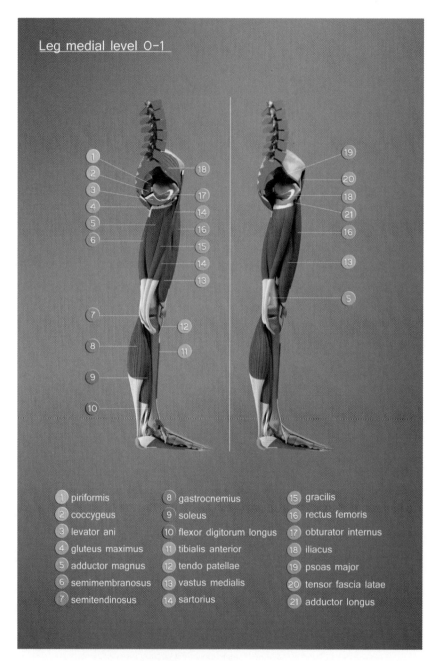

Fig. 13.31 Leg, medial view, level 0–1

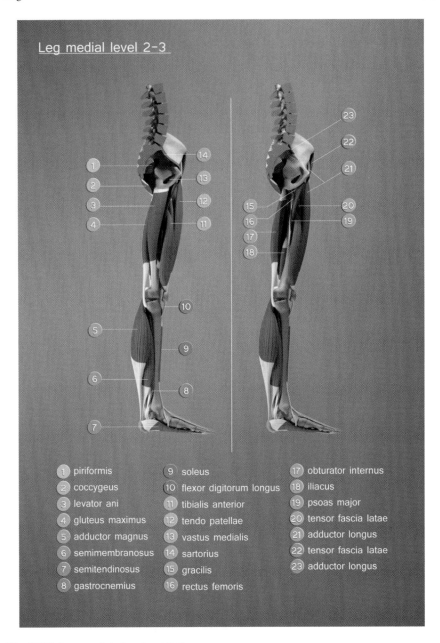

Fig. 13.32 Leg, medial view, level 2–3

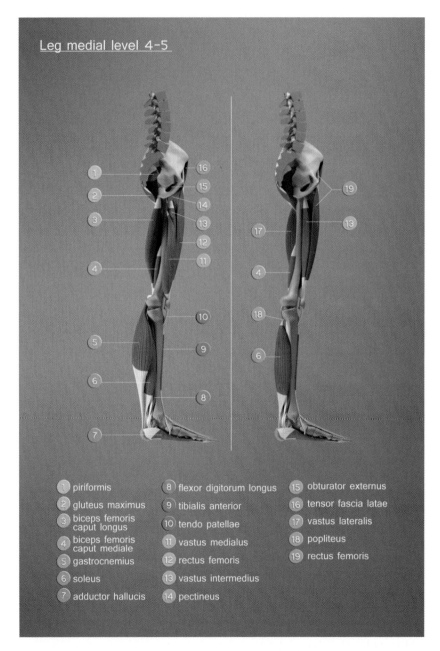

Fig. 13.33 Leg, medial view, level 4–5

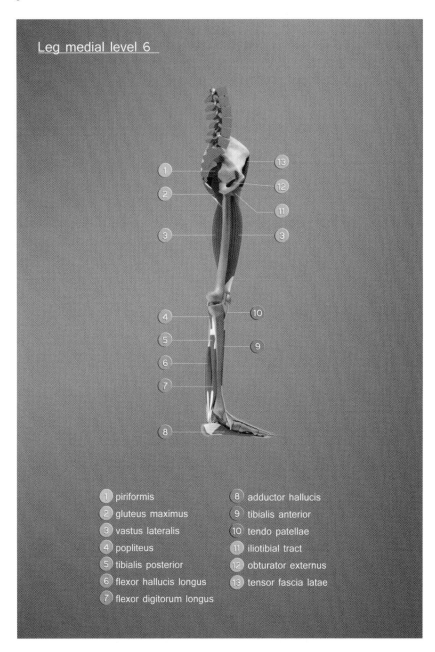

Leg medial level 6

1 piriformis
2 gluteus maximus
3 vastus lateralis
4 popliteus
5 tibialis posterior
6 flexor hallucis longus
7 flexor digitorum longus

8 adductor hallucis
9 tibialis anterior
10 tendo patellae
11 iliotibial tract
12 obturator externus
13 tensor fascia latae

Fig. 13.34 Leg, medial view, level 6

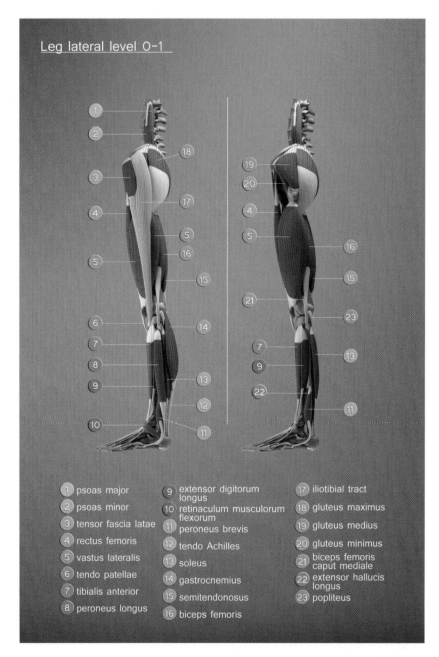

Leg lateral level 0–1

1 psoas major
2 psoas minor
3 tensor fascia latae
4 rectus femoris
5 vastus lateralis
6 tendo patellae
7 tibialis anterior
8 peroneus longus
9 extensor digitorum longus
10 retinaculum musculorum flexorum
11 peroneus brevis
12 tendo Achilles
13 soleus
14 gastrocnemius
15 semitendonosus
16 biceps femoris
17 iliotibial tract
18 gluteus maximus
19 gluteus medius
20 gluteus minimus
21 biceps femoris caput mediale
22 extensor hallucis longus
23 popliteus

Fig. 13.35 Leg, lateral view, level 0–1

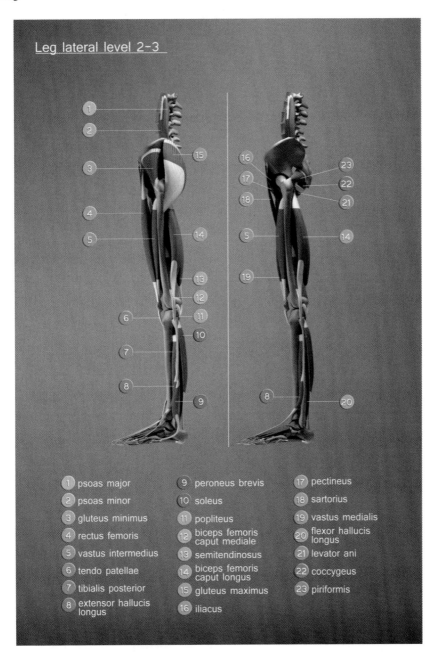

Fig. 13.36 Leg, lateral view, level 2–3

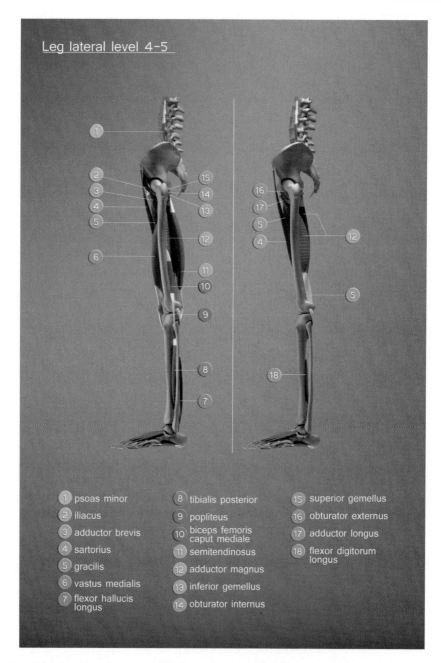

Fig. 13.37 Leg, lateral view, level 4–5

Foot

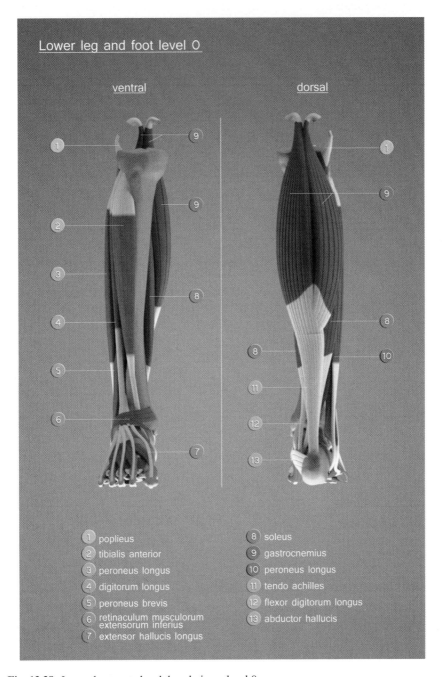

Lower leg and foot level 0

ventral   dorsal

1. poplieus
2. tibialis anterior
3. peroneus longus
4. digitorum longus
5. peroneus brevis
6. retinaculum musculorum extensorum inferius
7. extensor hallucis longus
8. soleus
9. gastrocnemius
10. peroneus longus
11. tendo achilles
12. flexor digitorum longus
13. abductor hallucis

Fig. 13.38 Lower leg, ventral and dorsal views, level 0

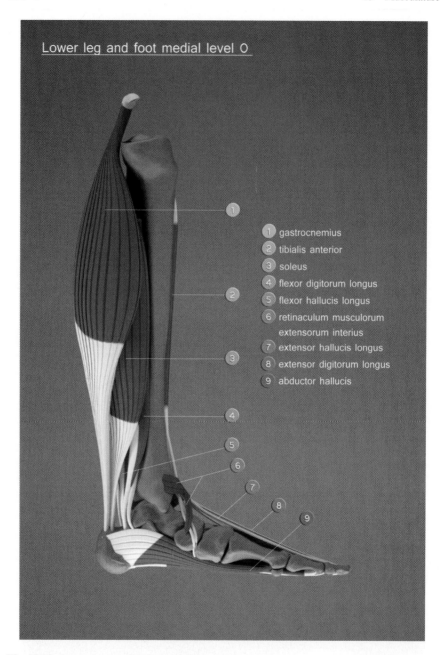

Fig. 13.39 Lower leg, medial view, level 0

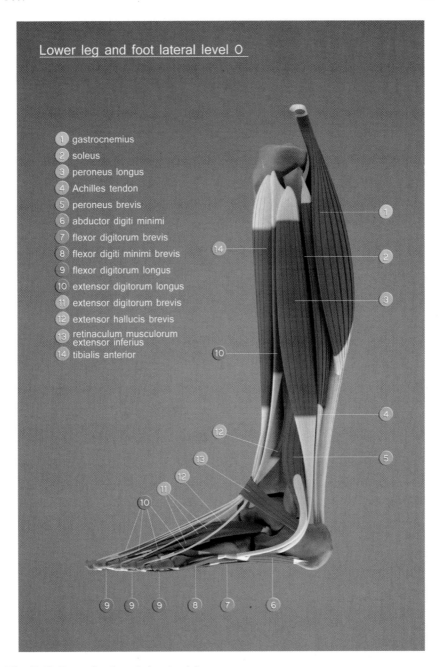

Lower leg and foot lateral level 0

1. gastrocnemius
2. soleus
3. peroneus longus
4. Achilles tendon
5. peroneus brevis
6. abductor digiti minimi
7. flexor digitorum brevis
8. flexor digiti minimi brevis
9. flexor digitorum longus
10. extensor digitorum longus
11. extensor digitorum brevis
12. extensor hallucis brevis
13. retinaculum musculorum extensor inferius
14. tibialis anterior

Fig. 13.40 Lower leg, lateral view, level 0

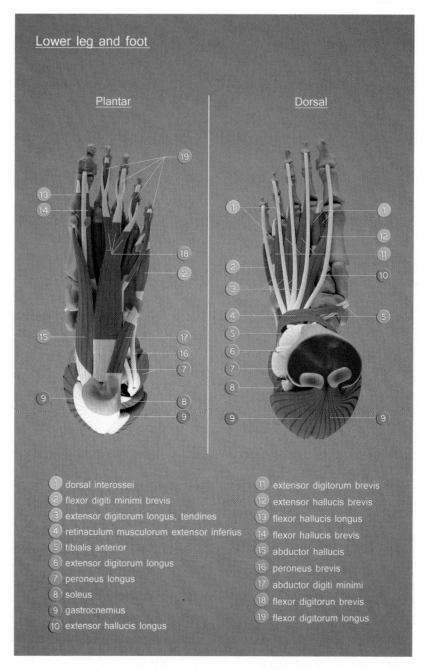

Lower leg and foot

Plantar   Dorsal

1   dorsal interossei   11 extensor digitorum brevis
2   flexor digiti minimi brevis   12 extensor hallucis brevis
3   extensor digitorum longus, tendines   13 flexor hallucis longus
4   retinaculum musculorum extensor inferius   14 flexor hallucis brevis
5   tibialis anterior   15 abductor hallucis
6   extensor digitorum longus   16 peroneus brevis
7   peroneus longus   17 abductor digiti minimi
8   soleus   18 flexor digitorun brevis
9   gastrocnemius   19 flexor digitorum longus
10 extensor hallucis longus

Fig. 13.41 Foot, plantar and dorsal views

Chapter 14
Joints

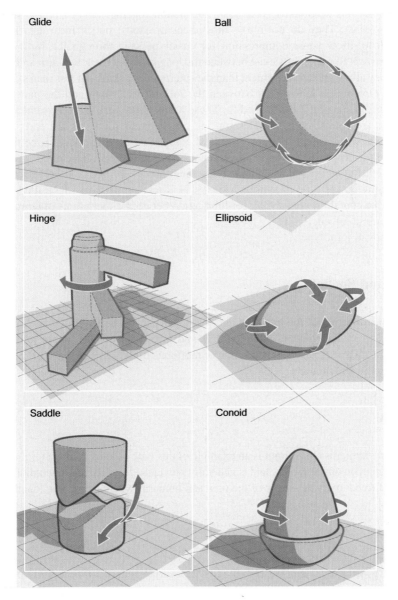

Fig. 14.1 These six skeletal joint types define motion differently from the most commonly used joint in CG, a pivot

A. Paquette, *Computer Graphics for Artists II: Environments and Characters,*
© Springer-Verlag London Limited 2009

In computer graphics, unless you make a special effort to define a joint differently, all joints are either pivot joints or modifications of pivot joints made by limiting the number of axes the joint will rotate in. As far as your software is concerned, this is not much of a distinction. Real skeletal anatomy has much more variety than this (Fig. 14.1). There are three structural types of joints: fibrous, cartilaginous, and synovial, and several varieties within each of these categories.

The various sections of your skull are bound together along *sutures* that are fibrous joints. They do not allow movement in adults, but at birth are flexible enough to allow some compression for easier passage through the birth canal. *Syndesmosis* fibrous joints exist between the long bones of the lower arm and lower leg. They allow greater movement than the sutures of the skull, but less than synovial joints. *Gomphosis* joints exist between the root of each tooth and the part of the mandible or maxilla it is attached to. These joints allow very little movement.

Ribs are connected to the sternum via cartilaginous joints, as are parts of the spine. These are tough sections of almost completely rigid cartilage. Like fibrous joints, they do not allow much movement, though they are slightly more flexible.

All other joints are synovial joints. These joints allow varying degrees of movement, depending on the type of synovial joint it is. These joints have sacs called *bursa sacks* that contain *synovial fluid* for lubrication between either points of contact for the bones involved.

Synovial joint types:

Ball and Socket

The upper portion of the humerus and the upper part of the femur are both part of a ball and socket joint, in the shoulders and hips, respectively. These joints can rotate on all three axes, but their range of motion is limited by the shape of the bone and muscle attachments.

Hinge

The ulna/humerus elbow joint is an example of this type of joint. A hinge joint allows for rotation on one axis only, and is generally prevented from having much more than 150° of freedom by the shape of the ulna and humerus where they come together.

Saddle

The carpometacarpal joint between the first metacarpal of the thumb and the trapezium of the wrist is the only saddle joint in the human body. It allows the metacarpal to slide along the carpal bone in two directions, following the shape of the bone itself, but does not allow rotation.

Pivot

The two bones of the forearm, ulna and radius, twist around each other to from a locked pivot near the elbow and are held in the same position relative to each other by the interosseous ligament.

Ellipsoid

Also known as a *condylitic joint*, an ellipsoid joint is similar to a ball and socket joint, but the bones of the joint are either elliptical or irregular in their shape, and as a result movement is more restricted. The side of the carpal bones *scaphoid*, *lunate*, and *triquetum* that face the radius of the lower arm, form an elliptical shape that fits neatly into a receiving concave ellipse on the radius. Between them is an *articular disk*, a plate of fibrous cartilage that separates both sides of this ellipsoid joint.

Plane

A plane joint is a joint where adjacent bones slide along each other's surfaces as in the midcarpal and midtarsal bones of the wrists and ankles.

The neck by itself is not "a" joint. In CG, it is often represented by a single bone that allows head rotation from between the ears at the superior end of the bone, and between either acromion at the proximal end. The neck, however, has joints between each of the seven cervical vertebrae, i.e., the first cervical vertebra (C1) with the occipital bone of the cranium, and the seventh cervical vertebra (C7) with the first thoracic vertebra (T1), for a total of eight joints (Fig. 14.2).

It is possible to imitate the motion of these eight joints with just one CG bone, but doing so requires considerable effort to make it fully convincing by careful *weighting*[1] of the vertices. If your joint budget allows it, using more than one of the joints that allow neck articulation will result in smoother neck movement than otherwise.

Each of the cervical vertebrae is capable of a limited amount of rotation in the transverse plane, of about 10°, depending on flexibility. In the coronal plane, the joint is markedly less flexible, capable of about 4° rotation to either side. In the sagittal plane, movement is limited to about 7° to either side. It is also possible to move the entire head by means of rotation in all three planes at once by all the joints in question, in a roughly circular motion around the transverse plane, a full 360°.

---

[1] Weighting vertices is a procedure for assigning various weight values to vertices relative to different bones. For example, the first row of vertices of the upper arm might be less strongly influenced by the moving bone than the fixed bone because it has a low weight on the moving bone and a high weight value on the fixed bone. This can gradually change as the vertices move down the bone, to blend vertex motion and avoid *vertex dislocation*, a condition where vertices at a joint move unnaturally and cause severe structural deformation due to rigid movement with a bone.

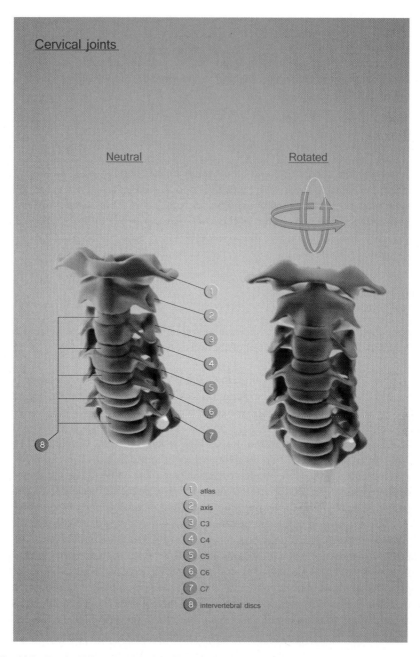

Fig. 14.2 Cervical joints, neutral and after rotation

If you multiply the number of joints by their individual rotation limits, it is easy to see why the neck is so flexible. Ten degrees multiplied by 8 is 80°, multiplied by 2, for movement away from the center on either side, is 160°. Although individual vertebrae are not capable of a great deal of movement, their numbers allow the spine to be very flexible.

The *shoulder joint* (Fig. 14.3) is made up of three separate joints. They are the *glenohumeral joint, acromioclavicular joint,* and the *sternoclavicular joint.* A large *capsule* surrounds the articulation surfaces of each of these joints. It is filled with synovial fluid, to lubricate the joint and provide smooth movement for the three bones involved. This joint is the most flexible of all the joints in the human body. It is also more prone to dislocation than any other joint, due to its comparatively light reinforcement. This is the reason it is so much more flexible than other joints.

The glenohumeral joint is most commonly associated with the shoulder joint, and is frequently mistaken for being the entire shoulder joint. It is made of the glenoid fossa of the scapula and the head of the humerus. This joint allows the humerus a great deal of freedom of movement, principally because the articulation surface of the fossa is so small that humeral movement is not constrained by the socket end of the joint. For animation purposes it is important to note that humeral movement alone does not fully express the potential of the shoulder joint. To animate it properly, the other joints of the shoulder must be understood as well.

The acromioclavicular joint is formed by the acromion process of the scapula and the distal end of the clavicle. This joint strengthens the connection between the acromion and clavicle with its joint capsule and also serves to increase the overall mobility of the shoulder joint.

The sternoclavicular joint is the pivot around which the majority of the shoulder moves when rotating the arm in the transverse plane. For animation, it is best to include this joint and the glenohumeral joint at a minimum, if convincing shoulder movement is expected. This joint is located where the proximal end of the clavicle meets the manubrium of the sternum.

The elbow joint (Fig. 14.4) is made up of three bones, humerus, ulna, and radius. Between each of these bones there are subordinate joints: the humeroulnar joint, humeroradial joint, and the proximal radial joint. All of the articular surfaces are encased in a large joint capsule containing synovial fluid and tough ligaments both to connect the bones and to lubricate their movements.

The humeroulnar joint is a hinge joint that allows most of the motion commonly associated with the elbow. It allows the lower arm and hand to rotate around the trochlea of the humerus to about 75°. Hinge motion is restricted on the anterior and posterior surface of the distal end of the humerus by fossi, the olecranon fossa, and the coranoid fossa of the humerus. In both cases, these depressions match the shape of the olecranon and coranoid process of the ulna in much the same way as a key fits into a lock, and prevent the ulna from rotating once the olecranon process is fully inserted into the olecranon fossa on the posterior side of the joint, or the coranoid process is fully inserted into the coranoid fossa on the anterior side.

In addition to the hinge-like motion associated with the elbow, it also allows a pivot-like articulation between the ulna and the radius, in cooperation with rotation

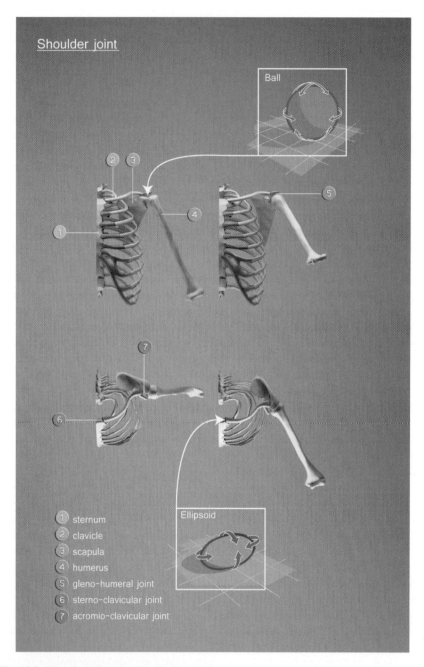

Fig. 14.3 Shoulder joint, neutral and after rotation

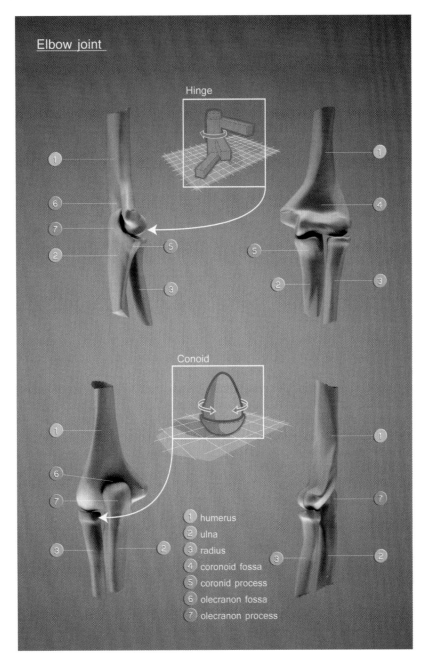

Fig. 14.4 Elbow joint, views

at the wrist. To accomplish this, when the wrist is rotated, the proximal head of the ulna is fixed at the humerus, but the radius can rotate around the ulna, which in some views can make it look as if it has crossed it as in the letter "X." This motion is allowed by the gliding joints at the humeroradial joint and the proximal radioulnar joint. In both cases, while the humerus remains fixed, these two joints allow the radius to smoothly glide over the ulna by rotating the carpal bones of the wrist. This movement is called *pronation*, and its opposite is *supination*, and allows the hand to be turned palm upwards or to be reversed with the palm down.

The wrist (Fig. 14.5) is an ellipsoidal joint formed of the distal end of the radius and the *articular disc* on one end, and the three carpal bones, the scaphoid, lunate, and triquetrum, on the other. The articular disk is a thin plate of fibrous cartilage that rests between the distal end of the ulna and the lunate and triquetrum bones. In combination with the radius, the pair forms the concave half of the ellipsoid joint of the wrist. The three carpal bones in communication with it are all gliding joints that move along the surface of the articular disk and each other, to provide a wide range of movement at the wrist.

Thumb

The saddle joint formed by the trapezium in the wrist and the first metacarpal of the hand is the only such joint in the human body. It is partly due to the unique shape of the bones in this joint that the thumb is opposable and may be brought into contact with the opposite side of the hand. The joint operates by allowing the bones on either side to glide along each other's surface. Because their contact surfaces are shaped differently, roughly in arcs that cross each other at about a 90° angle, the thumb is allowed to rotate in a nearly circular movement, and can also rotate in two planes at right angles to each other.

Fingers

The second row of carpal bones, the hamate, capitate, trapezium, and trapezoid, articulate with the second through the fifth metacarpals of the hand. The carpometacarpal joint formed by the hamate and fifth metacarpal at the base of the pinky finger, is the most flexible. As the joints move inward from the lateral aspect of the wrist, they become less flexible until they are almost immovable at the middle finger, or third metacarpal. These joints are all gliding joints.

Beyond the carpometacarpal joints between the wrist and individual fingers at their roots are the articulations of individual fingers. These begin with a row of metacarpophalangial joints between each metacarpal bone and the proximal phalange attached to it. These are very flexible gliding joints. The second and fifth of these joints, the index and pinky fingers, respectively, are the most flexible of the group. Because of the shape of the articulating surfaces, these joints allow circumduction and rotation in two planes. It is due to this that it is possible to spread the fingers of the hand in a fan shape.

The remaining finger joints, between each of the phalanges, are all hinge joints that allow limited rotation on one axis only. Their form closely resembles the humeroulnar

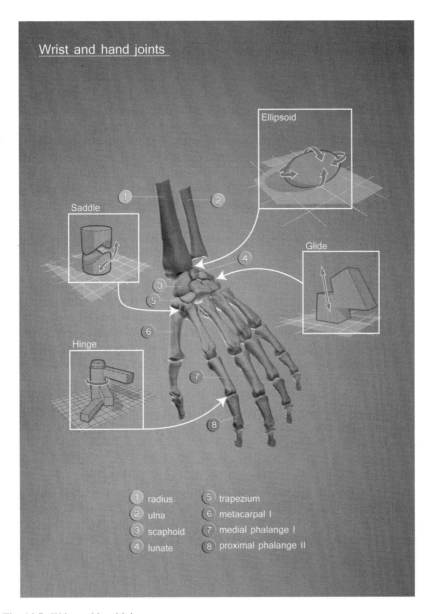

Fig. 14.5 Wrist and hand joints

joint, and they have about the same range of motion. Like the humeroulnar joint, their shape prevents motion beyond about 90°.

The superficial aspect of the hip is situated over the greater trochanter of the femur (Fig. 14.6). The location of the articulating joint is where the head of the femur rests within the acetabulum socket of the pelvis. The acetabulum is formed by three of the bones of the pelvis, the ilium, ischium, and pubis. The femoral head is somewhat detached from the body of the femur, and extends away from it by means of the femoral neck.

The angle of the femoral neck relative to the body of the femur varies during its lifetime, and even from one side to the other. It is the site of a number of femoral fractures, generally in elderly populations. One of the greatest stress factors is the angle of the neck to the body. This is measured by comparing the lateral rim of the acetabulum with a line projected into it from the center of the femoral neck. This angle varies a great deal, but is normally between 125° and 135°. The joint angle can also project forwards towards the anterior face of the body by about 12°. This Y-shaped structure puts a great deal of stress on the intersection of the two segments of the bone. When the *center edge angle* is less than 125°, the joint is considered unstable.[2] It is this angle that causes the legs to tilt inwards from the hips to the knees so that, while the hips are located at the lateral aspect of the body, the knees are nearer to the median line.

The hip joint has the second greatest range of movement in the body. It allows flexion and extension, abduction and adduction, internal and external pelvic rotation, and circumduction of the femur. Because of its great flexibility and that the majority of the weight of the body is carried by both hip joints, the acetabulum is a much larger, heavier structure than its counterpart in the shoulder, the glenoid fossa. In addition to this, there is a *labrum*, a fibro-cartilaginous rim that surrounds the lateral surface of the acetabulum and secures the joint. Around this are a number of tough ligaments, including the strongest ligament in the body, the iliofemoral ligament. Surrounding these is a large joint capsule filled with synovial fluid to lubricate the joint.

The shape of the hips is dramatically different between males and females because of the difference in the shape of the pelvic girdle, which is wider and deeper in females than in males. This displaces the position of the hip joint in women, resulting in wider hips.

The knee joint (Fig. 14.7) is formed by the distal end of the femur, the proximal ends of the tibia and fibula, and the patella. The femur and tibia are connected by a number of ligaments. The anterior cruciate ligament, posterior cruciate ligament, lateral collateral ligament, and medial collateral ligament form a tough group of connective structures, to bind the lower leg to the upper leg. The patellar tendon, sometimes called the patellar ligament, connects the patella to the tibia. On the superior

---

[2] *Mechanical analysis and computer simulation of the structure of the femoral neck*, by Jing Guang Qian, Yia-Wei Song, Xiao Tang, and Songning Zhang of the Nanjing Institute of physical education, Nanjing, China, and the University of Tennessee, Knoxville, TN, USA

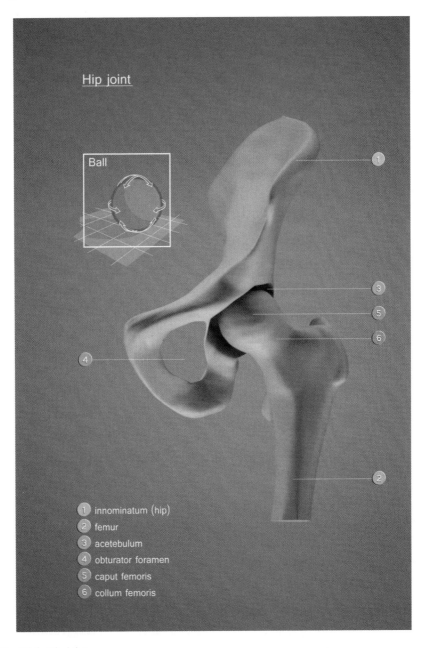

Fig. 14.6 Hip joint

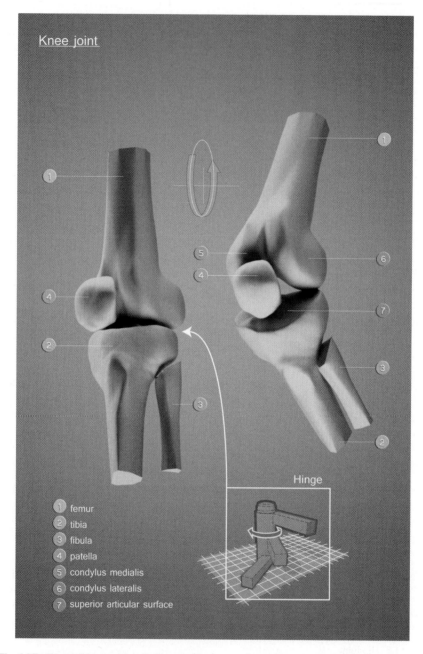

Fig. 14.7 Knee joint, neutral and after rotation

face of the patella, it is connected to the femur by the quadriceps tendon. The articular portions of the knee are surrounded by a joint capsule filled with synovial fluid for lubrication. Between them are two *menisci*, or C-shaped pads at the medial and lateral aspects of the joints, respectively, for shock absorption, more fluid rotation, and strengthening of the joint.

The knee is classified as a hinge joint, though it does allow slight medial or lateral rotation around a vertical axis. Its topological position in the body plan corresponds to that of the elbow in the arm, and its range of movement in the hinge axis is roughly similar. Depending on whether the hip is flexed or extended, it may rotate through between 120° and 160°. Rotation around its central axis is about 40°, with 30° of that from a neutral position towards the lateral side of the body, and 10° towards the medial line.

Unlike the twisting of the ulna and radius, made possible by the pivot joint at the olecranon, the lower leg cannot twist in the same manner, though it can rotate somewhat. In this respect, just as with the hip and shoulder, the knee is less flexible than the elbow. When the lower leg is rotated on its central axis, the tibia and fibula rotate together, without moving their position relative to each other.

To build a knee joint properly in CG, care must be taken to position the patella in relation to the leg's neutral position, and then to include controls to accommodate how the positional relationship with its neighbors in the knee joint is changed when the joint is flexed or extended. Failure to accommodate this feature can cause a CG knee to entirely collapse or to bulge unnaturally, depending on how it is handled.

The ankle is a hinge joint that allows upwards and rearwards rotation of the foot. It is responsible for dorsiflexion and plantar flexion of the foot, when the body's weight is either raised up onto the toes (dorsiflexion) or lowered onto the heels. The articulating surfaces of the joint belong to the distal end of the tibia and fibula, and the superior face of the talus, one of the tarsal bones. Because of the spinous processes of the fibula and tibia on either side of the talus, rotation along the lower leg's central axis is severely limited (Fig. 14.8).

Tarsal Joints

The tarsal joints are located relative to the foot and lower leg at the same position as the carpal bones are to the hand and lower arm. They are similar in some respects. For example, they are almost all gliding joints and are packed very tightly together in two rows, one on the ankle side of the foot, the other in contact with the metatarsals. They are dissimilar too, in that, unlike any of the carpal bones, the talus and calcaneous tarsal bones are much larger than any of the other tarsal bones, and they are each meant to carry a majority of the body's weight.

Much of the work of these bones is to distribute weight downwards from the body and into the plantar surface of the foot. This is accomplished by slight movement of the smaller tarsals, and by the calcaneous, or heel, which serves as a counterbalance.

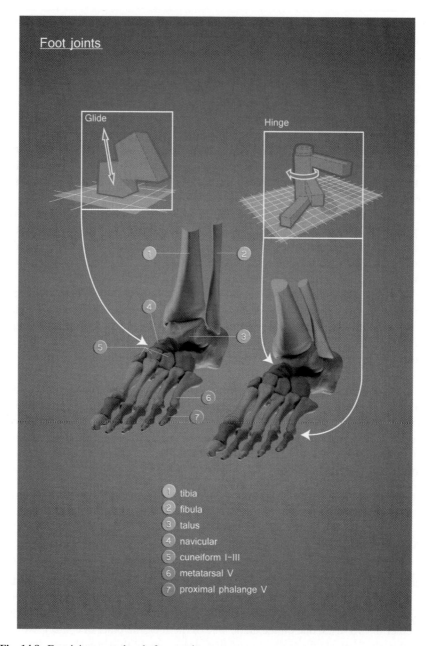

Foot joints

Glide

Hinge

1 tibia
2 fibula
3 talus
4 navicular
5 cuneiform I–III
6 metatarsal V
7 proximal phalange V

Fig. 14.8 Foot joint, neutral and after rotation

The talus allows rotation forwards or backwards at the ankle, either onto the calcaneous, or away from it and onto the plantar surface. Each of these joints has their own synovial joint capsule.

Toes

The bones of the toes, the metatarsals and phalanges, roughly correspond to the metacarpal and phalange joints of the hand. The biggest difference is that the first metatarsal is not part of a saddle joint, like the corresponding first metacarpal of the hand. The number of phalanges (two) attached to the first metatarsal, or big toe, is the same as for the first metacarpal, or root of the thumb. The second through fifth metatarsals are joints of the same type as the metacarpals, hinge joints, but they are attached to form a high arch where they connect to the metatarsals. This arch is known as the *transverse arch*.

Conclusion

The joints are important because they dictate how the body will move, and also because they strongly affect the shape of the body. In some cases, such as the knee and elbow, joint structure forms the primary defining features of superficial anatomy in those regions. Even more important, when a joint moves, the shape of the joint often changes. Knowledge of how a joint functions is crucial in understanding how to animate it and how to rig it so that when your character is animated, no unnatural or unwanted deformations occur at the joints.

Chapter 15
CG Anatomy

Fig. 15.1 Tori, by Steven Geisler (face), Francisco Cortina (hair and body), and Jake Rowell (body textures)

Anatomy tells us what a character is supposed to look like and how it moves, but it does not tell us exactly how to build it for use in a CG scene. Depending on your project, you may want anything from a highly detailed anatomical model such as the one described in the project for this section, or a very low-resolution polygonal model that uses texture maps to represent all superficial detail, such as muscles. The first fact that you must ascertain, then, is what type of model you desire to make (Figs. 15.1–15.9). The most common varieties are the following (in order of detail, from lowest level to highest):

- Lowest resolution game
  - 750 triangles, 1 texture map, usually about 512 × 512 pixels
- Low-resolution game
  - 2,000 triangles, one 1 k texture map, or multiple maps that in total would fit within a 1,024 1,024 area.

A. Paquette, *Computer Graphics for Artists II: Environments and Characters,*
© Springer-Verlag London Limited 2009

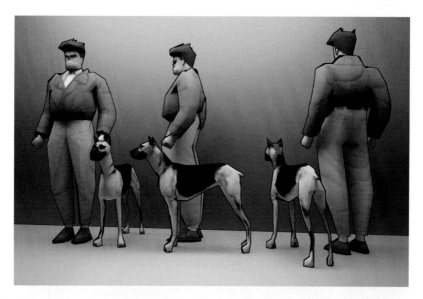

Fig. 15.2 Extremely low-resolution character models. The human has 634 triangles, the dog has 522

- Stand-in film
  - This type of model is used for blocking animation with a complete skeleton. Nurbs surfaces are often used for these, usually of perfect proportions but low detail. Patches will normally have no more than 12 isoparms each. Sometimes they have texture maps, more often if the stand-in is made of polygons.
  - Nurbs
    - Minimum of 6 patches for major limbs, 30 in total including hands and feet. No texture maps.
  - Polys
    - 3,000 triangles, if mapped, it is 1 k
- Medium-resolution game
  - 3,000–5,000 triangles, multiple 1 k maps for color, normals, and specularity
- Low-resolution film
  - Nurbs
    - Very similar to stand-in model, but with textures, sometimes with several layers of information represented by them
    - Polys
    - 5,000–7,500 triangles, multiple 1 k–2 k maps

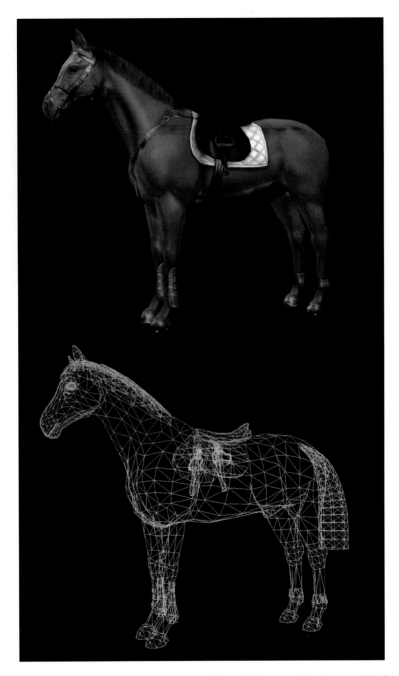

Fig. 15.3 A low-resolution horse and its wireframe (From *My Horse and Me*. Courtesy Wii Games)

Fig. 15.4 One horse becomes many, thanks to a good UV layout and multiple texture maps (From *My Horse and Me*. Courtesy Wii Games)

- High-resolution TV
  - Because of television screen resolution limits, characters rarely need to be of any higher resolution than this, except if the animation requires a long shot and extreme close-up of the same figure. Even then, the poly budget does not need to increase much beyond this level.
  - 7,500 triangles, multiple 1 k maps
- Medium-resolution film
  - Nurbs
    - Axial and appendicular musculature and all digits represented along with full complement of joint articulations, hair, and multiple tex maps between 1 k and 2 k in size. Face is modeled, but might have low-detail teeth and ears as well as simplified anatomical structure. This is the most common resolution for full figure character shots.
  - Polys
    - Same as above, but 7,500–10,000 polygons
- High-resolution game
  - 10,000–15,000 polygons, 3–8 layers of maps, up to 2 k each
- Highest-resolution game
  - 25,000 polygons, 5–10 layers of maps. This resolution is becoming less common because of normal map use as a substitute for high levels of poly gonal detail

Fig. 15.5 This character model has many millions of triangles, but will be reduced to much less after this uber-high-resolution model is converted to normal maps (Copyright © 1998–2008, Epic Games, Inc. All rights reserved)[1]

- High-resolution film
  - Nurbs
    - Up to several hundred complex patches, many layers of maps (3 minimum, to several dozen), up to 4 k in size
  - Polys
    - 50,000 triangles, many layers of maps (3 minimum, to several dozen)
  - Subdivided surfaces
    - May be only one patch, but subdivided for extremely fine detail, including knuckles, fingernails, muscle boundaries, eyelashes, and other small structures. Many maps.
- Medical simulation
  - Nurbs (unusual)
    - Thousands of patches to represent numerous small details, such as circulatory system, bones of inner ear, nervous system, and thickness of arterial walls. Texture maps are unusual, though not unheard of for this type of project.
  - Polys
    - Hundreds of thousands of polys (could be in the low millions), no texture maps.

---

[1] Epic, Epic Games, Unreal, the "Powered by Unreal Technology" logo, the Circle-U logo, and Gears of War are trademarks or registered Trademarks of Epic Games, Inc. in the United States of America and elsewhere.

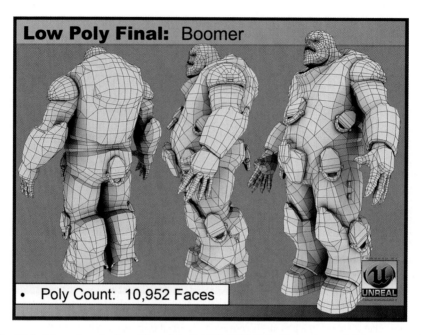

Fig. 15.6 After poly reductions (Copyright © 1998–2008, Epic Games, Inc. All rights reserved)[2]

- Highest-resolution film
  - This level of resolution is reserved for extreme close-ups of large creatures. They are not uncommon in the sense that some movies use models at this resolution, but they are reserved for a small number of shots of major characters only, usually when speaking. This resolution does not apply to most human or simplified character types because the level of detail is not needed to represent them. It is used for creatures that have an extraordinary amount of surface detail built into them, like characters with tentacles or horns.
  - Nurbs
    - A thousand or more patches, many layers of large maps
  - Polys
    - From 100,000 triangles to several hundred thousand. Many layers of complex maps.

- Stand-in normal map detail model, games
  - These models are used as an intermediate object during the modeling process, to generate normal maps only. They can be as high as 20 million polygons, but are more often around one million triangles. No texture maps.

---

[2]Epic, Epic Games, Unreal, the "Powered by Unreal Technology" logo, the Circle-U logo, and Gears of War are trademarks or registered Trademarks of Epic Games, Inc. in the United States of America and elsewhere.

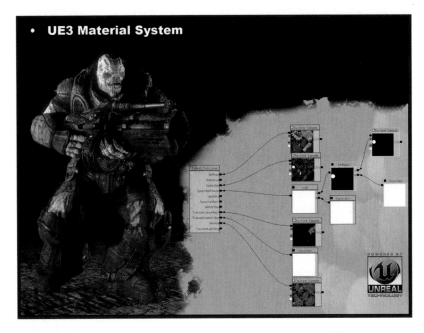

Fig. 15.7 The final character, with many maps applied. The importance of shaders to a character model should never be underestimated. Regardless of the level of detail in the model itself, shaders and maps can enhance it a great deal (Copyright © 1998–2008, Epic Games, Inc. All rights reserved)[3]

When you decide the resolution of your character model, it is a good idea to use the information listed above as a maximum number only, and to try and find a minimum number as well. It is true that, especially at higher polygon counts, additional polygons do not always visibly benefit the model, and they can be quite costly. If you use more polys than necessary in a game, you may have fewer characters or other objects in your environment than you would like, or the frame rate may be unacceptably slow. In a film or other pre-rendered product, render times may be extremely high, and interacting with the model may be extremely slow due to low screen redraw rates.

To arrive at a good budget for a character, you should keep in mind that the polygons primarily accomplish two things: higher curve detail and additional parts. For characters over about 5,000 triangles, additional polygons only add to curve detail, unless the character has extra arms, a complicated costume, or some other type of unusual detail. Here, then, is a list of minimums:

---

[3] Epic, Epic Games, Unreal, the "Powered by Unreal Technology" logo, the Circle-U logo, and Gears of War are trademarks or registered Trademarks of Epic Games, Inc. in the United States of America and elsewhere.

Fig. 15.8 Half a million triangles for a partial face scan, the starting point for a high-resolution treatment in film

Fig. 15.9 Convincing skin, hair, and other details are crucial to the success of your character model (Image courtesy Francisco A. Cortina – Cortina Digital)

- 2 triangles/1 polygon: A card, mapped with an alpha mapped image of a character, usually animated. Characters in crowd scenes of the film *Space Jam* were built like this. Careful viewing will also show that many of the characters are repeated in the same frame.
- 15 triangles: This is the smallest number of triangles needed to represent independent movement of limbs and hands (not fingers). With this type of geometry, alpha-mapped textures are used to improve the illusion of a three-dimensional character. This type of character can be found in some very old *Doom*-era video games or in the backgrounds of a few later games.
- 250 triangles: Characters built like this do not use alpha maps to enhance resolution of their silhouette, and have the appearance of origami. Curve detail is so low that they are not always convincing, nor do they move in a very credible manner, except at great distances.
- 750 triangles: This is a common triangle budget for a Playstation 1 era video game. These characters have hands simplified by fusing the second through fifth fingers, and reducing the number of joints per hand from 15 to 2. Facial features are painted on, except for the nose, and only rarely do they have an articulated jaw. Animated texture maps are used for eye and mouth movement. Characters built to this budget are not unusual in modern games that have hundreds of characters on screen simultaneously.
- 1,750 triangles: This is a standard budget for representing every major structure of the human body in the round. Therefore, a character with this budget will have every joint of every finger, a mouth that opens, simplified teeth, a nose, simple eyes, sculpted hair, knee joints, extra polys around shoulders and hips for animation, and feet represented with a minimum of three sections (ball, arch, and heel). A character in this budget range will not have a fully articulated spine, but will have at least the three major sections represented: cervical, thoracic, and lumbar. Curve detail remains low here, but skilled artists can disguise this fairly well within this budget.
- 3,500 triangles: A character that has extra appendages, unusual clothing, props, or fairly smooth curve detail may be built within this budget. The silhouette will have a faceted appearance, but only if looked for. Facial detail will include a full mouth, tongue, and teeth. Eyes may be built separate from head model, ears will have good detail, and most facial bones will be evident in geometry. Working at this budget requires some knowledge of anatomy and practice. Less experienced artists will be more comfortable at a higher poly count, but may find that their characters have less structural detail than those made by more skilled counterparts working at this resolution.
- 5,000 triangles: This is a comfortable budget for most artists, regardless of skill, because it is very easy to represent the major structures of a character within it. Skilled artists will be able to sculpt many individual muscles into the figure without any difficulty. Artists with less experience will instead rely on high resolution normal maps to inscribe muscle detail.
- 10,000 triangles: At this level of detail, most visible anatomical detail may be represented with sufficient curve detail that the model does not appear to be faceted except in extreme close-up, or at high resolution, such as on a

movie screen. In a game, to use more polygons than this for any character is only justified when there are numerous small details, such as complicated jewelry, clothing, hair, weapons, or other accoutrements in addition to the anatomy of the character itself.

- 50,000 triangles: This is a sufficient poly count to describe almost any character in fine detail, with smooth enough curve detail that even on a movie screen, no faceting will be evident. Higher poly counts than this is necessary only for shots that include both a long shot of the entire character and close-ups on complex details, such as the blades of individual teeth.
- 100,000 triangles and above: This is strictly for extremely complex characters that have either many more limbs than normal, or the equivalent. The Doctor Octopus character in *Spider-Man 2*, for instance, may have had a poly budget in this range (if he was a poly character) because he had four extra limbs, those limbs had a perfectly round cross-section, and each had dozens of joints.

The most common poly budget in use for games at the time of this writing is between 5,000 and 10,000 tris. Anything within that range is sufficient to accommodate all superficial anatomical details without resort to optimization beyond normal model cleanup. If you are working within that budget range and find that it is difficult to represent the superficial shape of a human body, it may be that you are spending more polygons on curve detail than on finding structural boundaries. This is an important distinction because it defines the difference between artists who prefer curve detail and artists who are able to include a high amount of part detail at the same or lower poly count.

The difference in working method can be apparent almost immediately. A wasteful artist will often start by extending edge loops along the length of every section of the body, without ever modifying the number of vertices around the edge loop to accommodate the amount of structural detail present at that location in the model. Models of this type tend to look as if they have been divided into evenly measured grids around every limb and digit. Sometimes this is done to improve animation by averaging the distance between vertices. This is a legitimate justification, but care should be taken that important structural detail isn't lost to accomplish it. If vertices are present, they should be used to add to the structural definition of the model. When this is not true, the model will suffer from an unnecessarily high poly count without any corresponding improvement in its appearance.

Skin

Depending on age, your character's skin should be either tightly or loosely bound to its muscles (Fig. 15.10). The skin will in most cases reduce definition between muscles at muscle borders by stretching from one muscle to the next at an angle. The end result is very much like a bevel operation performed on every edge. The sharpness

Fig. 15.10 Crouched Woman, by Francisco Cortina – Cortina Digital

of the angle is determined in your subject by the amount of muscle definition, and in the model by the depth of the bevel. If you keep this in mind, you should be able to make a credible character model by simply tracing off the shape of the muscles. Just be careful to keep the skin a constant thickness above the muscles, about half a centimeter, and avoid extremely sharp creases between muscles.

Subdivision Surfaces

Subdivision surfaces are a type of hybrid geometry that allows the user to modify a simple polygonal control mesh to define complex curved surfaces. The geometry type allows for progressive subdivision and multiple branchings, both of which are not allowed with nurbs surfaces. Subdivisions are an excellent geometry class for certain subjects, especially characters, because they can very quickly become complex, smooth, well-articulated forms without having to battle against the limitation of polygons (not smooth) or nurbs (achieving tangency or curvature continuity). In addition to those benefits, subdivision surfaces will convert to either polys or nurbs when you are done, or they can be rigged, textured, and rendered as is.

One defect of subdivision surfaces is that they can result in excessively dense geometry, so when using them, please be aware of this problem in order to avoid it with your model. The reason it happens is that each level of subdivision increases the poly count by four, making each successive level of subdivision much greater than the previous one.

To make a character with subdivision surfaces, you may make a cube and pull it into the basic shape of your character using basic editing tools and then convert the poly object into a subdivision surface. The other way is to make a subdivision surface primitive and model it with basic modeling tools. Some of the options will be different from poly modeling, but most are the same. You may also start with a nurbs object and convert to subdivisions, but this is not an efficient way to work, so it is not recommended.

Neutral Pose

Most character models are built with animation in mind. Exceptions, such as static statues, are not considered "characters" in the sense that they will never be more than a decoration in a scene. A statue that does move is a character. Because of this, modeling characters should always be done with some knowledge of the animator's needs. If not, you are likely to have the model returned for modification.

The first concern of the modeler is that the likeness of the character is good. Secondly, the geometry should be clean. The next most important factor is that the neutral pose of the model should be correct (Figs. 15.11–15.13). Some animators differ on what is the most efficient pose for a character. In the 1990s, the common pose was called the "T-pose," where the character stands erect, with feet spread slightly apart, arms outstretched straight to either side at shoulder height, palms forward, and fingers spread in a fan shape. The purpose of the pose was to aid the animator when attaching it to a skeleton and to provide a neutral start position for all joint animation. If moving parts are too close together, such as if the model were made with the arms at its sides, then the vertices of one half of the torso would become part of the same group of vertices attached to the humerus and lower arm bones and would move with them. Disentangling such errors led to the T-pose, and others like it.

Fig. 15.11 The "T" pose (Courtesy Arno Schmitz)

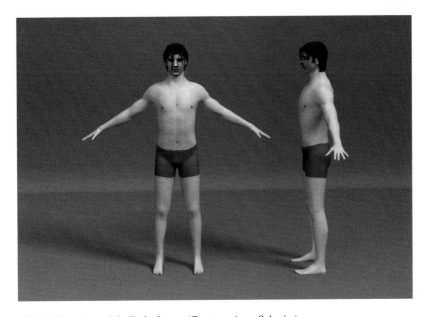

Fig. 15.12 Neutral, straight-limbed pose (Courtesy Arno Schmitz)

A more popular pose in recent years, used on the film *Spider-Man* and many others afterwards, is the arms and legs akimbo pose. With this pose, the character's spine is erect, but the legs and arms are bent to about the halfway point of their total rotation range, and the legs and arms are rotated slightly outwards from the hip and shoulder joints. The purpose of this pose accomplishes the goal of the T-pose, but adds something extra: because the major joints are rotated to about the midpoint of their range, it reduces the amount of distortion that must be accounted for in the rig because the limb will now only move half as far, in either direction, as it would in a straight-arm and straight-legged pose.

The akimbo pose is a bit more difficult to model because it is unnatural and each limb is rotated out of alignment with the global coordinate system. A solution for this is to build each part separately, and then assemble and stitch them together in the appropriate posture. It is here that knowledge of anatomy becomes very useful, especially if you have a pre-built skeleton to use as reference for positioning the different limbs.

Fig. 15.13   Mid-rotation posture (Courtesy Arno Schmitz)

Once you have the pose set properly, you may need to modify the edge loop pattern at all joints. This is because the surface definition of a character can be done fairly well without reference to how it is supposed to bend during joint rotation. If this is not kept in mind during the modeling process, there is a good chance you will need to modify the model to ensure there are enough vertices at every joint to maintain the shape of surrounding structures during limb rotation. For example, the extensor carpi radialis longus crosses over the elbow joint completely in almost a straight line, with no allowance made for the shape of the elbow. When the arm bends at the elbow, this muscle must also bend, but if does not have vertices aligned with the location of the elbow joint, it will not bend correctly. This same problem is present to differing degrees in many other joints.

The most common solution to joint flexibility issues is to add up to five edge loops at hips and shoulders, and then to have at least three rows at elbows and knees: one row at the top and bottom of the joint and another in the center.

UVs

UVs must be assigned prior to rigging (Fig. 15.4). This must be done because any UV errors may force the animator to throw away any work done up until the point when the UV error was discovered. One way this might occur is if there is an error

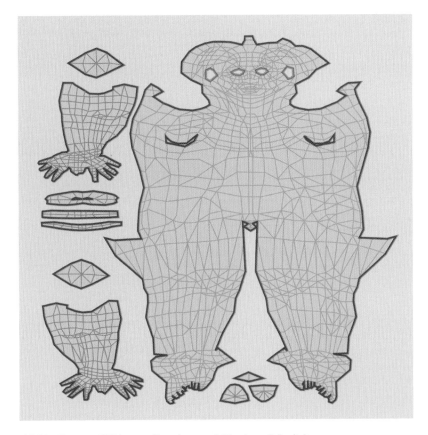

Fig. 15.14 Character UV layout (Based on model by Arno Schmitz)

in a part of the model that is not easily checked, like in the armpit. When the animator moves the arm to test his rig, he may find the mistake and then be forced to send it back to be fixed, and throw away the work he's done so far. One way to help prevent this problem is to use the arms and legs akimbo neutral pose because it is easier to see most faces of a model. You should always carefully triple-check your UVs before delivering the model for rigging (or rigging it yourself) or you risk losing a great deal of work.

Chapter 16
Projects and Conclusion

3D4
Project 1
Anatomy[1]

Supplies/materials required:
1. Anatomical reference

Instructions

1. Build low-resolution skeleton model (polygons or nurbs)
   (a) First take overall measurements of all bones at same scale. This can be done by using a photo or drawing of a full skeleton (but not a partial one) or by digitizing major measurements with a 3D digitizer or other measuring instrument, such as a ruler, tape measure, or calipers.
      (i) It is extremely important that these measurements be taken and that all measurements are taken not only at the same scale, but from the same subject. If you use bones from different skeletons, whether from different drawings, photos, or 3D reference, they are unlikely to match each other proportionately.
   (b) Construct each bone, taking care to ensure each bone matches the dimensions measured earlier. If this is done, the proportions of your bones will be correct.
      (i) The vertebrae must be measured very accurately. If not, their large numbers can exaggerate a small mistake to such a degree that the skull's vertical position is offset to a noticeable degree.
      (ii) Bones should be the lowest resolution possible, without losing important structural details needed for locating muscle origins and insertions.

---

[1] Note: this project may easily be split into two. The first is to build a skeleton, the second to build the muscles and skin

(c) After bones are built, assemble them into full skeleton.

   (i) This part of the project should be done very carefully. Proper positioning, alignment, and orientation of bones are required for a good result. Any errors in this area will be carried forward through every muscle attachment and result in some amount of distortion, often serious.

     1. Most common problem areas are:

       (a) Pelvis

       (b) Scapula

       (c) Thoracic cage

       (d) Skull

       (d) Optional step: Find and mark all muscle origin and insertion locations on bones. These can be marked with a named nurbs curve to define the area on the bone that is covered by any given muscle.

         (i) You can waste a lot of time by not making a simple skeleton. Correct insertion and origin locations are more important to the success of this project than a detailed skeleton. Please do not allow yourself to be trapped by an overly complex treatment of this part of the project. If the bones start and end in the right place, and contain correctly positioned attachment points for muscles, they will be fine.

   (b) Name all bones with correctly spelled Latin names

  2. Build nurbs muscles. Polys are illegal for this stage. Muscles must have correct shape, origin, and insertion. Solid muscles are preferred, but superficial surfaces will be accepted.

   (c) Muscle shapes will be of the following types:

     (i) Cylindrical (as in paired cylinders of biceps brachii)

     (ii) Sheet (as in pectoralis major)

     (iii) Belt (as in sartorius)

     (iv) Drape (as in ilio-psoas)

   (d) Name all muscles with correctly spelled Latin names

   (e) Be careful to avoid accidentally combining muscles, especially with the tensor fascia latae and gluteus maximus

   (f) Most sources identify 640–850 muscles in the human body, depending on how they are defined. There are about 320 superficial muscles. Because most of these are laterally repeated, there are only about 140 unique superficial muscles on either side of the body. For this project, quality will be negatively affected if a model contains less than 75 unique muscles. Grades may be positively affected if there are 100 or more unique muscles.

   (g) Be extremely careful to avoid exaggeration

     (i) Most muscles are very thin, but appear larger due to the presence of other muscles and tissue beneath them.

     (ii) If one muscle is exaggerated, it tends to throw off the proportions of every other muscle in the body

3. Build subdivision surface skin around muscles and bones
    (h) Skin model must be one piece
        (i) Please be careful when building this, to make sure the end result appears to be human
4. Add eyes, teeth, ears, and nose
5. Optional: Make low-resolution polygonal figure based on subdivision surface skin model.
6. Deliver an archived file containing the following:
    (j) 3D file containing:
        (i) Bones
        (ii) Nurbs muscles
        (iii) Sub-D skin
        (iv) Low poly model (if made)

Rules

1. Penetration not allowed for any reason
    (a) Insertions and origins must attach exactly on the required surface
2. Naming convention for intermediate hand-ins:
    (a) lastnameFirstnameProjectnameYearH#.rar/zip
        (i) "H" stands for "hand-in", "#" should be replaced with sequential number for hand-in, 1–6.

Expectations

1. Likeness is mandatory. Failure to achieve this goal will result in a failing grade, regardless of any other factor.
2. All models will be complete. Incomplete models will suffer significant point reductions

Delivery Schedule

This schedule is intended for use by students to improve their ability to determine whether their work will be sufficient or not, and as an aid in scheduling the progress of their project.

Hand-in Schedule

1. Measurements
   (a) Sufficient: file contains an object (probably a linear curve) to represent the dimensions of every skeletal object
       (i) This includes: all carpal and metacarpals, tarsals and metatarsals, cranial bones (inner ear bones not required), rib case shape, pelvic structure, scapula structure, mandible, and all long bones, such as the femur, etc.
       (ii) Fidelity to shape of target bone is not required, but dimensions must be accurate
2. All bones built and named
   (a) All bones represented in polys or nurbs
   (b) Bones may be stylized to reduce detail (but for no other reason)
       (i) If realistic bones are made, they must be built quickly enough that they do not interfere with finishing project on time
3. Bones assembled into skeleton
   (a) Orientation, position, and alignment are all correct.
       (i) This is vitally important. Any problems in the skeleton will be carried forward into each successive phase of the project
4. Axial musculature
   (a) All superficial axial muscles built
       (i) For extra credit, deep muscles also built
5. Appendicular musculature
   (a) All superficial appendicular muscles built
       (i) For extra credit, deep muscles also built
6. Cartilage, facial organs, and gender-specific details built
7. Subdivision surface skin model
   (a) Subdivision surface must completely enclose all muscles and skeletal elements
   (b) All joints, limbs, and protuberances (like knees, arms, and the nose) must be represented
   (c) Optional: build fingernails and toenails
2. Optimized poly model
   (a) 10,000 triangle limit
   (a) All joint edge loops setup properly
3. Optional: Hair is built

   • Polygonal optimization project
   • Hair project
   • Conclusion

Glossary

Abductor	A muscle that pulls a bone away from the medial plane. Abductors oppose the action of adductor muscles.
Active area	Any portion of a scene that allows interaction by the player.
Active camera range	The portion of an environment or scene that is visible to any given camera.
Adductor	A muscle that pulls a bone towards the medial plane of the body. Adductors oppose the action of abductor muscles.
Animatics	A sequence of images meant to represent a proposed animation, but in abbreviated form, for the purpose of planning an animation or presenting a proposed animation.
Anterior	The frontal plane of the body.
Articulation	A joint structure, as in knee or elbow.
Axillary bud	A bud that develops from the axil of a leaf or plant. These are located at the nodes from which new stems, branches, or flowers grow.
Axis of projection	A single direction relative to a global or local coordinate system. For example, a normal map receives information from an object's normals, however many there are, but a bump map will project in only one direction.
Background matte	An image used to represent a background. This is most often used to represent distant or complex landscapes, but can also be used with smaller-scale subjects.
Bare earth	A digital elevation map that provides elevation information without elevation noise from manmade structures, trees, and other things that projects upwards from the ground.
Bipinnate	Pinnate leaflets that grow opposite each other from a common stem. Twice pinnate.
Billboard	An alpha mapped textured plane, usually used to represent complex or distant objects, such as trees or mountains.
Biome	A region defined by similar climate and vegetation.

Biped	A two-footed animal.
Blend map	A texture map that defines how two or more other textures will blend together, by assigning two or more colors to the maps to be blended, and then manipulating the intensity of each to define the opacity of corresponding maps.
Brachial	Of the arm.
Body plan	The topological network or layout of a biological organism.
Calcaneus	The heel bone.
Calibration, monitor	The act of adjusting a monitor so that its display matches a desired absolute color standard.
Capitate	The largest of the carpal bones.
Carpal	Of the wrist.
Cartilage	A type of connective tissue that is found throughout the body, in forms of differing toughness and elasticity. It is found in the nose, ears, between ribs, in the bronchial tubes, and between articulating ends of bones.
Cervical	Of the neck.
Channel interference	A mixture of information related to different information filter types, when viewed simultaneously, renders unclear information related to any one filter, such as when soft shadows, which belong to the shadow layer of an image, must be extracted from the dirt layer, which might be difficult to distinguish from the shadow layer.
Civil engineering	The design of structures of various types, generally of a public utility nature, such as roads, dams, sewers, light-houses, harbors, and other works.
Circumduction	A circular motion.
Clavicle	The collar bone.
Color shift	When lighting or other factors influence the overall color of an image, usually found in photographs.
Compound leaf	A leaf made up of a number of leaflets attached to a common stem.
Conifer	A cone-bearing plant, usually a tree. Cedar, pine, redwood, and yews are all examples of coniferous trees.
Continental drift theory	The movement of the earth's continents relative to each other.
Contrast edge	An edge defined by any pair of distinguishably different elements, such as brightness levels, hue change, change of saturation, or even of contrast.
Cranium	The portion of the skull containing the brain.
Cuboid	A bone of the foot, with articulations to the fourth and fifth metatarsal joints.
Cuneiform, bones	The medial, intermediate, and lateral cuneiform bones articulate with the first, second, and third metatarsal, respectively. The lateral cuneiform is adjacent to the cuboid bone. All three are distal to the navicular bone.

Dicot	A broad category of plants defined by having two seed leaves instead of one, as in the monocot family of plants. Most fruits, vegetables, and other important food plants are dicots.
Digital elevation map	Also known as a DEM, this is a type of image that uses color to define varying elevations in a landscape. These images may be converted to a three-dimensional object, usually extremely detailed, to represent terrain with a very high level of accuracy.
Dimension contrast	This occurs when objects that fall within differing dimension ranges are in near proximity to each other. For instance, a building that is made primarily in full or half meter units has decorations built of objects that never exceed 10 cm in any direction.
Displacement map	A type of texture map that is used to create polygonal geometry at render time to modify the appearance of the surface or polygons it is attached to. Unlike a normal map, a displacement map only projects in one direction from the surface of an object. Unlike a bump map, a displacement map will affect the silhouette of an object because it modifies its geometry.
Distal	At the far end, distant, at the end farthest from the root.
Event boundary	A structural boundary that may be linked to a distinct geologic event, such as a landslide, earthquake, or slump. The boundary defines a region within which a change relative to its surroundings has taken place.

Earthquake	A movement of the earth's crust, precipitated by a sudden release of energy. Earthquake types are defined by the type of movement caused.
	
	Normal
	    An earthquake that causes land to drop
	Thrust
	    An earthquake that causes land to rise
	Megathrust
	    An earthquake occurring in one of the earth's subduction zones, where a tectonic plate subducts beneath another. There are the world's largest earthquakes.

Elevation	The height above sea level for any given part of a landmass, such as a road on a mountain.
Esker	The trail left by a glacier as it slides downwards. Eskers tend to be smooth and meandering in shape, and are bordered by moraine to either side and at their leading edge, just in front of the glacier.
Erosion	To carry away or displace solids in an environment by any or more of a variety of agents, such as wind, water, and gravity.

Ethmoid	A facial bone of the skull, located between either maxilla bones, and above the vomer.
Even pinnate	A pinnate leaf that ends in a pair of leaflets.
Extension, set	A CG element meant to enlarge upon an existing practical set.
Extensor	A muscle that serves to open, or increase, the angle of a joint.
Façade	The front of a building or any side of a building that has been given a special architectural treatment, especially if it contains a prominent entrance.
Fault line	A fracture between rocks that evidences movement of either side relative to each other.
Fibonacci numbers	A series of numbers, defined by a mathematician called Fibonacci, that are found in many biological organisms, such as in the number of leaves on a plant.
Fibonacci sequence	See *Fibonacci numbers*
Flagged polygons	A face or group of faces that have an attribute attached, known as a *flag*. Flags are often generated to customize information contained within a dataset. For example, a video game might be written to interpret every occurrence of the word "door" in a polyset to define a location of a given size that will trigger, if crossed by a player character, another event, usually that of switching exterior geometry for interior geometry. In this case, the flag is the names of the doors in combination with code that allows them to be recognized by this naming convention.
Flashing	An object designed to prevent water from entering a structure by deflecting its passage away from exterior joints. Flashing can be placed beneath or on top of other roofing materials, and is most often made of long strips of weather-resistant metal.
Flexion	A bending at a joint that causes the joint angle to decrease.
Flexor	A muscle that accomplishes flexion.
Foramen	A natural opening, usually through bone.
Fossa	In anatomy, a shallow depression.
Frames	Any set of static images which, when played in sequence, describe motion or convey a sequential description of information or an event.
Geometric subdivision	A type of measurement where all dimensions are derived from a single geometric primitive, usually a square or circle.
Glacial ice	A type of highly compressed, blue-tinged ice that is found in glaciers.
Glaciation	The creation and movement of glaciers.
Grade	The pitch of a slope, or steepness of a hill.

Growth limit	The maximum size a biological organism may attain.
Growth patterns	The arrangement of leaves relative to their stalk. Some common patterns are: alternate, opposed, and whorled.
Hamate	A bone of the wrist that forms one half of a joint with the fourth and fifth metacarpal bones. The hamate is distinguished by a hook-like process on its volar surface.
Height map	Also known as a *bump map* or *displacement map*. This is an image that is used during a render to either displace geometry or adjust how light falls on a surface, according to gray scale values that define relative height.
High contrast adjacent pixels	Any pair of pixels of distinctly different hue, luminosity, or saturation. Often, high contrast adjacent pixels occur in large clusters that number in the thousands. When such a condition exists, a camouflage-like noise may be created.
Horizon	An edge defined by the location where the sky is blocked by the earth. This is normally understood to be the horizon, as defined above, regardless of intervening structures that might obstruct the view.
Humerus	The bone of the upper arm.
Hyoid	A floating bone of the throat, held in place by a number of muscles and located directly in front of the esophagus.
Ilium	The largest and uppermost of the three bones that make up the innominatum, or one half of the pelvis.
Ischium	The bottommost and posterior of the three bones of the innominatum, or one half of the pelvis.
Inferior	Below.
Infrastructure, civilian	The most basic structures necessary to service the needs of a community, especially large ones as in a town or city.
Insertion, muscle	The part of a muscle that connects to the free bone of a pair of bones, one fixed and one free.
Intrinsic color	The inherent color of an object, regardless of light or other adulterants capable of modifying that color.
Lacrimal	A small bone on the medial anterior side of the maxilla, and at the inferior medial portion of the orbit, that allows passage of the lacrimal gland.
Land use map	A map that is coded for different types of use, such as to distinguish between civilian and military, or commercial from residential.
Lateral	Side.
Leaflet	A part of a compound leaf that resembles a leaf, but grows out of the vein of a leaf rather than a stem. Abcordate

Leaf shape, types	Shaped like an inverted heart.
	Cordate
	Heart-shaped.
	Elliptic
	Elliptical.
	Flabellate
	Fan-shaped.
	Kidney
	Kidney-shaped.
	Lanceolate
	Broadest at its base, about four times longer than it is ide, like a lance.
	Ovate
	Oval, broader at the base than the tip.
	Oblong
	Rectangular, with rounded edgers.
	Obovate
	Oval, broader at the tip than the base.
	Round
	Circular.
	Subulate
	Tapering to a point; awl-shaped.
	Truncate
	A square end, as if cut.
Lens distortion	An effect caused by the focal length of a lens. The shorter a lens is, the more distortion is evident, where straight lines are progressively more curved.
Lumbar	The lower portion of the spine, below the thoracic section and above the sacrum.
Lunate	A carpal bone located in the center of the proximal row of carpal bones, between the scaphoid and triquetrum.
Mandible	The jawbone.
Manubrium	A portion of the sternum bone on its superior end, distinguishable by a deep crevice between it and the main body of the sternum.
Margin, of a leaf	The shape of the edge of a leaf.
Margo	An edge shared by two bones.
Mass wasting	The down-slope movement of soil and rock by the force of gravity.
Maxilla	The largest of the facial bones, one on either side of the medial line, and containing eight teeth on either side.
Medial	Closest to the middle of the body, in opposition to lateral, which is the furthest from the middle.

Metacarpal	Bones of the hand located between the carpal bones and phalanges.
Metatarsal	Bones of the foot located between the tarsals and phalanges.
Milestone	An intermediate delivery, meant to assess or prove progress on a project.
Monitor calibration	The act of matching a monitor's display to a desired color standard, usually either for color printing or to match other monitors.
Monocot	A plant with one embryonic leaf in its seed. Grasses and orchids are both examples of common monocot plants.
Moraine	Material moved aside or deposited by a glacier as it moves.
Mountain-building	The elevation of rock and soil through a variety of forces acting on plate tectonics.
Muscle	Cardiac
	Muscle of the heart.
	Skeletal
	Striated muscle attached to bones, to effect skeletal movement.
	Smooth
	Non-striated muscle, found in numerous places throughout the body; organs, veins, arteries, gastro-intestinal tract and respiratory tract. Smooth muscle can either maintain volume or force movement through contraction, such as durnig digestion.
Natural detail	Full detail, without optimization.
Natural slope	Also known as *angle of repose*, the angle at which stacked dry material will rest, without sliding due to the force of gravity. For most granular materials, the natural slope is between 30° and 37°.
Navicular	A tarsal bone located on the medial side of the foot, between the talus and the three cuneiform bones.
Node, of a leaf	The place on a stem that a leaf grows from.
Nonvascular plant	A plant without venation.
Normal map	An image that represents normal vectors as colors that can be interpreted by a renderer to reproduce a high level of normal detail without requiring the original geometry the data are derived from.
Occipital	A bone at the base of the cranium that rests on the atlas bone, or first vertebra of the neck.
Odd-pinnate	A pinnate leaf structure that ends in a single leaf.

Origin, muscle	The place where a muscle attaches to the fixed bone of an articulation.
Os coxae	The ribs.
Palatine	A bone posterior to the maxilla that forms a part of the hard palate.
Palmate	A pattern where five rays extend outwards from a common point.
Parallax	An effect where, when two distant objects are compared for relative position, different results will be obtained depending on the viewpoint from which the comparison is made. Because the effect is consistent, it can be used to make accurate distance measurements, as is commonly done in astronomy.
Parietal	Two bones of the cranium, positioned between the frontal and occipital bones, with one parietal bone to either side of the medial line.
Perspective distortion	Two-dimensional distortion, usually in a photograph or a drawing, where the perspective of the image modifies true dimensions of the subject. With photographs, this can also be called *lens distortion*.
Petiole	The stalk of a leaf.
Petiolate	To have a stalk or petiole.
Phalange	Distal
	The phalanges most distant from the metacarpals.
	Medial
	The phalanges between the most distant and least distant phalanges from the metacarpals.
	Proximal
	The phalanges nearest to the metacarpals.
Pinnate	Like a feather, where leaflets are symmetrically arranged on either side of a stalk.
Pisiform	A bone of the wrist, lying against the anterior surface of the triquetrum.
Plant classification	A system by which different plants are organized and identified based on a number of different factors, or ranks, such as: *kingdom, division, class, order, family, genus,* and *species*.
Posterior	Located behind, or to the back of. Dorsal.
Pre-rendered	An image that is rendered and stored as an image, to be recalled on demand as in a video game. This is in opposition to *real-time graphics* where images are generated and discarded during play based on unique factors in the game.
Pressure ridge	A ridge forced by the collision of two opposing tectonic plates.

Procedural	A method of creating various effects in computer graphics by using variables to control the effect. For example, by pre-defining a growth pattern for a CG plant, variables could include: plant height, leaf type, and number of branches. By adjusting these variables, a variety of different plants may result.
Procedural variables	The variables by which a procedurally generated object is described and controlled.
Pronator	A muscle that *pronates* a limb, as in when a hand is turned so that the palm is facing downwards, or the corresponding motion in the foot.
Proportion	The size of one thing relative to another.
Proximal	Nearest.
Pubis	The anterior inferior bone of three bones that together form one half of the bilaterally symmetrical pelvis.
Quadruped	A four-legged animal.
Quoining	A type of architectural decoration used to define an edge between two angles in a structure.
Rachii	A series of stem-like veins of a leaf, from which leaflets grow in compound leaves.
Radius, bone	A bone of the lower arm, located between the humerus and carpal bones, that in combination with the ulna, allows supination and pronation of the hand.
Ramus	A branch, or offshoot, as in the ramus of the mandible.
RGBA image	A four-channel image where the four channels are: red, green, blue, and alpha, respectively.
Real-time renderer	A renderer that calculates, or *renders*, an image as a player manipulates it, usually at a very high frame rate, or number of renders per second.
Rotator	A muscle that causes rotation.
Sagittal	An imaginary plane, used as a means of defining the location of anatomical subjects, that divides the body in the medial plane, and oriented to face laterally on either side.
Scaphoid	The largest of the proximal row of carpal bones, located adjacent to the radius.
Scapula	Also known as the *shoulder blade*, a bone that connects the humerus to the clavicle, and that contains the glenoid fossa, or shoulder socket.
Sediment	Mineral or organic matter deposited by water.
Sedimentary rock	Rock formed by *sedimentation*.
Sedimentation	A process where solids are first deposited by a variety of mediums, such as wind or water, and are then compacted and cemented together in a process called *lithification* to form new rock.
Sessile	A flower or leaf without a stalk that grows directly from its stem.

Set extension	A CG element meant to enlarge upon an existing practical set.
Shot list	In filmmaking, a summary of every continuous filmed sequence needed for a story sequence; for example: a sequence designed to show a man leaving a building may be made of multiple shots: he approaches the door, his hand in close-up as it pushes against it, a wide shot as he walks away from the camera and through the door.
Signage	Signs, such as traffic signs, in an environment.
Simple leaf	A leaf without leaflets.
Skeletal muscle	Striated muscle attached to bones by tendons that cause skeletal movement by contraction and release of tissue.
Slope	The steepness or grade of a straight line.
Slump	To fall or sink suddenly. In geology, this is a mass-wasting event when a portion of material that makes up a slope collapses.
Spatial pattern	The natural pattern in which plants of the same variety grow.
Sphenoid	A bone of the cranium that connects the occipital bone with the frontal bone and forms a part of the posterior portion of the orbits.
Spine	The vertebral column.
Sternum	Also known as the *breastbone*, a bone located between the os coxae at the anterior midline of the thoracic cage.
Subduct	The movement of one tectonic plate beneath another.
Subduction	When something *subducts*.
Subduction zone	A region where the major geological formations are made by *subduction*.
Subsurface anatomy	Anatomical structures, such as muscle and bone, located beneath the epidermis, or skin.
Supinator	A muscle that causes *supination*, as in the supinator muscle of the lower arm, which allows the hand to be turned so that the palm faces upwards.
Strike-slip fault	A type of fracture where two sections of rock move away from each other horizontally due to vertical cracks between either side.
Sulcus	A depression or fissure, like a channel, found in many bones, particularly in the cranium.
Superior	Above.
Superstructure	Anything that rests above a foundation. In architecture and engineering, the term can be used to describe the walls and roof of a house, which rests on a foundation, or the struts of a bridge, which rest on large piers or abutments.

Switchback	A type of road design meant to reduce steepness of slope for vehicles by traversing a distance in a zigzag pattern instead of a straight line to the destination.
Talus	The second largest of the tarsal bones of the foot, the talus articulates with the tibia, fibula, calcaneus, and navicular.
Tarsal	Of the foot.
Tectonic plate	A massive slab of rock, from hundreds to thousands of kilometers across and anywhere from 5 to several hundred kilometers thick. The earth's crust is made of many tectonic plates.
Temporal	A bone of the cranium, containing the opening for the ear.
Terrain	The part of a CG environment meant to represent the ground and other landscape features, but exclusive of such things as buildings, plants, and props.
Terrain mesh	The polygonal geometry used to represent *terrain* in a CG environment.
Tetrapod	Four-footed, or four-limbed creatures, such as humans, reptiles, dinosaurs, and birds.
Thoracic	A section of the body that generally corresponds to the chest and that is protected by a bony cage, within which many critical internal organs, such as the heart and lungs, are contained.
Tilable	An image that may be symmetrically repeated to create a larger pattern. Although this can be said to be true of any pattern, this word is generally used to describe images that are purposely created to produce patterns that either disguise or emphasize the seams between each tile. Square bathroom tiles emphasize the boundary between tiles, but some Islamic tile patterns hide the boundary by creating larger patterns out of smaller pieces.
Tile	A single image, usually square, designed to be repeated in a scene.
Tile set	A group of tiles that together form patterns that would be impossible for any single tile.
Transform fault	A strike-slip fault whose primary motion is horizontal and occurs at tectonic plate boundaries.
Transverse	At a right angle to the long axis of a body, as in the transverse arch of the foot.
Tree line	An arbitrary elevation, above or below which trees will not grow.
Polar	Pertaining to the pole, or either end, of a sphere.
Desert	Arid land with sparse vegetation and low rainfall.
Elevation	An orthographic view of something, usually from the side. The height of any point relative to the ground. The elevation of Black Mountain at its summit is 4,811 ft.

Trifoliate	Having three leaflets.
Triquetrum	Also called the *triquetral* bone, one of eight carpal bones. It is roughly pyramidal in shape, and is located on the medial side of the proximal row of carpal bones. It articulates with the pisiform, hamate, and lunate bones.
Ulna	One of the two long bones of the forearm, located between the humerus and carpal bones and medial to the forearm.
Vascular plant	A plant with venation.
Venation	Arrangement of veins in a leaf or other structure containing veins.
Vertebra	Any of the articulating bones of the spine.
Vomer	An unpaired facial bone located within the nasal septum.
Walk zone	A region in a game where players are allowed to navigate their characters or other game objects, such as vehicles.
Windbreak	Also known as a *shelterbelt*, it is one or more files of trees planted to block wind. Windbreaks can be very large civil infrastructure projects, for instance, along highways.
World ocean	A continuous body of water encircling the earth, usually broken into five sub-oceans: Atlantic, Pacific, Indian, Arctic, and Southern.

Bibliography

Binney, Marcus. *Airport Builders*. New York: Wiley, 1999.

Brickell, Christopher, ed. et al. *The American Horticultural Society Encyclopedia of Gardening*. New York: Dorley Kinderley, 2003.

Chen, Wai-Fah and J.Y. Richard Liew, eds. *The Civil Engineering Handbook*. Boca Raton, FL: CRC Press, 2002.

Doczi, Gyorgy. *Power of Limits : Proportional Harmonies in Nature, Art and Architecture*. Boulder, CO: Shambala, 1981.

Fazzio, Michael, Marian Moffett and Laurence Wodehouse. *A World History of Architecture*. New York: McGraw-Hill, 2008.

Goldsmith, Ben and Tom O'Regan. *The Film Studio: Film Production in the Global Economy*. Lanham, MD: Rowman & Littlefield, 2005.

Gray, Henry. *Gray's Anatomy*. New York: Gramercy, 1988.

Kent, Steven L. *The Ultimate History of Video Games: From Pong to Pokemon – The Story Behind the Craze that Touched Our Lives and Changed the World*. New York: Three Rivers Press, 2001.

Kuennecke, Bernd H. *Temperate Forest Biomes—Greenwood guides to Biomes of the World*. Westport, CT: Greenwood Press, 2008.

Netter, Frank H. *Atlas of Human Anatomy*. Philadelphia, PA: Saunders Elsevier, 2006.

Olson, Robert. *Art Direction for Film and Video*. Boston: Focal Press, 1993.

Phillips, Roger. *Trees of North America and Europe*. New York: Random House, 1978.

Putz, R. and R. Pabst, eds. *Sobotta Atlas of Human Anatomy*. Munich: Urban & Fischer, 2006.

Robinson, Andrew. *Earthshock: Hurricanes, Volcanoes, Earthquakes, Tornadoes and Other Forces of Nature*. London: Thames & Hudson, 1993.

Sandler, Kevin S. and Gaylyn Studler. *Titanic: Anatomy of a Blockbuster*. Rutgers, NJ: Rutgers University Press, 1999.

Stedman, Thomas L. *Stedman's Medical Dictionary*. Baltimore, MD: Lippincott Williams & Wilkins, 2006.

Index